Windows Application Development Cookbook

Discover over 125 solution-based recipes to help you build applications for smartphones, tablets, and desktops

Marcin Jamro

BIRMINGHAM - MUMBAI

Windows Application Development Cookbook

First published: December 2016

Production reference: 1151216

Published by Packt Publishing Ltd.
Livery Place
35 Livery Street
Birmingham
B3 2PB, UK.

ISBN 978-1-78646-772-0

www.packtpub.com

Credits

Author

Marcin Jamro

Reviewer

Melania Andrisan

Commissioning Editor

Kunal Parikh

Acquisition Editor

Chaitanya Nair

Content Development Editor

Rohit Singh

Technical Editor

Pratish Shetty

Copy Editors

Gladson Monteiro

Muktikant Garimella

Project Coordinator

Izzat Contractor

Proofreader

Safis Editing

Indexer

Rekha Nair

Graphics

Jason Monteiro

Production Coordinator

Shraddha Falebhai

About the Author

Marcin Jamro, PhD, is an entrepreneur and researcher as well as a developer and architect of various kinds of application, such as web, mobile, and distributed ones. He is interested in many aspects of computer science, including software engineering and project management. Marcin is passionate about C#, C++, and C languages in general, design patterns, new technologies, and mobile devices, especially the Windows platform.

He has significant practical experience in project development and holds the position of the President of the Board at TITUTO Sp. z o.o. [Ltd.] in Rzeszów, Poland. His company develops various IT projects, including mobile and web applications. To add to this, TITUTO Sp. z o.o. [Ltd.] has a set of its own products dedicated to hotels and tour operators. You can read more about them at `http://tituto.com`.

Marcin has published several papers, taken part in many conferences, organized a few of them, and participated in two internships at Microsoft in Redmond, USA. He has Microsoft Certified Professional, Microsoft Certified Technology Specialist, and Microsoft Certified Professional Developer certificates.

You can find out more about Marcin on his website, `http://jamro.biz`, and you can easily contact him by sending an e-mail to `marcin@jamro.biz`.

Acknowledgements

I would like to dedicate this book to my parents – Dorota and Jozef.

Of course, I cannot forget the employees at Packt for their support while writing this book. I would like to thank the reviewer for her valuable feedback regarding the content and for pointing out the topics that required additional clarification or modification. Last but not least, I would really want to thank you for reading this book. I hope that you will enjoy it and it will become a source of useful knowledge when developing applications for various platforms with the Windows 10 operating system.

About the Reviewer

Melania Andrisan was interested in technology from an early age, so pursuing computer science was a natural fit for her. During college in Timisoara, she was involved in a lot of Microsoft-related community events, discussing topics such as WPF, Silverlight, and ASP.NET. Her involvement continued after joining the Haufe Group as she talked at various national and international developer conferences about Microsoft-related technologies. For Haufe Group, Melania is part of Haufe Group's CTO office as a Cross Domain Solution Architect and she has architected several of their internal and consumer-facing projects. At the moment, she is a proud mother of a little girl, but she's eager to get back to work soon.

You can find out more about Melania on her website, `http://mela.ro` or on Twitter at `@melaniadanciu`.

www.PacktPub.com

For support files and downloads related to your book, please visit www.PacktPub.com.

Did you know that Packt offers eBook versions of every book published, with PDF and ePub files available? You can upgrade to the eBook version at www.PacktPub.com and as a print book customer, you are entitled to a discount on the eBook copy. Get in touch with us at service@packtpub.com for more details.

At www.PacktPub.com, you can also read a collection of free technical articles, sign up for a range of free newsletters and receive exclusive discounts and offers on Packt books and eBooks.

https://www.packtpub.com/mapt

Get the most in-demand software skills with Mapt. Mapt gives you full access to all Packt books and video courses, as well as industry-leading tools to help you plan your personal development and advance your career.

Why subscribe?

- Fully searchable across every book published by Packt
- Copy and paste, print, and bookmark content
- On demand and accessible via a web browser

Table of Contents

Preface

Nowadays, there are various types of devices available on the market, such as smartphones, tablets, and desktops. You can use them every day to perform common tasks, such as browsing the Internet, sending e-mail messages, recording movies, sharing photos using social media, and playing games. It is not unusual to use even more than one device, for instance, a smartphone, which we carry in our pockets almost all the time, a tablet that we use to perform various tasks at home, and a desktop at work. Of course, these devices can differ significantly from each other not only in terms of screen resolution, but also about available sensors and performance. However, does it mean that you cannot develop your own application for all of them in a simple way? Do you need to create a separate application from scratch for smartphones, tablets, and desktops?

If such devices use the Windows 10 operating system, the answer to both these questions is no! This platform allows you to develop a Universal Windows Platform (UWP) application that can be run on various device families. Such a task is really simplified because you can use the same programming language, technologies, as well as the Integrated Development Environment (IDE).

Despite supporting a wide range of devices, the UWP applications can be equipped with an attractive User Interface (UI) created using the Extensible Application Markup Language (XAML). With the availability of a set of predefined controls and animations, your work can be significantly reduced. What is more, you can take advantage of the Model - View - ViewModel (MVVM) design pattern and data binding to improve quality of the code and make its maintenance easier. The UWP applications can also use multimedia, read data from built-in sensors, and store data in various ways. Internet-based scenarios are supported and you can also download a file or get data from an Application Programming Interface (API). Many devices allow obtaining the current Global Positioning System (GPS) location, which can be used to show a marker in a suitable place on the map or to launch the GPS-based navigation. When the solution is developed, it can be submitted to the Windows Store. Thus, it can be downloaded and used by people all over the world!

Are you ready to learn how to develop an application for Windows 10-based smartphones, tablets, and desktops? If so, let's start reading and writing the code!

What this book covers

Chapter 1, *Getting Started*, presents setting up a suitable IDE, creating a project, adding pages to the application, designing a user interface, and handling navigation. You will learn how to run the application in an emulator and on a real device as well as how to debug it and measure performance.

Chapter 2, *Designing a User Interface*, shows how to design pages using various controls, such as textboxes and buttons, as well as how to arrange them in various variants, either vertically, horizontally, or in a grid. You will also get to know how to prepare user controls, apply styles, localize the project, and prepare dedicated versions of pages for various device families.

Chapter 3, *MVVM and Data Binding*, covers the application of the MVVM design pattern, which divides the project into three parts, namely, model, view, and view model. The topic of the data binding mechanism, together with commands, is also taken into account. You will see how to display a collection of items and how to use value converters.

Chapter 4, *Data Storage*, deals with managing directories and files along with writing and reading a few types of files, such as with plain text, XML, and JSON-formatted content, as well as binary files with content in the user-defined format. You will also learn how to use a SQLite database in your application.

Chapter 5, *Animations and Graphics*, explains how to improve the user interface by introducing animations. They can be applied to display a control as well as change its size, position, or even rotation. This chapter also shows how to handle a few touch events and introduces the topic of rendering 3D graphics using DirectX, XAML, and C++ language.

Chapter 6, *Multimedia*, describes how to support multimedia content in an application, such as by playing a movie clip, listening to an audio file, and presenting a collection of photos. The subject of modifying images in a programmatic way is also taken into account. You will see how to take an image or record a movie using a camera, scan QR codes, and synthesize and recognize speech.

Chapter 7, *Built-in Sensors*, presents how to use various sensors to obtain a set of data, such as G-force values using an accelerometer, a heading of magnetic north using a compass, a current value of ambient light using a light sensor, as well as a current orientation of a device. To add to this, you will learn how to control vibrations of a phone and how to obtain the current GPS location.

`Chapter 8`, *Internet-based Scenarios*, covers various scenarios related to the Internet, such as opening a website, composing an e-mail message, as well as opening a map in the external tool and directly in your application. You will also see how to get and send some data to an API, as well as how to download files from the Internet.

`Chapter 9`, *Testing and Submission*, introduces unit testing and the process of configuring and submitting the project to the Windows Store. You will get to know how to adjust the configuration, prepare the necessary files, submit and update the application, as well as browse reviews and ratings regarding the published application.

What you need for this book

This book presents development of UWP applications for various devices running on the Windows 10 operating system. Thus, you need a set of tools that allow designing the user interface, writing supporting code, as well as running the application and testing it. Fortunately, all of these features are available in the Microsoft Visual Studio Community 2015, which you can use while reading this book. The process of its installation and configuration is presented in detail in `Chapter 1`, *Getting Started*.

To step through all recipes presented in this book, especially to publish an application in the Windows Store, it is necessary to have a developer account. What is more, it is recommended to have a real smartphone or tablet with the Windows 10 operating system to test the developed applications on a real device. If you do not have one, you can use the built-in emulators, but not all recipes can be checked in practice.

Who this book is for

The book is dedicated to programmers with various experience in developing applications for Windows-based smartphones, tablets, and desktops. Thus, even beginners can find suitable content to learn how to develop their first application!

However, it is recommended to have some basic knowledge of the C# language and object-oriented programming to understand code snippets presented in the book. Prior experience in developing mobile and desktop applications and using the XAML language is not necessary.

This book is organized in the form of solution-based recipes to present various features that could be interesting for developers. To make it even more useful, the code is attached to each chapter. Thus, you can easily download the code and run the application without the need of typing the code on your own.

It is worth mentioning that some code has been simplified. For this reason, it could differ from the *best practices* and may have significantly limited, or even removed, security checks and functionalities. Before publishing your application, it should be thoroughly tested to ensure that is works correctly in various circumstances.

Sections

In this book, you will find several headings that appear frequently (*Getting ready, How to do it..., How it works..., There's more...*, and *See also*).

To give clear instructions on how to complete a recipe, we use these sections as follows:

Getting ready

This section tells you what to expect in the recipe, and describes how to set up any software or any preliminary settings required for the recipe.

How to do it...

This section contains the steps required to follow the recipe.

How it works...

This section usually consists of a detailed explanation of what happened in the previous section.

There's more...

This section consists of additional information about the recipe in order to make the reader more knowledgeable about the recipe.

See also

This section provides helpful links to other useful information for the recipe.

Conventions

In this book, you will find a number of text styles that distinguish between different kinds of information. Here are some examples of these styles and an explanation of their meaning.

Code words in text, database table names, folder names, filenames, file extensions, pathnames, dummy URLs, user input, and Twitter handles are shown as follows: "The files regarding the default page, both .xaml and .xaml.cs, are automatically added to the main directory."

A block of code is set as follows:

```
private void button_Click(object sender, RoutedEventArgs e)
{
    Frame.Navigate(typeof(ProductsPage), 0);
}
```

When we wish to draw your attention to a particular part of a code block, the relevant lines or items are set in bold:

```
private void button_Click(object sender, RoutedEventArgs e)
{
    if (Frame.CanGoBack)
    {
        Frame.GoBack();
    }
}
```

New terms and **important words** are shown in bold. Words that you see on the screen, for example, in menus or dialog boxes, appear in the text like this: "Verify a list within the **Selected features** group and click on **Install**."

Warnings or important notes appear in a box like this.

Tips and tricks appear like this.

Reader feedback

Feedback from our readers is always welcome. Let us know what you think about this book--what you liked or disliked. Reader feedback is important for us as it helps us develop titles that you will really get the most out of. To send us general feedback, simply e-mail feedback@packtpub.com, and mention the book's title in the subject of your message. If there is a topic that you have expertise in and you are interested in either writing or contributing to a book, see our author guide at www.packtpub.com/authors.

Customer support

Now that you are the proud owner of a Packt book, we have a number of things to help you to get the most from your purchase.

Downloading the example code

You can download the example code files for this book from your account at http://www.packtpub.com. If you purchased this book elsewhere, you can visit http://www.packtpub.com/support and register to have the files e-mailed directly to you.

You can download the code files by following these steps:

1. Log in or register to our website using your e-mail address and password.
2. Hover the mouse pointer on the **SUPPORT** tab at the top.
3. Click on **Code Downloads & Errata**.
4. Enter the name of the book in the **Search** box.
5. Select the book for which you're looking to download the code files.
6. Choose from the drop-down menu where you purchased this book from.
7. Click on **Code Download**.

Once the file is downloaded, please make sure that you unzip or extract the folder using the latest version of:

- WinRAR / 7-Zip for Windows
- Zipeg / iZip / UnRarX for Mac
- 7-Zip / PeaZip for Linux

The code bundle for the book is also hosted on GitHub at `https://github.com/PacktPubl ishing/Windows-Application-Development-Cookbook`. We also have other code bundles from our rich catalog of books and videos available at `https://github.com/PacktPublish ing/`. Check them out!

Downloading the color images of this book

We also provide you with a PDF file that has color images of the screenshots/diagrams used in this book. The color images will help you better understand the changes in the output. You can download this file from `http://www.packtpub.com/sites/default/files/downl oads/WindowsApplicationDevelopmentCookbook_ColorImages.pdf`.

Errata

Although we have taken every care to ensure the accuracy of our content, mistakes do happen. If you find a mistake in one of our books-maybe a mistake in the text or the code-we would be grateful if you could report this to us. By doing so, you can save other readers from frustration and help us improve subsequent versions of this book. If you find any errata, please report them by visiting `http://www.packtpub.com/submit-errata`, selecting your book, clicking on the **Errata Submission Form** link, and entering the details of your errata. Once your errata are verified, your submission will be accepted and the errata will be uploaded to our website or added to any list of existing errata under the Errata section of that title.

To view the previously submitted errata, go to `https://www.packtpub.com/books/conten t/support` and enter the name of the book in the search field. The required information will appear under the **Errata** section.

Piracy

Piracy of copyrighted material on the Internet is an ongoing problem across all media. At Packt, we take the protection of our copyright and licenses very seriously. If you come across any illegal copies of our works in any form on the Internet, please provide us with the location address or website name immediately so that we can pursue a remedy.

Please contact us at `copyright@packtpub.com` with a link to the suspected pirated material.

We appreciate your help in protecting our authors and our ability to bring you valuable content.

Questions

If you have a problem with any aspect of this book, you can contact us at questions@packtpub.com, and we will do our best to address the problem.

1
Getting Started

In this chapter, we will cover the following recipes:

- Setting up the IDE
- Arranging windows
- Creating a new project
- Running the application
- Adding a new page
- Placing a control
- Handling events
- Navigating between pages
- Passing data between pages
- Handling the back button
- Changing a default page
- Modifying the back stack
- Utilizing additional features of the emulator
- Breakpoints-based debugging
- Step-by-step debugging
- Executing code while debugging
- Logging information while debugging
- Monitoring the CPU and memory usage

Introduction

Application development is certainly an exciting task that allows you to create amazing solutions that may be used by people all over the world! What is more, with the usage of the Windows 10 platform, you can develop **Universal Windows Platform** (**UWP**) applications that run on various devices, including smartphones, tablets, and desktops. The availability of great tools and a lot of interesting resources make such a task significantly easier. Additionally, they shorten the time required for preparing the product. So, why not try developing another great solution that could be known and used in various regions of the world?

However, before developing amazing applications and sharing them with others, you need to perform a set of necessary steps, such as setting up a suitable **Integrated Development Environment** (**IDE**), creating a project, or adding pages to your application. Then, you need to design a **User Interface** (**UI**) as well as handle suitable navigation within the application. You also need to write supporting code in a programming language as well as test the newly created application in an emulator and a real device.

Unfortunately, sometimes not everything works exactly as you plan. Therefore, it is important to learn how to debug your solution and find the source of the problem as well as measure performance to ensure that the application will work smoothly on various devices.

In the case of this book, we will use **Extensible Application Markup Language** (**XAML**) for UI definition as well as the C# programming language to specify the interaction with the UI and to prepare business logic.

If you are already aware of the previously mentioned topics, you could skip this chapter. Otherwise, it is strongly recommended that you read it thoroughly because the information will be used in the remaining part of this book as well. Let's start!

You can find more information about various topics presented in the book at `https://developer.microsoft.com/en-us/windows/apps/develop`. This website contains a lot of interesting resources regarding developing UWP applications for Windows 10, such as about:

- The XAML platform (`https://msdn.microsoft.com/windows/uwp/xaml-platform/index`)
- Controls (`https://msdn.microsoft.com/windows/uwp/controls-and-patterns/index`)
- Data binding (`https://msdn.microsoft.com/windows/uwp/data-binding/index`)
- Files and folders (`https://msdn.microsoft.com/windows/uwp`

/files/index)
- Sensors (https://msdn.microsoft.com/windows/uwp/devices -sensors/sensors)
- Graphics and animation (https://msdn.microsoft.com/windo ws/uwp/graphics/index)
- Maps and location (https://msdn.microsoft.com/windows/uw p/maps-and-location/index)
- Audio, video, and camera (https://msdn.microsoft.com/wind ows/uwp/audio-video-camera/index)

Setting up the IDE

Downloading, launching, and configuring an IDE is the first step that you should perform to start developing applications for smartphones, tablets, and desktops running on the Windows 10 operating system. With the usage of a convenient environment, a developer can easily design UI, write code, debug the application, as well as deploy it on an emulator or a real device.

In this book, we will use Microsoft Visual Studio Community 2015.

Of course, Microsoft Visual Studio Community 2015 is not the only IDE that one can use to develop solutions for Windows 10. There are also other versions of Microsoft Visual Studio that you could use, such as Professional and Enterprise. You can take a look at the comparison between the various versions of Microsoft Visual Studio 2015 at:
https://www.visualstudio.com/en-us/vs-2015-product-editions.

Getting ready

To step through this recipe, you need a PC that meets the requirements that are necessary to run Microsoft Visual Studio Community 2015.

How to do it…

To install the IDE, you need to perform the following steps:

1. Download the installation file of Microsoft Visual Studio Community 2015 from: `https://www.visualstudio.com/en-us/products/visual-studio-community-vs`.

2. Open the downloaded file and wait until the installer is started.

3. Choose the **Custom** installation type, as presented in the following image (on the left). Then, click on the **Next** button.

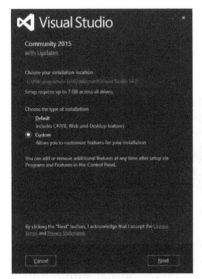 

4. Check all the options within the **Universal Windows App Development Tools** group in the **Select features** part, as shown in the image (on the right). Then, click on **Next**.

5. Verify a list within the **Selected features** group and click on **Install**.

6. Wait until the Microsoft Visual Studio Community 2015 is installed and the **Setup Completed** message is presented. You can monitor the progress of the installation and the downloading of necessary data using the **Acquiring** and **Applying** progress bars presented by the installer.

There's more…

Microsoft Visual Studio Community 2015 allows you to develop various kinds of applications, not only solutions running on devices with the Windows 10 operating system. What is interesting is that it is also possible to develop applications for Android and iOS platforms using the same IDE, by applying the Xamarin platform. A set of suitable tools for this purpose can be installed by selecting the **Cross Platform Mobile Development** option while installing the IDE, as shown in the preceding screenshot (on the right). If you want to learn more about Xamarin, you could visit https://www.xamarin.com/.

What is more, Microsoft Visual Studio Community 2015 also supports other types of applications, such as web and desktop applications, as well as allows to use various languages, including C#, C++, and even F#. If you want to learn more about the various possibilities of the IDE, let's take a look at https://www.visualstudio.com/.

Of course, during the installation of the IDE, you can select more features than mentioned in this recipe. In such a case, apart from developing Windows 10-based solutions, you can use the same IDE for other development scenarios.

See also

- The *Arranging windows* recipe

Arranging windows

Microsoft Visual Studio Community 2015 is a really powerful and advanced IDE. However, it can be adjusted even further by a developer. For instance, one can easily show or hide particular windows as well as arrange them in a few variants, such as floating, docked, or tabbed. In this recipe, you will learn how to open additional windows and place them in suitable areas.

Getting ready

To use this recipe, you just need Microsoft Visual Studio Community 2015 installed, as explained in the previous recipe. No other prerequisites are required.

How to do it...

To arrange windows, you need to perform the following steps:

1. Launch Microsoft Visual Studio Community 2015.

2. To open an additional window, such as **Solution Explorer** or **Class View**, choose a suitable option from the **View** menu, as shown in the following screenshot:

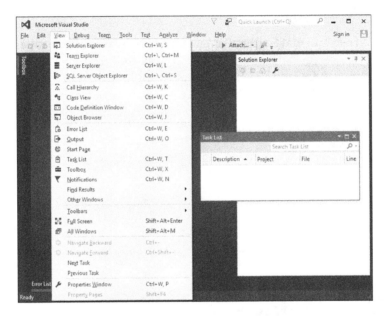

3. To make a window floatable, either drag its title bar and drop it in the empty space, or choose the **Float** option from the context menu of the title bar.

4. To make a window docked, either drag its title bar and drop it in the location specified by the special indicator that appears on the screen, as shown in the following screenshot, or choose the **Dock** option from the context menu of the title bar.

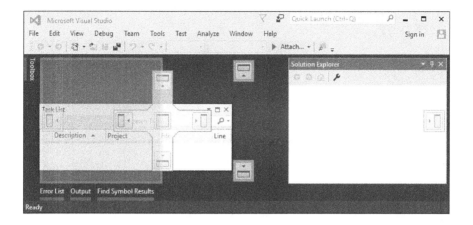

There's more...

It is important to prepare a suitable arrangement of windows that allows you to work with projects in a comfortable way. What is worth mentioning is that the arrangement of windows will automatically change in some special scenarios, such as debugging, and some new windows, strictly related to the given scenario, could appear on the screen. Their aim is to help a developer perform some specific tasks. You will learn how to run the application in the debug mode in the following part of this chapter.

See also

- The *Running the application* recipe

Creating a new project

Once you have the IDE installed, you can proceed to creating a new **project**. A project consists of a set of files that specify, for instance, the configuration of an application, or the design of particular pages, as well as code defining the interaction with the user interface.

Getting ready

To use this recipe, you just need Microsoft Visual Studio Community 2015 installed, as explained earlier in this chapter. No other prerequisites are required.

How to do it...

To create a new project, you need to perform the following steps:

1. Launch Microsoft Visual Studio Community 2015.
2. Navigate to **File** | **New** | **Project...** from the menu.
3. Click on the **Installed** group on the left-hand side. Then, navigate to **Templates** | **Visual C#** | **Windows** | **Universal** from the tree.
4. Select **Blank App (Universal Windows)** on the right-hand side, as shown in the following screenshot.
5. Type a name of the project (**Name**, such as CH01), choose a suitable location (**Location**), as well as type a name of the solution (**Solution name**).

6. Click on **OK**. If an additional window with the possibility of choosing the target and minimum supported platform versions appears, choose proper values and click on **OK**. The project will then be created automatically.

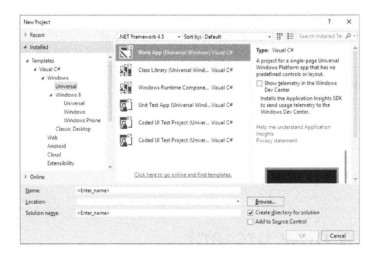

There's more...

It is worth mentioning the structure of the automatically generated solution to learn more about the various files that you will see while developing UWP applications for the Windows 10 platform. You could easily browse through the solution with the **Solution Explorer** window, which you can open by navigating to the **View** | **Solution Explorer** option from the menu.

The automatically generated structure of the solution is shown as follows:

At the top, you have the **CH01** solution that contains only one project, also named **CH01**. Just after its name, there is an indicator that it is the **Universal Windows** project, thus it should work on various devices, such as smartphones, tablets, and desktops.

The first group within the project is named **Properties**. It contains two files, namely `AssemblyInfo.cs` and `Default.rd.xml`. This group provides information about the assembly with your application along with runtime directives. In most cases, you will not need to modify such files on your own.

 You can open the graphical configuration tool by double-clicking on the **Properties** group.

The **References** group performs a very important role because it informs which additional references are used by the application. Such references may include your own class libraries or pre-prepared solutions available for developers. By using packages from the huge number of available ones, it is possible to significantly speed up development as well as limit the chance of introducing bugs while developing such software on your own. What is more, the IDE is supported by the NuGet Package Manager and can find and install packages. You will learn how to use it in the *Creating and using a user control* recipe in `Chapter 2`, *Designing a User Interface*.

The third group is named **Assets** and contains a set of images necessary for the application, such as for the splash screen, tiles, or logo. Of course, you need to prepare suitable graphics before submitting the application to the store.

The `App.xaml` file uses the XAML language. You can use this file to define the resources that will be shared between various pages of the application, not to define them multiple times in various files, as shown in the *Defining a global style* recipe in `Chapter 2`, *Designing a User Interface*. Apart from the `App.xaml` file, there is the `App.xaml.cs` file, which contains C# code handling a few scenarios regarding the application, such as its launching.

The `MainPage.xaml` file is another file with XAML-based content. It represents the first page added automatically to the project. By default, it does not contain any controls, except a grid with a specified background color. You will learn more about this control in `Chapter 2`, *Designing a User Interface*. Similarly, as in the case of the `App.xaml` file, the `MainPage.xaml` file is supported by the dedicated `.xaml.cs` file, namely `MainPage.xaml.cs`. It contains the C# code regarding this page.

Among other files, you can also find `Package.appxmanifest`. It specifies the various properties regarding the application. You will take a look at the various settings available in this file in the *Adjusting the manifest file* recipe in `Chapter 9`, *Testing and Submission*. At the end, it is worth mentioning the `project.json` file with configuration of the project, including dependency to `Microsoft.NETCore.UniversalWindowsPlatform`.

See also

- The *Adding a new page* recipe
- The *Arranging controls in a grid*, *Defining a global style*, and *Creating and using a user control* recipes in `Chapter 2`, *Designing a User Interface*
- The *Creating the view model for a page* recipe in `Chapter 3`, *MVVM and Data Binding*
- The *Adding a project to the Windows Dev Center*, *Associating an application with the store*, and *Adjusting the manifest file* recipes in `Chapter 9`, *Testing and Submission*

Running the application

While developing the application, it is necessary to run it to check whether it operates as expected. You can run the application on various devices, including a development machine, smartphone, or a set of emulators available within the IDE. In this recipe, you will learn how to build and run the application.

Getting ready

To step through this recipe, you only need the automatically generated project.

How to do it...

To run the application either on an emulator or on a real device, you need to perform the following steps:

1. Choose a proper configuration mode, either **Debug** or **Release**, from the drop-down list in the toolbar.

During development, the **Debug** configuration mode is recommended. However, it is also important to test the application in the **Release** mode before submitting it to the store.

2. Click on the small black arrow located in the toolbar, next to the option with the green triangle, as shown in the following image:

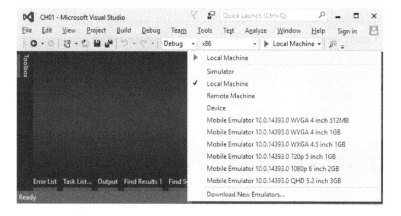

3. Choose a suitable option from the list:

- **Simulator**: This is used to test the application in the dedicated simulator of tablets and desktops with the Windows 10 operating system and different screen sizes, from 7" to 27". It is also possible to easily check various touch modes, namely basic, pinch/zoom, and rotation.
- **Local Machine**: This is used to test the application on the development machine currently used for development.
- **Remote Machine**: This is used to test the application on the external device available in the network.
- **Device**: This is used to test the application on a smartphone directly connected to the development machine.
- **Mobile Emulators**: This is used to test the application on an emulator with various screen resolutions (WVGA, WXGA, 720p, 1080p, or QHD) and memory sizes (from 512 MB to 3 GB).

See also

- The *Utilizing additional features of the emulator* recipe
- The *Breakpoints-based debugging* recipe
- The *Step-by-step debugging* recipe

- The *Executing code while debugging* recipe
- The *Logging information while debugging* recipe
- The *Monitoring the CPU and memory usage* recipe

Adding a new page

Each application contains pages with controls that allow the user to interact with the application. However, only one page is added to the project by default, so in this recipe, you will learn how to add another one.

Getting ready

To step through this recipe, you only need the automatically generated project.

How to do it...

To add a new page to the project, you need to perform the following steps:

1. Right-click on the project node in the **Solution Explorer** window and navigate to the **Add** | **New Item...** option from the context menu. The **Add New Item** window is opened.
2. Click on the **Installed** section on the left-hand side. Then, select **Visual C#** | **XAML**. Choose **Blank Page** on the right-hand side, as shown in the next screenshot.

3. Type a suitable name (**Name**) for the `.xaml` file, representing the new page. The `.xaml.cs` file will be generated automatically. As an example, you could set the name as `AboutPage.xaml`.

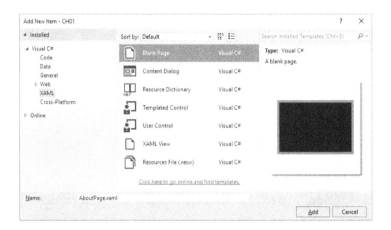

There's more...

The files regarding the default page, both `.xaml` and `.xaml.cs`, are automatically added to the main directory. However, you do not need to place the files that represent the page here. You could locate such files in a dedicated directory, such as **Views**. You will learn how to create a new directory as well as place the `.xaml` and `.xaml.cs` files there in the *Creating the view model for a page* recipe in `Chapter 3`, *MVVM and Data Binding*.

See also

- The *Placing a control* recipe
- The *Navigating between pages* recipe
- The *Passing data between pages* recipe
- The *Changing a default page* recipe
- The *Creating the view model for a page* recipe in `Chapter 3`, *MVVM and Data Binding*

Placing a control

The automatically generated page does not contain any content that could be interesting to a user. For this reason, it is important to learn how to place a new control.

By default, you have access to many controls that are available out of the box, such as a button, textbox, checkbox, list view, progress bar, calendar, or web view. Of course, these are only examples of the available controls. You can browse the full list in the **Toolbox** window within the IDE.

In this recipe, you will learn how to add the first button to the page.

Getting ready

To step through this recipe, you only need the automatically generated project.

How to do it...

To place a control on the page, you need to perform the following steps:

1. Double-click on the `MainPage.xaml` file in the **Solution Explorer** window.
2. Open the **Toolbox** window by navigating to **View** | **Toolbox** from the menu.

3. Drag and drop the **Button** item from the **Toolbox** window to the graphical designer in the `MainPage.xaml` file. The control is now added, and you can easily adjust its location and size, as shown in the following image:

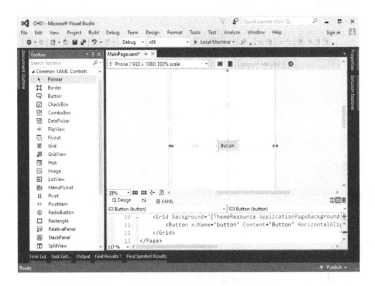

How it works...

Adding controls by dragging them from the **Toolbox** window causes the creation of a suitable part of the XAML code. In the case of the exemplary button, the following code is generated automatically:

```
<Page
 x:Class="CH01.MainPage"
 xmlns="http://schemas.microsoft.com/winfx/2006/xaml/presentation"
 xmlns:x="http://schemas.microsoft.com/winfx/2006/xaml"
 xmlns:local="using:CH01"
 xmlns:d="http://schemas.microsoft.com/expression/blend/2008"
 xmlns:mc="http://schemas.openxmlformats.org/markup-
           compatibility/2006"
 mc:Ignorable="d">
    <Grid Background="{ThemeResource
          ApplicationPageBackgroundThemeBrush}">
        <Button
         x:Name="button"
         Content="Button"
         HorizontalAlignment="Left"
         Margin="164,242,0,0"
```

```
        VerticalAlignment="Top" />
    </Grid>
</Page>
```

As you can see, the Button control is added within Grid. Its name is set to button (x:Name) and its content is set to the Button text (Content). Its location within the grid is specified by margins (Margin), given in the following order: left (164 pixels), top (242 pixels), right (0 pixels), and bottom (0 pixels). What is more, horizontal and vertical alignments are set (HorizontalAlignment and VerticalAlignment, respectively).

 Try to adjust the values of Margin, HorizontalAlignment, and VerticalAlignment on your own to get to know the impact of such properties on the button layout. You will learn more about various ways to place controls in the next chapter.

There's more...

The graphical editor available in Microsoft Visual Studio Community 2015 has a set of really useful features, such as the presentation of a UI for various screen resolutions. It is beneficial to learn more about such features in order to design a UI in a more efficient way.

See also

- The *Handling events* recipe
- The *Adding a button, Adding a text block, Adding a textbox, Adding a password box, Adding a checkbox, Adding a combobox, Adding a listbox, Adding an image, Adding controls programmatically*, and *Creating and using a user control* recipes in Chapter 2, *Designing a User Interface*

Handling events

Apart from adding controls to the page, it is necessary to introduce interaction with them, such as performing some actions after clicking on a button or choosing an item from a drop-down list. In this recipe, you will learn how to handle the event of pressing the button.

Getting ready

To use this recipe, you need the project from the previous recipe. It should contain the `MainPage.xaml` file with the added button.

How to do it...

To handle the `Click` event, you need to perform the following steps:

1. Double-click on the `MainPage.xaml` file in the **Solution Explorer** window.

2. To generate a method that handles the situation of the button being pressed, double-click on the added button. Alternatively, click on the button (either in a graphical designer or the XAML code) and then double-click on the **Click** field in the **Properties** window with the **Event handlers for the selected element** option (the lightning icon) selected, as shown in the following screenshot:

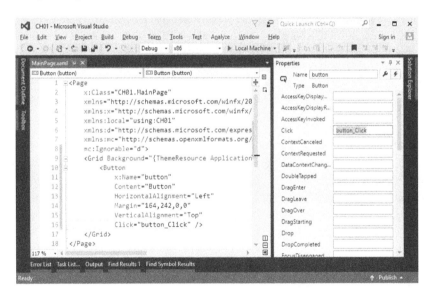

How it works...

Generating the method for handling the event of the button being clicked causes a modification, which is automatically introduced in both the `MainPage.xaml` and `MainPage.xaml.cs` files.

In the first file, with the XAML code describing the UI of the page, the `Click` property is automatically added to the `Button` element. It specifies the name of the method that is called when the user clicks on the button. The exemplary code is as follows:

```
<Page (...)>
    <Grid (...)>
        <Button
         x:Name="button"
         Content="Button"
         HorizontalAlignment="Left"
         Margin="164,242,0,0"
         VerticalAlignment="Top"
         Click="button_Click" />
    </Grid>
</Page>
```

It is worth mentioning that the `button_Click` method must exist in the `MainPage` class (name set as `x:Class` in the `Page` element). This method is also automatically generated in the `MainPage.xaml.cs` file, as follows:

```
private void button_Click(object sender, RoutedEventArgs e) { }
```

The method has a name that contains the name of the button (`button`) as well as information about the kind of event (`Click`). It has two parameters:

- `sender`: This is an object that represents the clicked element, which you can cast to `Button` as `(Button)sender`
- `e`: This represents the additional arguments regarding the operation

To specify operations that should be performed after pressing the button, you just need to add suitable C# code as the body of the `button_Click` method.

 You could easily jump from the editor with the XAML code to the C#-based method definition by right-clicking its name defined in the `.xaml` file (within `Click`) and choosing **Go To Definition** from the context menu. Another solution is to click on such a name and press *F12*.

This way of handling the button being pressed is not the only possible one. Later in the book, you will learn how to use the data binding mechanism together with commands and the MVVM design pattern to improve the solution.

See also

- The *Placing a control* recipe
- The *Creating the view model for a page* and *Introducing bindings and commands* recipes in `Chapter 3`, *MVVM and Data Binding*

Navigating between pages

It is quite difficult to imagine an application with only one page. Thus, it is crucial to know how to navigate from one page to another. In this recipe, you will learn how to navigate to another page after pressing the button as well as how to go back to the previous page after pressing the button on the other page.

Getting ready

To complete this recipe, you need the project with two pages, represented by the `MainPage` and `AboutPage` classes. Let's imagine that the first page operates as a main menu of the application with a set of buttons. After clicking on each of them, a user should be navigated to a particular page, such as with information about the company, with a list of products, or with contact data.

As an example, the `Button` control should be added to both the pages, namely `MainPage` and `AboutPage`. However, they should present different content, such as **About us** (in `MainPage`) and **Go back** (in `AboutPage`), as graphically explained as follows:

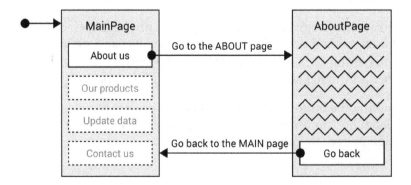

How to do it...

To prepare an example that shows how to navigate between pages, you need to perform the following steps:

1. To navigate from `MainPage` to `AboutPage`, modify the code of the `button_Click` method in the `MainPage.xaml.cs` file, as follows:

```
private void button_Click(object sender, RoutedEventArgs e)
{
    Frame.Navigate(typeof(AboutPage));
}
```

2. To go back to the previous page from `AboutPage`, modify the code of the `button_Click` method in the `AboutPage.xaml.cs` file, as follows:

```
private void button_Click(object sender, RoutedEventArgs e)
{
    if (Frame.CanGoBack)
    {
        Frame.GoBack();
    }
}
```

How it works...

Navigation to another page is possible using the `Frame` property of the `Frame` type. It provides developers with a few methods, including `Navigate` and `GoBack`.

The first method (`Navigate`) is used to navigate the user to another page with or without additional parameters (take a look at the next recipe), while the other (`GoBack`) allows the user to go back to the previous page. In such a case, it is recommended that you check whether you can go back to the previous page by verifying whether the `CanGoBack` property has a value equal to `true`.

See also

- The *Passing data between pages* recipe
- The *Handling the back button* recipe

- The *Changing a default page* recipe
- The *Modifying the back stack* recipe

Passing data between pages

It is often necessary to pass some data from one page to another. It can be accomplished easily using another version of the `Navigate` method, called on the `Frame` property, as explained in this recipe.

Getting ready

To complete this recipe, you need the project with two pages, represented by `MainPage` and `ProductsPage` classes. The first page should contain the button with the **Our products** caption, while the other–the list of products and categories as well as the **Go back** button. The structure of pages is presented as follows:

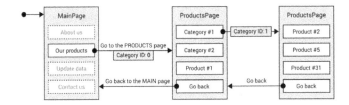

It is worth mentioning that the page with products requires an identifier of the category, which should be presented. Such an identifier needs to be passed as a parameter. To show products and subcategories from the root category, 0 is passed. If you want to open a particular category, its identifier is passed instead, as shown on the right-hand side of the image.

How to do it...

To prepare an example that shows how to pass data between pages, you need to perform the following steps:

1. To pass an integer value (namely 0) from `MainPage` to `ProductsPage`, modify the code of the `button_Click` method in the `MainPage.xaml.cs` file, as follows:

```
private void button_Click(object sender, RoutedEventArgs e)
{
    Frame.Navigate(typeof(ProductsPage), 0);
}
```

2. To read the passed integer value, add the `OnNavigatedTo` method to the `ProductsPage.xaml.cs` file, as follows:

```
protected override void OnNavigatedTo(
    NavigationEventArgs e)
{
    base.OnNavigatedTo(e);
    int categoryId = (int)e.Parameter;
    List<string> products = GetProductsByCategory(categoryId);
}
```

 To keep simplicity of the example, the scenario of showing a list of subcategories and products from a given category is not presented. If you want to develop it, you can use one of the items controls, as described in Chapter 3, *MVVM and Data Binding*.

How it works...

Navigating to another page by passing a value is possible in a way that is similar to the approach presented in the previous recipe. However, in such a case, you should use another version of the `Navigate` method with two parameters. The second is an object that is passed to another page. Of course, it could be an object of any type, not only an integer value as shown in the example.

A bit more explanation is necessary in the case of reading the parameter in the target page. To do so, you need to override the `OnNavigatedTo` method, which has a parameter that is an instance of the `NavigationEventArgs` class. Such a class contains the `Parameter` property. However, it is not strongly typed, so you need to cast it to a suitable type, such as `int`, as shown in the following code snippet:

```
int categoryId = (int)e.Parameter;
```

There's more...

Apart from passing an integer, a floating point, or even string values, it is often necessary and convenient to pass more complex data, such as instances of user defined classes, between pages. This task can be achieved with the same approach as described in detail in the current recipe. Of course, you should not forget about specifying the values of particular properties of the class instance before passing it to another page as well as casting the parameter to a proper type in the code of the target page.

See also

- The *Navigating between pages* recipe
- The *Handling the back button* recipe
- The *Changing a default page* recipe
- The *Modifying the back stack* recipe

Handling the back button

The UWP applications can be run on various devices that differ, for example, by availability of the back button. As you can see, such a button exists in the case of smartphones, but it is not available for tablets and desktops. Fortunately, it is possible to use the `SystemNavigationManager` class to handle pressing the back button on a smartphone to navigate to the previous page in the application. What is more, the mechanism allows you to present the additional back button, at the top of the window, in case of a tablet or desktop-based version. You will learn how to do it in the current recipe.

Getting ready

To complete this recipe, you need the project with two pages, represented by the `MainPage` and `AboutPage` classes. Let's imagine that the first page operates as the main menu of the application with a set of menu items. After clicking on the first of them, the user should be navigated to the page with information about the company.

How to do it…

To handle the back button on a smartphone, as well as present an additional back button on tablets and desktops, you need to perform the following steps:

1. Specify the visibility of the additional back button (on devices without such a button), as well as handle an event of using it. To do so, modify the code of the OnLaunched method in the App.xaml.cs file, as shown as follows:

```
protected override void OnLaunched(
    LaunchActivatedEventArgs e)
{ (...)
    if (rootFrame == null)
    {
        rootFrame = new Frame(); (...)
        Window.Current.Content = rootFrame;
        rootFrame.Navigated += (s, ev) =>
        {
            SystemNavigationManager.GetForCurrentView()
                .AppViewBackButtonVisibility =
                    ((Frame)s).CanGoBack ?
                    AppViewBackButtonVisibility.Visible :
                    AppViewBackButtonVisibility.Collapsed;
        };
        SystemNavigationManager.GetForCurrentView()
            .BackRequested += OnBackRequested;
    } (...)
}
```

2. Go back to the previous page when the back button is used, by adding the OnBackRequested method in the App.xaml.cs file, as shown as follows:

```
private void OnBackRequested(object sender,
    BackRequestedEventArgs e)
{
    Frame rootFrame = (Frame)Window.Current.Content;
    if (rootFrame.CanGoBack)
    {
        e.Handled = true;
        rootFrame.GoBack();
    }
}
```

How it works...

By adding the necessary code directly in the `App.xaml.cs` file, you do not need to specify the same operations in all `.xaml.cs` files representing pages. The required lines of code are not very complicated and are explained in the following part of this recipe.

First of all, you handle the `Navigated` event on an instance representing the frame (the `roomFrame` variable of the `Frame` type). When a user navigates to some page, the visibility of the back button is specified. Of course, it should be visible only when it is possible to go back from the current page, as specified in the following part of code:

```
SystemNavigationManager.GetForCurrentView()
    .AppViewBackButtonVisibility = ((Frame)s).CanGoBack ?
        AppViewBackButtonVisibility.Visible :
        AppViewBackButtonVisibility.Collapsed;
```

Then, you handle an event of the back button being clicked, namely `BackRequested`. Of course, it supports a scenario of both pressing the hardware-based version and clicking on the additional back button added in the top-left corner of the window, as presented in the following screenshot of mobile and desktop-based versions:

When a user clicks on the back button, the `OnBackRequested` method is called. Within it, you check whether it is possible to go back from the current page. In such a case, you indicate that the event is handled and call the `GoBack` method. The operation of such a method is explained in detail in the *Navigating between pages* recipe.

See also

- The *Navigating between pages* recipe
- The *Passing data between pages* recipe
- The *Changing a default page* recipe
- The *Modifying the back stack* recipe

Changing a default page

By default, the automatically added page is shown after you launch the application. However, you may want to start with another page. Of course, such a change is possible and does not require significant modifications. You will learn how to do it in this recipe.

Getting ready

To step through this recipe, you need a project with two pages, represented by the `MainPage` and `DefaultPage` classes. Of course, you should manually add the second one.

How to do it...

To change a default page, shown when the application is launched, you need to perform the following steps:

1. Open the `App.xaml.cs` file by expanding the `App.xaml` node in the **Solution Explorer** window and double-clicking on `App.xaml.cs`.
2. Take the line in the `OnLaunched` method (line #75):

    ```
    rootFrame.Navigate(typeof(MainPage), e.Arguments);
    ```

3. Change this line to the following:

```
rootFrame.Navigate(typeof(DefaultPage), e.Arguments);
```

How it works...

Changing the default page requires a small modification in the `App.xaml.cs` file, in the part related to the launching of the application. As you can see, such a part also uses the `Navigate` method (on the `Frame` instance), so changing the default page requires just a modification of its first parameter.

There's more...

It is also possible to conditionally change the default page, for instance, depending on a value that indicates whether the user is currently logged in. The exemplary line of code is shown as follows:

```
rootFrame.Navigate(isLogged ? typeof(UserPage) :
    typeof(AnonymousPage), e.Arguments);
```

In this example, if the user is logged in (`isLogged` equals to `true`), the user will be navigated to `UserPage`. Otherwise, `AnonymousPage` is used instead.

See also

- The *Navigating between pages* recipe
- The *Passing data between pages* recipe
- The *Handling the back button* recipe
- The *Modifying the back stack* recipe

Modifying the back stack

While navigating from one page to another, the previous page is pushed to the **back stack** to allow the user to go back. However, in some scenarios, it could be necessary to programmatically read the back stack in order to know what the previously visited pages are. What is more, you can manually modify the back stack, for instance, to go back two pages instead of one. In this recipe, you will learn how to do it.

As an example, you will analyze the scenario presented in the following image:

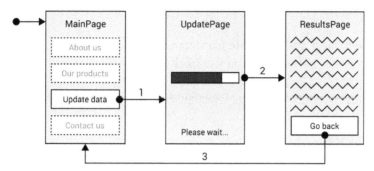

On the dashboard (`MainPage`), the user clicks on the **Update data** button. It navigates the user to `UpdatePage` with the progress bar informing him/her about the progress of downloading necessary data. As soon as the download process is completed, the user is navigated to `ResultsPage` with the **Go back** button. After pressing it, the user should go back directly to the dashboard, not to the previous page (`UpdatePage`).

Getting ready

To use this recipe, you need a project with three pages, namely `MainPage`, `UpdatePage`, and `ResultsPage`. On the first, you should place the **Update data** button navigating to `UpdatePage`. Just as an example, the `UpdatePage` could be equipped with the button, which will navigate the user to the last page. On `ResultsPage`, let's place the **Go back** button. You should have an empty method handling the event of clicking on this button. Its code will be modified later in this recipe.

How to do it...

To modify the back stack to omit one page while going back, you need to perform the following steps:

1. Modify the body of the method handling clicking on the **Go back** button in the `ResultsPage.xaml.cs` file, as follows:

```
if (Frame.BackStackDepth > 1)
{
    Frame.BackStack.RemoveAt(Frame.BackStack.Count - 1);
}
```

```
if (Frame.CanGoBack)
{
    Frame.GoBack();
}
```

2. Run the project and navigate from `MainPage` to `UpdatePage` and to `ResultsPage`. Then, click on **Go back** and ensure that you have been navigated directly to `MainPage`, not to `UpdatePage`.

How it works...

At the beginning, you check whether the back stack has a suitable number of elements, which is at least two. Only in such a case, you are able to skip one entry while going back. If the mentioned condition is satisfied, the last entry from the back stack is removed using the following line of code:

```
Frame.BackStack.RemoveAt(Frame.BackStack.Count - 1);
```

Then, it is necessary to go back using the `GoBack` method, already explained in one of the previous recipes in this chapter.

There's more...

The back stack performs a really important role while navigating between pages within an application. For this reason, it is beneficial to learn how it works and what information is stored in the back stack. You can check this with the following code snippet:

```
for (int i = 0; i < Frame.BackStack.Count; i++)
{
    PageStackEntry entry = Frame.BackStack[i];
    Type pageType = entry.SourcePageType;
    object pageParameter = entry.Parameter;
}
```

This code fragment iterates through the back stack using the `for` loop. In each iteration, you get a `PageStackEntry` instance (named `entry`) that contains various information about a visited page, such as its type and parameter.

 You can display a value while debugging using the code presented in the *Logging information while debugging* recipe.

In the exemplary scenario, analyzed in this recipe, the back stack contains two entries: regarding `MainPage` (index 0) and `UpdatePage` (index 1).

See also

- The *Navigating between pages* recipe
- The *Passing data between pages* recipe
- The *Handling the back button* recipe
- The *Changing a default page* recipe
- The *Modifying the back stack* recipe

Utilizing additional features of the emulator

The provided emulators are equipped with some additional features that simplify the testing of applications. In this recipe, you will learn how to use such features of the smartphone-based emulators available within the IDE.

Getting ready

To complete this recipe, you need an automatically generated project.

How to do it...

To utilize additional features provided by the emulator of a smartphone, you need to perform the following steps:

1. Select `Fit to Screen` to automatically adjust the size of the emulator. You could specify zoom directly using the `Zoom` option.
2. Use the `Rotate Left` and `Rotate Right` options to rotate the emulator, either counterclockwise or clockwise, respectively.
3. Check various input modes by clicking on the small icons located on the right-hand side of the emulator, such as:
    - `Single Point Mouse Input`
    - `Single Point Touch Input`
    - `Multi-touch Input`

4. Run the application in **Mobile Emulator (…) WXGA 4.5 inch 1GB**. Then, wait until the application is loaded.

5. Click on the `Tools` option (double arrow) to open the window with the additional features available within the emulator, which are organized into tabs, such as:

   - **Accelerometer**: This is used to simulate data from the accelerometer sensor
   - **Location**: This is used to simulate the current GPS location
   - **Screenshot**: This is used to capture and save the screenshot from the emulator
   - **Network** : This is used to enable or disable the network for an emulator as well as to specify the network speed and signal strength
   - **SD Card**: This uses the local folder as an SD card within the phone
   - **Checkpoints**: This is used to manage the saving states of the emulator
   - **Optional Settings**: This is used to mark which hardware should be emulated
   - **Notifications**: This is used to simulate push notifications sent to the application
   - **NFC**: This is used to emulate NFC-based scenarios

See also

- The *Running the application* recipe
- The *Creating a unit test* and *Running a set of tests* recipes in `Chapter 9`, *Testing and Submission*

Breakpoints-based debugging

Unfortunately, sometimes the prepared application does not work as expected. In such a case, it is useful to debug the solution to see how the application is executed. There are various ways of debugging, such as performing step-by-step execution or using breakpoints to stop the execution of a particular line of code. In this recipe, you will learn how to use both unconditional and conditional breakpoints.

Getting ready

To complete this recipe, you need the project with two pages, represented by the `MainPage` and `ProductsPage` classes. It is necessary to pass a category identifier while navigating from `MainPage` to `ProductsPage`.

How to do it...

To perform the breakpoints-based debugging, you need to follow the given steps:

1. Open the `ProductsPage.xaml.cs` file.
2. To place an unconditional breakpoint, click on the gray margin on the left-hand side of the code line or click on the code line and press *F9*. As an example, you could place a breakpoint in the following line:

   ```
   categoryName = categoryNames[categoryId];
   ```

3. Run the application in the emulator in the **Debug** mode by pressing *F5* or by navigating to **Debug** | **Start Debugging** from the menu.

4. Navigate to the second page. The execution of the application should be stopped on the line of code with a breakpoint. Such a line is marked in the IDE with the yellow background, as shown as follows:

```
CH01 - ProductsPage.xaml.cs                                              —  □  ×

ProductsPage.xaml.cs  ⊸  ×
C# CH01                              ▾ ⁴⁵ CH01.ProductsPage        ▾ ⁰⁺ OnNavigatedTo(NavigationEventArgs e)  ▾
   14                 protected override void OnNavigatedTo(NavigationEventArgs e)
   15                 {
   16                     Dictionary<int, string> categoryNames = new Dictionary<int, string>()
   17                     {
   18                         [0] = "All products",
   19                         [1] = "Food & drinks",
   20                         [2] = "Sport",
   21                         [3] = "Hobby"
   22                     };
   23                     int categoryId = (int)e.Parameter;
   24                     string categoryName = "-";
   25                     if (categoryNames.ContainsKey(categoryId))
   26                     {
 ◑ 27                         categoryName = categoryNames[categoryId];
   28                     }
   29                 }
   30             }
   31         }
117 %  ▾
```

5. Place the mouse over `categoryId` to show a popup with the current value of the variable.

6. To stop the execution of the application conditionally, right-click on the image of the breakpoint and choose the **Conditions...** option from the context menu. Then, specify the condition in the **Breakpoint Settings** window by providing the expression that must be evaluated to `true` to stop the execution, such as:

```
categoryId > 0
```

7. Run the application in the emulator and see that its execution is stopped because the condition associated with the breakpoint is satisfied, as shown in the following screenshot:

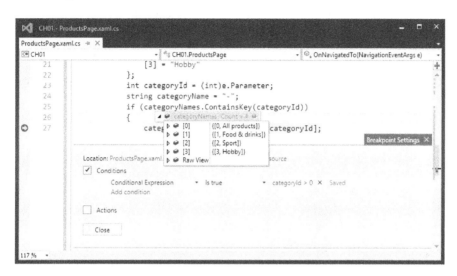

See also

- The *Step-by-step debugging* recipe
- The *Executing code while debugging* recipe
- The *Logging information while debugging* recipe
- The *Creating a unit test* and *Running a set of tests* recipes in `Chapter 9`, *Testing and Submission*

Step-by-step debugging

Debugging with breakpoints is a powerful technique that you can use to find a source of the problem in your applications. However, it is also useful to check its execution line by line. Of course, such a task can be accomplished by placing a breakpoint in each line, but this may be cumbersome for a developer. For this reason, this recipe will show you how to debug the application with step-by-step debugging.

Getting ready

To complete this recipe, you need the project with two pages, represented by the `MainPage` and `ProductsPage` classes. It is necessary to pass a category identifier while navigating from `MainPage` to `ProductsPage`. You should start the debugging of the project and stop it at any breakpoint.

How to do it...

To perform the step-by-step debugging, you need to perform the following steps:

1. To execute a single line and stop in the following line, press *F10* or click on the **Step Over** icon in the toolbar. As a result, the next line will be marked with the yellow background, as shown in the following screenshot.
2. To step into a method that is called within the line, where debugging has stopped, press *F11* or click on the **Step Into** icon in the toolbar.
3. To go to the line where the cursor is currently located, press *Ctrl* + *F10* or choose the **Run To Cursor** option from the context menu of the line with the cursor.

There's more...

The values of variables can be checked in a few ways, such as by placing the cursor over the name of the variable. However, when you want to see the values of a few variables in the following iterations within a loop, it is much more convenient to *pin* tooltips with their current values so they are automatically refreshed in each iteration. You can *pin* the tooltip by placing the cursor over the name of the variable and then pressing the pin icon. The exemplary result is shown in the preceding screenshot.

See also

- The *Breakpoint-based debugging* recipe
- The *Executing code while debugging* recipe
- The *Logging information while debugging* recipe
- The *Creating a unit test* and *Running a set of tests* recipes in `Chapter 9`, *Testing and Submission*

Executing code while debugging

When the execution of the application is stopped, you can easily check the values of the variables by moving the cursor over them. However, sometimes it may be useful to execute some parts of code, such as checking the length of a string. In such a case, you do not need to modify the application code and add some additional variables because you can use the **Immediate Window** feature that allows you to execute particular lines of code and present results. In this recipe, you will learn how to do this.

Getting ready

To complete this recipe, you need the project with two pages, represented by the `MainPage` and `ProductsPage` classes. It is necessary to pass a category identifier while navigating from `MainPage` to `ProductsPage`. You should start the debugging of the project and stop it at any breakpoint.

How to do it...

To execute some code while debugging, you need to perform the following steps:

1. Open **Immediate Window** by navigating to **Debug** | **Window** | **Immediate** from the menu.
2. Type an expression in **Immediate Window** and press Enter. The calculated result will be presented in the next line, as shown in the following screenshot:

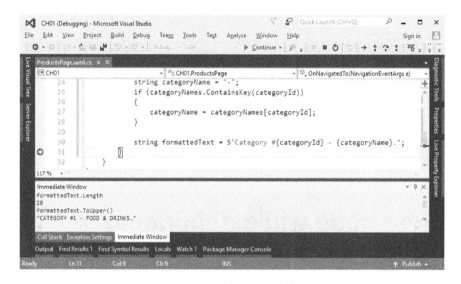

How it works...

The example from the screenshot you just saw shows a result of the following expression in **Immediate Window**:

```
formattedText.Length
```

It is evaluated using the values of the variables from the current state of debugging. In the example, the `formattedText` variable is equal to `Category #1 - Food & drinks.`, thus the string has 28 characters and such a result is shown in the window.

The next expression is as follows:

```
formattedText.ToUpper()
```

It presents the current value of the `formattedText` variable, but in the uppercase version.

See also

- The *Breakpoints-based debugging* recipe
- The *Step-by-step debugging* recipe
- The *Logging information while debugging* recipe
- The *Creating a unit test* and *Running a set of tests* recipes in Chapter 9, *Testing and Submission*

Logging information while debugging

Sometimes, it is inconvenient to place many breakpoints in the code to see how the application, or its particular module, is being executed. In such a case, it is a good idea to log various information and present it to the developer in the IDE in real time.

In this recipe, you will learn how to perform such a task using the `Debug` class from the `System.Diagnostics` namespace as well as present logs in the IDE within the **Output** window.

Getting ready

To complete this recipe, you need the project with two pages, represented by the `MainPage` and `ProductsPage` classes. It is necessary to pass a category identifier while navigating from `MainPage` to `ProductsPage`.

How to do it...

To prepare an example that shows how to log some data while debugging, you need to perform the following steps:

1. Open the `ProductsPage.xaml.cs` file.

2. To log information after clicking on the button, but before coming back to the dashboard, modify the code of the `Button_Click` method, as follows:

```
private void Button_Click(object sender, RoutedEventArgs e)
{
    Debug.WriteLine("Coming back to the dashboard");
    Frame.GoBack();
}
```

Do not forget to add the `using` statement for the `System.Diagnostics` namespace, using the following line of code:

`using System.Diagnostics;`

The IDE is equipped with a really nice feature that allows you to automatically insert a missing `using` statement. To do so, just left-click on the name of the unrecognized type and press *Ctrl + .* (dot). In the pop-up window, you can find an option to automatically add a proper `using` statement.

3. To add conditional logging, activated only if the associated Boolean expression is evaluated to `true`, modify the code of the `OnNavigatedTo` method in the `ProductsPage.xaml.cs` file, as follows:

```
protected override void OnNavigatedTo(
    NavigationEventArgs e)
{ (...)
    Debug.WriteLine($"Presenting a list of products
        from category #{categoryId}");
    Debug.WriteLineIf(categoryId < 0, $"Incorrect category
        identifier, namely {categoryId}");
}
```

5. Start debugging the application.
6. Open the **Output** window by navigating to **Debug | Windows | Output** from the menu. Then, click on the button in the emulator to see how the logs appear in the **Output** window. The exemplary result is shown as follows:

```
Presenting a list of products from category #1
Coming back to the dashboard.
```

See also

- The *Breakpoints-based debugging* recipe
- The *Step-by-step debugging* recipe
- The *Executing code while debugging* recipe
- The *Creating a unit test* and *Running a set of tests* recipes in `Chapter 9`, *Testing and Submission*

Monitoring the CPU and memory usage

Applications, even for smartphones, can perform operations that intensively use resources. For this reason, it is possible that an application behaves differentially on various devices. This could lead to some problems with the operation, such as a poor user experience. With the usage of Microsoft Visual Studio Community 2015, a developer could measure CPU and memory usage in real time while running the application. In this recipe, you will learn how to use such a mechanism in your projects.

Getting ready

To complete this recipe, you need an automatically generated project.

How to do it...

To monitor the CPU and memory usage while debugging the application, you need to perform the following steps:

1. Start debugging the application.
2. Open the **Diagnostic Tools** window by navigating to **Debug** | **Show Diagnostic Tools** from the menu.

3. Observe the process memory and CPU usage in charts, shown as follows:

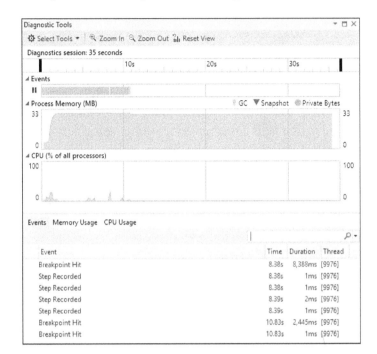

How it works...

The **Diagnostic Tools** window presents a set of useful information, not only about the used MB of the memory and percentage of CPU used. It also informs about moments when **Garbage Collector** (**GC**) is launched. What is more, you can see some steps of debugging, such as hitting a breakpoint.

It is really important to check the execution of the application on the slowest supported device to ensure that it will not have any problems with performance. Reaching the maximum acceptable values of CPU or memory usage is a sign that the code needs to be optimized. By modifying the code and checking its performance in an iterative way, you will see the impact of your changes on the final result.

2
Designing a User Interface

In this chapter, we will cover the following recipes:

- Adding a button
- Adding a text block
- Adding a textbox
- Adding a password box
- Adding a checkbox
- Adding a combobox
- Adding a listbox
- Adding an image
- Adding controls programmatically
- Arranging controls vertically
- Arranging controls horizontally
- Arranging controls in a scrollable view
- Defining a page-limited style
- Defining a global style
- Applying styles programmatically
- Arranging controls in a grid
- Arranging controls in absolute positions
- Choosing date and time
- Adding icons to app bars
- Creating and using a user control
- Presenting a message dialog
- Adjusting design based on the device type
- Localizing content in XAML

- Localizing content programmatically
- Forcing the current language

Introduction

In the previous chapter, you learned how to start your adventure of developing applications for smartphones, tablets, and desktops running on the Windows 10 operating system. In the next step, it is crucial to get to know how to design particular pages within the application to provide the user with a convenient user interface that works smoothly on screens with various resolutions.

Fortunately, designing the user interface is really simple using the XAML language and Microsoft Visual Studio Community 2015. You can use a set of predefined controls, such as textboxes, checkboxes, images, or buttons. What is more, you can easily arrange controls in various variants, either vertically, horizontally, or in a grid. This is not all, because you can prepare your own controls that could be placed on many pages within the application. It is also possible to prepare dedicated versions of particular pages for various **device families**, such as mobile or desktop.

You have already learned how to place a new control on a page by dragging it from the **Toolbox** window. In this chapter, you will see how to add a control and specify its appearance directly in the XAML language, as well as how to programmatically handle controls. Thus, some controls could either change their appearance, or the new controls could be added to the page when some specific conditions are met.

Another important question is how to provide the user with a consistent user interface within the whole application. While developing solutions for the Windows 10 operating system, such a task could be easily accomplished by applying styles. In this chapter, you will learn how to specify both page-limited and application-limited styles that could be applied to either particular controls or to all the controls of a given type.

In the remaining part of the chapter, you will see how to introduce more interaction with the user. By using simple code snippets, you can easily allow a user to choose a date or time in a convenient way, as well as present message dialogs, for example, confirming some important operations.

At the end, you could ask yourself a simple question, *Why should I restrict access to my new awesome application only to people who know a particular language in which the user interface is prepared?* You should not! And in this chapter, you will also learn how to localize content and present it in various languages. Of course, the localization will use additional resource files, so translations could be prepared not by a developer, but by a specialist who knows the given language well.

Adding a button

When developing applications, you can use a set of predefined controls among which a button exists. It allows you to handle the event of pressing the button by a user. Of course, the appearance of the button can be easily adjusted, for instance, by choosing a proper background or border, as you will see in this recipe.

The button can present textual content. However, it can also be adjusted to the user's needs, for instance, by choosing a proper color or font size. This is not all, because the content shown on the button does not have to be only textual. For instance, you can prepare a button that presents an image instead of text, text over an image, or text located next to the small icon that visually informs about the operation. Such modifications are presented in the following part of this recipe as well.

Getting ready

To step through this recipe, you only need the automatically generated project.

How to do it...

To add a button to the page and handle the `Click` event, perform the following steps:

1. Place a button on the page and adjust its appearance by modifying the content of the `MainPage.xaml` file as follows:

```
<Page (...)>
    <Grid (...)>
        <Button
            Content="Click me!"
            Foreground="#0a0a0a"
            FontWeight="SemiBold"
            FontSize="20"
            FontStyle="Italic"
```

```
                    Background="LightBlue"
                    BorderBrush="RoyalBlue"
                    BorderThickness="5"
                    Padding="20 10"
                    VerticalAlignment="Center"
                    HorizontalAlignment="Center" />
        </Grid>
    </Page>
```

2. Generate a method for handling the event of clicking on the button by pressing the button (either in a graphical designer or in the XAML code) and double-clicking on the **Click** field in the **Properties** window with the **Event handlers for the selected element** option (the lightning icon) selected. The automatically generated method is as follows:

```
private void Button_Click(object sender,
    RoutedEventArgs e) { }
```

How it works...

In the example, the Button control is placed within a grid. It is centered both vertically and horizontally, as specified by the VerticalAlignment and HorizontalAlignment properties that are set to Center. The background color (Background) is set to LightBlue. The border is specified by two properties, namely BorderBrush and BorderThickness. The first property chooses its color (RoyalBlue), while the other represents its thickness (5 pixels). What is more, the padding (Padding) is set to 20 pixels on the left and right-hand side, and 10 pixels at the top and bottom.

The button presents the **Click me!** text defined as a value of the Content property. The text is shown in the color #0a0a0a with semi-bold italic font with size 20, as specified by the Foreground, FontWeight, FontStyle, and FontSize properties, respectively.

If you run the application, you should see the following result:

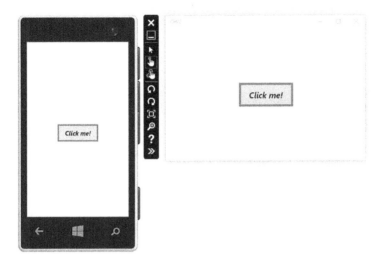

It is worth mentioning that the IDE supports a *live* preview of the designed page. So, you can modify the values of particular properties and have real-time feedback regarding the target appearance directly in the graphical designer. It is a really great feature that does not require you to run the application to see the impact of each introduced change.

There's more...

As already mentioned, even the Button control has many advanced features. For example, you could place an image instead of text, present text over an image, or show an icon next to the text. Such scenarios are presented and explained in this section.

First, let's focus on replacing the textual content with an image by modifying the XAML code that represents the Button control as follows:

```
<Button
    MaxWidth="300"
    VerticalAlignment="Center"
    HorizontalAlignment="Center">
    <Image Source="/Assets/Image.jpg" />
</Button>
```

Of course, you should also add the `Image.jpg` file to the `Assets` directory. To do so, navigate to **Add | Existing Item...** from the context menu of the `Assets` node in the **Solution Explorer** window, as follows:

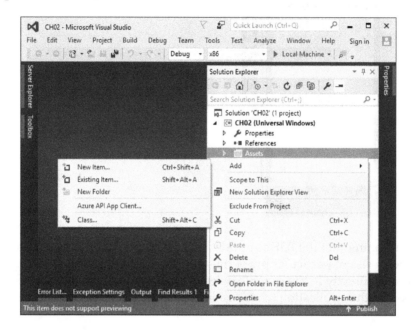

In the **Add Existing Item** window, choose the `Image.jpg` file and click on the **Add** button.

 As you can see, the example uses the `Image` control. In this recipe, no more information about such a control is presented because it is the topic of one of the next recipes, namely *Adding an image*.

If you run the application, you should see a result similar to the following:

The second additional example presents a button with text over an image. To do so, let's modify the XAML code as follows:

```
<Button
    MaxWidth="300"
    VerticalAlignment="Center"
    HorizontalAlignment="Center">
    <Grid>
        <Image Source="/Assets/Image.jpg" />
        <TextBlock
            Text="Click me!"
            Foreground="White"
            FontWeight="Bold"
            FontSize="28"
            VerticalAlignment="Bottom"
            HorizontalAlignment="Center"
            Margin="10" />
    </Grid>
</Button>
```

You will find more information about the `Grid`, `Image`, and `TextBlock` controls in the next recipes, namely *Arranging controls in a grid* and *Adding an image*. For this reason, the usage of such controls is not explained in the current recipe.

If you run the application, you should see a result similar to the following:

As the last example, you will see a button that contains both a textual label and an icon. Such a solution could be accomplished using the `StackPanel`, `TextBlock`, and `Image` controls, as you can see in the following code snippet:

```xml
<Button
    Background="#353535"
    VerticalAlignment="Center"
    HorizontalAlignment="Center"
    Padding="20">
    <StackPanel Orientation="Horizontal">
        <Image
            Source="/Assets/Icon.png"
            MaxHeight="32" />
        <TextBlock
            Text="Accept"
            Foreground="White"
            FontSize="28"
            Margin="20 0 0 0" />
    </StackPanel>
</Button>
```

You can find more information about the `StackPanel` control in the *Arranging controls vertically* and *Arranging controls horizontally* recipes.

Of course, you should not forget to add the `Icon.png` file to the `Assets` directory, as already explained in this recipe. The result should be similar to the following:

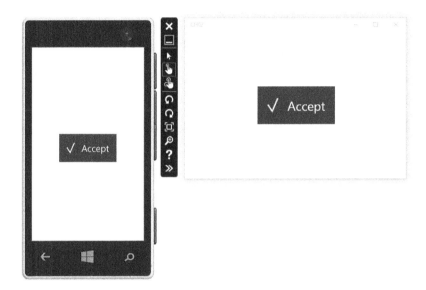

See also

- The *Adding a text block* recipe
- The *Adding a textbox* recipe
- The *Adding a password box* recipe
- The *Adding a checkbox* recipe
- The *Adding a combobox* recipe
- The *Adding a listbox* recipe
- The *Adding an image* recipe
- The *Adding controls programmatically* recipe
- The *Arranging controls in a grid* recipe
- The *Arranging controls vertically* recipe
- The *Arranging controls horizontally* recipe

Adding a text block

Very often, it is necessary to show some labels on the page. Such a task can be accomplished using the TextBlock control, which is the main subject of this recipe. Here, you will learn how to display static text on the page as well as how to format it.

Getting ready

To step through this recipe, you only need the automatically generated project.

How to do it...

To add a text block and handle the Tapped event, perform the following steps:

1. Place the TextBlock control on the page and adjust its appearance by modifying the content of the MainPage.xaml file as follows:

```
<Page (...)>
    <Grid (...)>
        <TextBlock
            Text="Exemplary justified content (...)"
            TextAlignment="Justify"
            MaxLines="3"
            TextTrimming="CharacterEllipsis"
            TextWrapping="Wrap"
            LineHeight="30"
            Foreground="RoyalBlue"
            FontSize="20"
            FontWeight="Thin"
            Margin="20" />
    </Grid>
</Page>
```

2. If you want to perform some operations after clicking on the TextBlock control, handle the Tapped event. The method is as follows:

```
private void TextBlock_Tapped(
    object sender, TappedRoutedEventArgs e) { }
```

How it works...

This example presents a text starting with **Exemplary justified content** (the `Text` property), which is justified (`TextAlignment`). The text is automatically wrapped if it is longer than one line (`TextWrapping`). The maximum length of the text is limited to three lines (`MaxLines`), and the remaining part of the text will be removed and replaced with three dots (`TextTrimming`). What is more, a height of each line is set to 30 pixels (`LineHeight`). A blue (`Foreground`) and thin (`FontWeight`) font of the size 20 (`FontSize`) is used. The whole control has a margin equal to 20 pixels (`Margin`).

If you run the application, you should see the following result:

Let's resize the window to see how the text is automatically moved to take up the necessary number of lines, which is of course limited to a maximum of three.

As already mentioned, it is possible to handle the scenario of pressing the `TextBlock` control by the user. Such a task could be accomplished by using the `Tapped` event. However, this event should be used with caution because the user could not expect that it is necessary to click on the static text to perform some additional operations.

> The `Tapped` event is not limited only to the `TextBlock` control and can be used with other ones as well.

There's more...

While the current recipe shows formatting of the text presented in the `TextBlock` control, it is also possible to vary formatting even within the control. Thus, you do not need to place a few `TextBlock` controls to distinguish the formatting of their content. To learn how to adjust the design of particular fragments of the content, let's modify the XAML code as follows:

```
<TextBlock
    FontSize="18"
    TextWrapping="Wrap"
    Margin="20">
    <Run Text="Hello!"
        FontWeight="SemiBold"
        FontSize="24" />
    <LineBreak />
    <Run Text="The TextBlock control allows to adjust design of
            particular fragments of its content, "
        FontWeight="Thin"
        Foreground="Gray" />
    <Run Text="even within one line."
        Foreground="Red" />
</TextBlock>
```

Now if you run the application, you should get the following result:

In this case, the content of TextBlock is organized as follows:

- The text **Hello!** is presented with semi-bold font of size 24, represented by Run
- The line break is represented by LineBreak
- The text **The TextBlock control allows to adjust design of particular fragments of its content** is presented with thin gray font of size 18 (inherited from a value of the FontSize property of TextBlock), represented by Run
- The text **even within one line** is presented with regular red font of size 18 (inherited from a value of the FontSize property of TextBlock), represented by Run

As you can see, it is possible to specify the formatting of particular text fragments as values of the properties of Run elements. Of course, formatting is first inherited from TextBlock properties, so you do not need to specify all values in each Run element.

See also

- The *Adding a button* recipe
- The *Adding a textbox* recipe
- The *Adding a password box* recipe
- The *Adding a checkbox* recipe

- The *Adding a combobox* recipe
- The *Adding a listbox* recipe
- The *Adding an image* recipe
- The *Adding controls programmatically* recipe

Adding a textbox

Another task that is frequently performed in applications is entering different types of information, such as a first or last name, an e-mail address, or a phone number. You could easily allow a user to type a text using the TextBox control. In this recipe, you will learn how to place it on the page, modify its appearance, as well as handle events related to typing data within such a control.

Getting ready

To step through this recipe, you only need the automatically generated project.

How to do it...

To add a textbox and handle some of its events, perform the following steps:

1. Place the TextBox control on the page and adjust its appearance by modifying the content of the MainPage.xaml file as follows:

```
<Page (...)>
    <Grid (...)>
        <TextBox
            PlaceholderText="Type a first name..."
            BorderBrush="#4a4a4a"
            BorderThickness="3"
            Foreground="#4a4a4a"
            Background="#efefef"
            FontSize="20"
            FontWeight="SemiBold"
            Padding="10"
            VerticalAlignment="Center"
            HorizontalAlignment="Stretch"
            Margin="20" />
    </Grid>
</Page>
```

2. If you want to perform some operations after pressing a key, but before modifying the content of the `TextBox` control, handle the `TextChanging` event. The method is as follows:

```
private void TextBox_TextChanging(TextBox sender,
    TextBoxTextChangingEventArgs args)
{
    string text = sender.Text;
}
```

3. If you want to perform some operations after modifying the content of the `TextBox` control, handle the `TextChanged` event. The method is as follows:

```
private void TextBox_TextChanged(object sender,
    TextChangedEventArgs e)
{
    TextBox textBox = (TextBox)sender;
    string text = textBox.Text;
}
```

How it works...

The preceding XAML code allows you to place a textbox on the page. It has a light gray (`#efefef`) background (the `Background` property), 3-pixel dark gray (`#4a4a4a`) border (`BorderThickness` and `BorderBrush`), as well as padding that is equal to 10 pixels (`Padding`) and margin equal to 10 pixels (`Margin`). The control is centered both vertically and horizontally, as specified by the values of `VerticalAlignment` and `HorizontalAlignment`.

The content in the `TextBox` control, such as entered by the user, is presented in a dark gray (`Foreground`) semi-bold (`FontWeight`) font of size 20 (`FontSize`). When no data is entered by the user, the control shows the **Type a first name...** text (`PlaceholderText`). The text automatically disappears when the user types anything within the textbox.

The result is shown in the following screenshot:

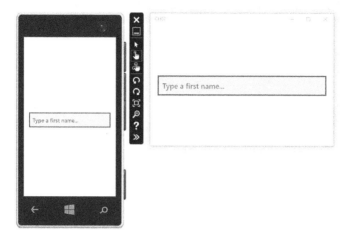

There's more...

The `TextBox` control can also be equipped with a header that could inform the user about the content that should be entered in the textbox. To learn how to specify a header as well as its appearance, let's modify the code as follows:

```
<TextBox (...)
    Header="First name">
    <TextBox.HeaderTemplate>
        <DataTemplate>
            <TextBlock
                Text="{Binding}"
                FontSize="16"
                Foreground="#4a4a4a"
                FontWeight="SemiBold" />
        </DataTemplate>
    </TextBox.HeaderTemplate>
</TextBox>
```

The text of the header is specified as the value of the `Header` property. However, in many scenarios, it may be necessary to modify the default appearance of the header. To do so, you can specify `HeaderTemplate` and define a proper **data template**. In the example you just saw, only the `TextBlock` control is shown with dark gray semi-bold font of size 16. Its content is bound to the value of the `Header` property, using the binding mechanism, which is explained in `Chapter 3`, *MVVM and Data Binding*.

Data templates are important and powerful mechanisms, which are presented in various places of the book, such as in the *Binding a collection to a list view*, *Binding a collection to a grid view*, *Binding a collection to a combobox*, and *Binding a collection to a hub* recipes in `Chapter 3`, *MVVM and Data Binding*.

The result is as follows:

What is interesting is that the `TextBox` control allows you to present various kinds of keyboards, depending on the selection made by a developer using the `InputScope` property. An example is presented in the *Arranging controls vertically* recipe.

See also

- The *Adding a button* recipe
- The *Adding a text block* recipe
- The *Adding a password box* recipe
- The *Adding a checkbox* recipe
- The *Adding a combobox* recipe
- The *Adding a listbox* recipe
- The *Adding an image* recipe
- The *Adding controls programmatically* recipe
- The *Arranging controls vertically* recipe

Adding a password box

The previously described TextBox control is great for entering various kinds of information. However, it is not a perfect solution for typing passwords. To handle this type of information, the PasswordBox control is available. You will learn how to use it in this recipe.

Getting ready

To step through this recipe, you only need the automatically generated project.

How to do it...

To add a password box and handle the PasswordChanged event, perform the following steps:

1. Place the PasswordBox control on the page and adjust its appearance by modifying the content of the MainPage.xaml file as follows:

```
<Page (...)>
    <Grid (...)>
        <PasswordBox
            PlaceholderText="Type a password..."
            VerticalAlignment="Center"
            HorizontalAlignment="Stretch"
            Margin="20" />
    </Grid>
</Page>
```

2. If you want to perform some operations after changing the entered password, handle the PasswordChanged event. The method is as follows:

```
private void PasswordBox_PasswordChanged(object sender,
    RoutedEventArgs e)
{
    PasswordBox passwordBox = (PasswordBox)sender;
    string password = passwordBox.Password;
}
```

How it works...

The preceding XAML code allows you to present the password box, as follows:

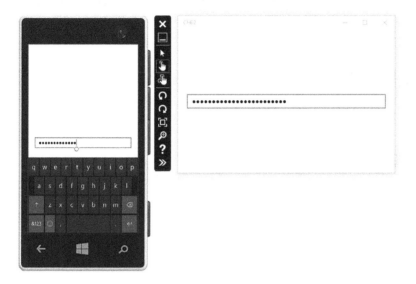

The password box is centered vertically within the Grid control, but its width is set to the width of Grid, using Stretch as a value of the HorizontalAlignment property. When the user does not enter a password, the **Type a password...** text is shown, as specified by the PlaceholderText property.

See also

- The *Adding a button* recipe
- The *Adding a text block* recipe
- The *Adding a textbox* recipe
- The *Adding a checkbox* recipe
- The *Adding a combobox* recipe
- The *Adding a listbox* recipe
- The *Adding an image* recipe
- The *Adding controls programmatically* recipe

Adding a checkbox

In the previous recipes, you learned how a user can type text values and passwords within your application. But what about other types of data, such as a confirmation of accepting the rules? In such a case, the CheckBox control can be used, as you will see in this recipe.

Getting ready

To step through this recipe, you only need the automatically generated project.

How to do it...

To add a checkbox and handle some of its events, perform the following steps:

1. Place the CheckBox control on the page and adjust its appearance by modifying the content of the MainPage.xaml file as follows:

```
<Page (...)>
    <Grid (...)>
        <CheckBox
            Content="I have read and accepted the rules."
            IsChecked="True"
            Foreground="RoyalBlue"
            FontSize="16"
            VerticalAlignment="Center"
            HorizontalAlignment="Center" />
    </Grid>
</Page>
```

2. If you want to perform some operations after checking the checkbox, handle the Checked event. The method is as follows:

```
private void CheckBox_Checked(object sender,
    RoutedEventArgs e) { }
```

3. If you want to perform some operations after unchecking the checkbox, handle the Unchecked event. The method is as follows:

```
private void CheckBox_Unchecked(object sender,
    RoutedEventArgs e) { }
```

How it works...

According to the XAML code you just saw, the checkbox is shown at the center (VerticalAlignment and HorizontalAlignment properties). Its content is set to **I have read and accepted the rules.** (Content) and, by default, the checkbox is checked (IsChecked). The appearance of the text is specified by the Foreground and FontSize properties.

The result is shown in the following screenshot:

See also

- The *Adding a button* recipe
- The *Adding a text block* recipe
- The *Adding a textbox* recipe
- The *Adding a password box* recipe
- The *Adding a combobox* recipe
- The *Adding a listbox* recipe
- The *Adding an image* recipe
- The *Adding controls programmatically* recipe

Adding a combobox

In many forms, it is necessary to choose a value from a predefined set, for example, in the case of a category of news or a supported language. Such a task can be accomplished using the ComboBox control. It allows you to choose a particular value from a drop-down list. In this recipe, you will learn how to use it and adjust its appearance.

Getting ready

To step through this recipe, you only need the automatically generated project.

How to do it...

To add a combobox and handle the SelectionChanged event, perform the following steps:

1. Place the ComboBox control with supported languages on the page and adjust its appearance by modifying the content of the MainPage.xaml file as follows:

```
<Page (...)>
    <Grid (...)>
        <ComboBox
            SelectedIndex="1"
            Header="Language"
            Foreground="RoyalBlue"
            BorderBrush="RoyalBlue"
            BorderThickness="2"
            VerticalAlignment="Center"
            HorizontalAlignment="Stretch"
            Margin="20">
            <ComboBoxItem Content="Polish" Tag="PL" />
            <ComboBoxItem Content="English" Tag="EN" />
            <ComboBoxItem Content="German" Tag="DE" />
        </ComboBox>
    </Grid>
</Page>
```

2. If you want to perform some operations after changing a selection, handle the SelectionChanged event. The method is as follows:

```
private void ComboBox_SelectionChanged(object sender,
    SelectionChangedEventArgs e)
{
    ComboBox comboBox = (ComboBox)sender;
```

```
int selectedIndex = comboBox.SelectedIndex;
ComboBoxItem selectedItem =
    (ComboBoxItem)comboBox.SelectedItem;
string selectedTag = (string)selectedItem.Tag;
}
```

How it works...

The combobox contains three items, specified as ComboBoxItem elements. For each of them, a language name is provided as Content and language code (such as PL) as Tag. Tag is used to easily identify a chosen element without the necessity of comparing language names or indices within the list.

By default, the second item of the combobox is chosen, as set by the SelectedIndex property. It is worth mentioning that indices are zero-based, which means that the first element has an index equal to 0, while the last one's index would be the count of items minus 1.

Other properties specify the appearance of ComboBox, including its header (Header), text color (Foreground), border (BorderBrush and BorderThickness), as well as the arrangement within the parent control (VerticalAlignment and HorizontalAlignment).

The result is as follows:

See also

- The *Adding a button* recipe
- The *Adding a text block* recipe
- The *Adding a textbox* recipe
- The *Adding a password box* recipe
- The *Adding a checkbox* recipe
- The *Adding a listbox* recipe
- The *Adding an image* recipe
- The *Adding controls programmatically* recipe

Adding a listbox

In the case of the collapsed ComboBox control, only one item is presented. However, if you want to show more items as well as allow to select multiple elements in the same time, you can use ListBox. The usage of this control is explained in this recipe.

Getting ready

To step through this recipe, you only need the automatically generated project.

How to do it...

To add a listbox and handle the SelectionChanged event, perform the following steps:

1. Place the ListBox control with the supported languages on the page and adjust its appearance by modifying the content of the MainPage.xaml file as follows:

```
<Page (...)>
    <Grid (...)>
        <ListBox
            SelectedIndex="1"
            SelectionMode="Single"
            VerticalAlignment="Center"
            HorizontalAlignment="Center">
            <ListBoxItem Content="Polish" Tag="PL" />
            <ListBoxItem Content="English" Tag="EN" />
            <ListBoxItem Content="German" Tag="DE" />
```

```
        </ListBox>
    </Grid>
</Page>
```

2. If you want to perform some operations after changing a selection, handle the
   `SelectionChanged` event. The method is as follows:

```
private void ListBox_SelectionChanged(object sender,
    SelectionChangedEventArgs e)
{
    ListBox listBox = (ListBox)sender;
    int selectedIndex = listBox.SelectedIndex;
    ListBoxItem selectedItem =
        (ListBoxItem)listBox.SelectedItem;
    string selectedTag = (string)selectedItem.Tag;
    switch (selectedTag)
    {
        case "PL": /* ... */ break;
        case "EN": /* ... */ break;
        case "DE": /* ... */ break;
    }
}
```

How it works...

The listbox contains three items that represent the languages supported by the application.
Each item presents a language name (`Content`) and specifies a language code as a value of
the `Tag` property. This value is used to programmatically distinguish a selected item from
the C# code, as shown in the `ListBox_SelectionChanged` method.

By default, the second item is selected, as set in the `SelectedIndex` property. It is worth
mentioning that indices are zero-based, which means that the first element has an index
equal to 0, while the last one's index would be the count of items minus 1.

An important role is also performed by the `SelectionMode` property. In the example, it has
a value that is equal to `Single`, which means that only one element can be selected at
each time. However, the control also supports scenarios when more than one element is
chosen by the user.

If you run the application now, you should see the following result:

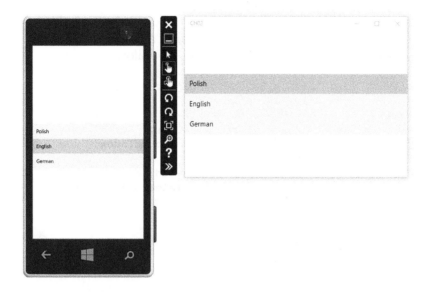

See also

- The *Adding a button* recipe
- The *Adding a text block* recipe
- The *Adding a textbox* recipe
- The *Adding a password box* recipe
- The *Adding a checkbox* recipe
- The *Adding a combobox* recipe
- The *Adding an image* recipe
- The *Adding controls programmatically* recipe

Adding an image

Modern applications often contain attractive designs that include images. In this recipe, you will learn how to present images in your application using the Image control.

Getting ready

To step through this recipe, you only need the automatically generated project.

How to do it...

To add a .jpg file to the project, add the Image control, and handle the Tapped event, perform the following steps:

1. Add the Image.jpg file to the Assets directory within the project. To do so, refer to these steps:
   1. Navigate to **Add** | **Existing Item...** from the context menu of the **Assets** node in the **Solution Explorer** window.
   2. Choose the file in the **Add Existing Item** window.
   3. Click on the **Add** button.

2. Place the Image control on the page and adjust its appearance by modifying the content of the MainPage.xaml file as follows:

```
<Page (...) Background="Black">
    <Grid (...)>
        <Image
            Source="/Assets/Image.jpg"
            Stretch="UniformToFill"
            HorizontalAlignment="Center"
            VerticalAlignment="Center" />
    </Grid>
</Page>
```

3. If you want to perform some operations after clicking on the image, handle the Tapped event. The method is as follows:

```
private void Image_Tapped(object sender,
    TappedRoutedEventArgs e) { }
```

How it works...

The image is added to the Grid control and is centered both horizontally and vertically within it (the HorizontalAlignment and VerticalAlignment properties). The source of the image is specified as /Assets/Image.jpg (Source). This means that the Image.jpg file from the Assets directory should be shown on the page.

Do not forget to add a slash (/) before `Assets` in the `Source` property.

Another important property is `Stretch`. It can take four values that define the way in which the image is presented. In the example, `UniformToFill` is chosen, and the image always occupies all of the available area (in this case, the `Grid` control) while keeping a constant width/height ratio. When the whole image cannot be shown, only a part of it is presented, taking into account the values of the `HorizontalAlignment` and `VerticalAlignment` properties. In the example, the center part (both vertically and horizontally) will always be shown, while the regions located at the top or bottom or on the left- or right-hand side of the image could disappear while resizing the window.

The result in both mobile and desktop-based versions is as follows:

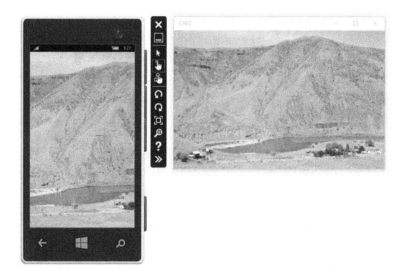

It is worth mentioning all other possible values of the `Stretch` property. Differences between them are presented in the following image (from the left: `Fill`, `None`, `Uniform`, and `UniformToFill`):

As you can see, the `Fill` value means that the image is always stretched (both vertically and horizontally) to take all the available space, thus the width/height ratio is not constant and the image may look unnatural in some cases. The `None` value just presents the image without resizing. The last unexplained value, `Uniform`, resizes it to take all the available space, but it does not clip parts of the image, which is a visible difference between `Uniform` and `UniformToFill`.

See also

- The *Adding a button* recipe
- The *Adding a text block* recipe
- The *Adding a textbox* recipe
- The *Adding a password box* recipe
- The *Adding a checkbox* recipe
- The *Adding a combobox* recipe
- The *Adding a listbox* recipe
- The *Adding controls programmatically* recipe

Adding controls programmatically

You have learned how to use the XAML language to place controls on the page and configure them. However, it does not mean that controls must only be created in a declarative way using XAML. In this recipe, you will learn how to create a button and add it to the `Grid` control programmatically, using the C# language.

Getting ready

To step through this recipe, you only need the automatically generated project.

How to do it...

To add a button and adjust its appearance programmatically, perform the following steps:

1. Specify the name of the `Grid` control by modifying the content of the `MainPage.xaml` file as follows:

```
<Page (...)>
    <Grid
        Name="Grid"
        Background="{ThemeResource
            ApplicationPageBackgroundThemeBrush}">
    </Grid>
</Page>
```

2. Create and configure a new button and add it to the `Grid` control by modifying the constructor of the `MainPage` class, in the `MainPage.xaml.cs` file, as follows:

```
public MainPage()
{
    InitializeComponent();
    Button button = new Button()
    {
        Content = "Click me!",
        Background = new SolidColorBrush(Colors.LightGray),
        Foreground = new SolidColorBrush(Colors.RoyalBlue),
        VerticalAlignment = VerticalAlignment.Center,
        HorizontalAlignment = HorizontalAlignment.Center,
        BorderBrush = new SolidColorBrush(Colors.RoyalBlue),
        BorderThickness = new Thickness(3),
        FontSize = 20
    };
    Grid.Children.Add(button);
}
```

Do not forget to add the necessary `using` statements, such as for `Windows.UI`, `Windows.UI.Xaml`, and `Windows.UI.Xaml.Media` namespaces.

3. Handle the event of clicking on the button by modifying the constructor of the MainPage class, in the `MainPage.xaml.cs` file, as follows:

```
public MainPage()
{ (...)
    Button button = new Button() { (...) };
    button.Click += Button_Click;
    Grid.Children.Add(button);
}
```

4. To modify the appearance of the button after clicking on it, define the `Button_Click` method in the `MainPage.xaml.cs` file, as follows:

```
private void Button_Click(object sender, RoutedEventArgs e)
{
    Button button = (Button)Grid.Children[0];
    button.Background = new SolidColorBrush(Colors.Red);
    button.Foreground = new SolidColorBrush(Colors.White);
    button.BorderBrush = new SolidColorBrush(Colors.Black);
}
```

How it works...

The most important part of the code is located in the constructor of the MainPage class, representing a page with the Grid control. Within the constructor, a new instance of the Button class is created and the values of its various properties are set:

- Content: Set by assigning the string value equal to Click me!
- Background, Foreground, and BorderBrush: Set by assigning new instances of SolidColorBrush to specify colors
- VerticalAlignment and HorizontalAlignment: Set by assigning enumeration values
- BorderThickness: Set by assigning a new instance of the Thickness class
- FontSize: Set by assigning a numerical value, such as double or int

In the next part of the constructor, the instance of the Button class (represented by the button variable) is added to the collection of children elements of the Grid control with the following line of code:

```
Grid.Children.Add(button);
```

It is worth mentioning that `Grid` in the line is not the name of the class but the name of a particular `Grid` control located on the page, as specified in the `MainPage.xaml` file.

Let's take a look at how to handle events in a code-behind file. The process of specifying a method that is called after clicking on the button is performed as follows:

```
button.Click += Button_Click;
```

Each time the `Click` event is fired, the `Button_Click` method is called.

Of course, you can also programmatically get access to the elements located within the grid, iterate through them, or simply get an element using the zero-based index, as follows:

```
Button button = (Button)Grid.Children[0];
```

Then, it is possible to adjust the appearance of the control just by assigning new values to its various properties, such as `Background` or `Foreground`, as shown in the example.

The final design of the button, before and after clicking on it (on the left and right, respectively), is presented in the following screenshot:

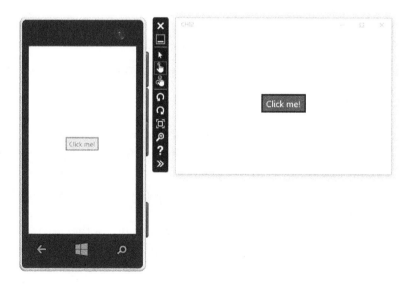

See also

- The *Adding a button* recipe

Arranging controls vertically

Pages often contain many controls that must be arranged in some way. One of the most natural ways is arranging them vertically, one below another. This linear method is supported by the StackPanel control. In this recipe, you will learn how to use it to prepare the page with a registration form consisting of a few other controls, namely TextBlock, TextBox, PasswordBox, ComboBox, CheckBox, and Button.

Getting ready

To step through this recipe, you only need the automatically generated project.

How to do it...

To arrange controls vertically to create a simple registration form, modify the content of the MainPage.xaml file as follows:

```xml
<Page (...)>
    <StackPanel Background="White" Padding="20">
        <TextBlock
            Text="Create an account"
            FontSize="26"
            Margin="0 0 0 20" />
        <TextBox
            Header="Login"
            PlaceholderText="Type a login..."
            InputScope="AlphanumericFullWidth"
            Margin="0 0 0 20" />
        <PasswordBox
            Header="Password"
            PlaceholderText="Type a password..."
            Margin="0 0 0 20" />
        <TextBox
            Header="E-mail address"
            PlaceholderText="Type an e-mail address..."
            InputScope="EmailNameOrAddress"
```

```
                    Margin="0 0 0 20" />
                <ComboBox
                    Header="Country"
                    PlaceholderText="Choose a country..."
                    HorizontalAlignment="Stretch"
                    Margin="0 0 0 20">
                    <ComboBoxItem Content="Poland" />
                    <ComboBoxItem Content="United States" />
                    <ComboBoxItem Content="England" />
                    <ComboBoxItem Content="Germany" />
                    <ComboBoxItem Content="France" />
                </ComboBox>
                <CheckBox Margin="0 0 0 20">
                    <TextBlock Text="I have accepted the rules" />
                </CheckBox>
                <Button
                    Content="Register"
                    HorizontalAlignment="Stretch"
                    BorderBrush="Black"
                    BorderThickness="1"
                    Padding="10"/>
            </StackPanel>
        </Page>
```

The `StackPanel` control can be placed directly within `Page`. It is not necessary that you place it in `Grid`, but such a scenario is also correct.

How it works...

The most important part of the XAML code is `StackPanel`. It has a white background as well as padding set to 20 pixels. All the controls located within `StackPanel` are arranged linearly in a vertical way. That means, `TextBox` (with **Login** as header) is located directly below `TextBlock` (with the **Create an account** content). Of course, you can specify the distance between the following controls by setting a proper margin.

If you run the application either on a smartphone or a desktop, you should see the following result:

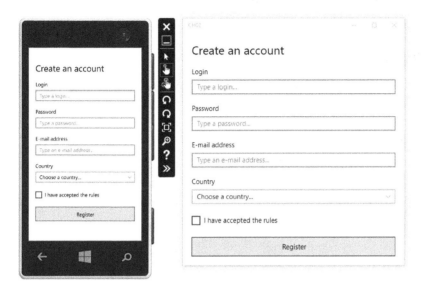

What is important, the content of `StackPanel` is not scrollable. Thus, if the height of the page is too small, the remaining part of `StackPanel` will just be invisible. Of course, it is also possible to make such a layout scrollable, but it is a topic of another recipe, namely *Arranging controls in a scrollable view*.

See also

- The *Arranging controls horizontally* recipe
- The *Arranging controls in a scrollable view* recipe
- The *Arranging controls in a grid* recipe
- The *Arranging controls in absolute positions* recipe

Arranging controls horizontally

Apart from arranging controls vertically, it is possible to place them in a linear horizontal way, where a control is placed on the right-hand side of the previous one. This task can be accomplished using `StackPanel` as well, as shown in this recipe.

Getting ready

To step through this recipe, you only need the automatically generated project.

How to do it...

To arrange controls horizontally, modify the content of the `MainPage.xaml` file, as shown in the following code:

```
<Page (...)>
    <StackPanel
        Orientation="Horizontal"
        Background="White"
        Padding="20">
        <TextBlock
            Text="Grade:"
            VerticalAlignment="Center" />
        <Button Content="1" Margin="20 0 10 0" />
        <Button Content="2" Margin="10 0" />
        <Button Content="3" Margin="10 0" />
        <Button Content="4" Margin="10 0" />
        <Button Content="5" Margin="10 0" />
    </StackPanel>
</Page>
```

How it works...

The most important change between the vertical and horizontal alignment is the value of the `Orientation` property. Here, the `Horizontal` value is used, which informs that the controls located within `StackPanel` should be placed one next to the other. It means that `TextBlock` should be located on the left-hand side, followed by five `Button` controls.

If you run the application, you should get the following result:

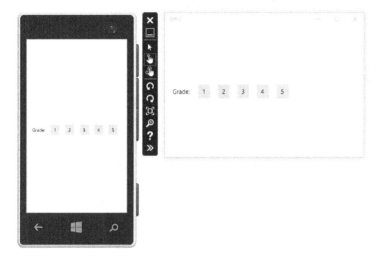

Another example of horizontal alignment has been presented in one of the previous recipes, namely *Adding a button*, where you learned how to create a button that contains both an icon and a textual label.

See also

- The *Arranging controls vertically* recipe
- The *Arranging controls in a scrollable view* recipe
- The *Arranging controls in a grid* recipe
- The *Arranging controls in absolute positions* recipe

Arranging controls in a scrollable view

As already mentioned, the StackPanel control does not automatically allow you to scroll its content. For this reason, when the screen is not big enough, some parts could just disappear. Of course, such a situation should not occur. For this reason, in this recipe, you will learn how to use ScrollViewer to scroll the photo gallery created as a collection of images, presented in StackPanel.

Getting ready

To step through this recipe, you only need the automatically generated project.

How to do it...

To arrange controls in a scrollable view to form a simple photo gallery, perform the following steps:

1. Add four images (named `Gallery1.jpg`, `Gallery2.jpg`, `Gallery3.jpg`, and `Gallery4.jpg`) to the `Assets` directory, as explained in the *Adding an image* recipe.
2. Modify the content of the `MainPage.xaml` file as follows:

```xaml
<Page (...)>
    <ScrollViewer
        Padding="10"
        ScrollViewer.VerticalScrollBarVisibility="Auto">
        <StackPanel>
            <Image
                Source="/Assets/Gallery1.jpg"
                Margin="10" />
            <Image
                Source="/Assets/Gallery2.jpg"
                Margin="10" />
            <Image
                Source="/Assets/Gallery3.jpg"
                Margin="10" />
            <Image
                Source="/Assets/Gallery4.jpg"
                Margin="10" />
        </StackPanel>
    </ScrollViewer>
</Page>
```

How it works...

Making a `StackPanel` scrollable requires placing it within `ScrollViewer`, as shown in the XAML code you just saw. You also have a possibility of setting the visibility of particular scroll bars. In the example, the vertical scroll bar will be presented only when it is necessary, as specified by `VerticalScrollBarVisibility`. If the content does not have enough height, the vertical scroll bar will be hidden.

The result is as follows:

See also

- The *Arranging controls vertically* recipe
- The *Arranging controls horizontally* recipe
- The *Arranging controls in a grid* recipe
- The *Arranging controls in absolute positions* recipe

Defining a page-limited style

One of the important tasks while developing applications is to ensure the design is consistent within the whole solution. However, copying and pasting the same code in several places, for instance, for each button located on the page, is not a suitable solution. In the case of any modifications, you will need to perform many changes and ensure that all the occurrences of a previous value have been replaced correctly. For this reason, it is a beneficial approach to use styles.

In this recipe, you will learn how to apply page-limited styles to the controls on the page. What is more, two kinds of styles will be taken into account: styles applied automatically to all the controls of a given type and styles applied only to a particular subset of controls.

As an example, you will create a photo gallery with the header. Each photo is represented by an `Image` control placed within `Border`. A style should be automatically applied to all `Border` elements to set its borders and margins. What is more, a style with a given key will be applied to the text block representing the header.

Getting ready

To step through this recipe, you only need the automatically generated project.

How to do it...

To adjust design of the photo gallery using styles, perform the following steps:

1. Define a style that is automatically applied to all `Border` controls located on the page. Do this by modifying the content of the `MainPage.xaml` file as follows:

```
<Page (...)>
    <Page.Resources>
        <Style TargetType="Border">
            <Setter Property="BorderBrush" Value="Black" />
            <Setter Property="BorderThickness" Value="2" />
            <Setter Property="Margin" Value="10" />
        </Style>
    </Page.Resources>
</Page>
```

2. Define a style that is applied to particular `TextBlock` controls on the page. Do this by modifying the content of the `MainPage.xaml` file as follows:

```
<Page (...)>
    <Page.Resources> (...)
        <Style x:Key="TxtHeader" TargetType="TextBlock">
            <Setter Property="HorizontalAlignment"
                    Value="Center" />
            <Setter Property="FontSize" Value="30" />
            <Setter Property="FontWeight" Value="SemiBold" />
            <Setter Property="Margin" Value="0 0 0 10" />
        </Style>
    </Page.Resources>
</Page>
```

3. Add necessary controls on the page and apply the style to the `TextBlock` control by modifying the content of the `MainPage.xaml` file, as shown in the following code snippet:

```
<Page (...)>
    <Page.Resources> (...)
    </Page.Resources>
    <ScrollViewer
        Padding="10"
        ScrollViewer.VerticalScrollBarVisibility="Auto">
        <StackPanel>
            <TextBlock
                Text="Photo gallery"
                Style="{StaticResource TxtHeader}" />
            <Border>
                <Image Source="/Assets/Gallery1.jpg" />
            </Border>
            <Border>
                <Image Source="/Assets/Gallery2.jpg" />
            </Border>
            <Border>
                <Image Source="/Assets/Gallery3.jpg" />
            </Border>
            <Border>
                <Image Source="/Assets/Gallery4.jpg"/>
            </Border>
        </StackPanel>
    </ScrollViewer>
</Page>
```

How it works...

The page-limited styles are defined within the resources of the page. Each style is represented by the `Style` element with `TargetType` indicating the type of the control for which the style is applied.

If there is no key (`x:Key`) specified, the style is applied automatically to all the controls of a given type. In the example, the first style is automatically applied to all `Border` controls to set a border of 2 pixels width and with a black color, as well as a margin of 10 pixels.

Specifying a key changes the way in which the style is applied to controls. In such a case, it is necessary to set the `Style` property of the control, which should use the style. In the example, the second style has `TxtHeader` set as a key and can be applied to `TextBlock` controls. To indicate that the header should have a given style, the value of its `Style` property is set, as shown in the following line of code:

```
<TextBlock (...) Style="{StaticResource TxtHeader}" />
```

If you run the application, you should see the following result:

See also

- The *Defining a global style* recipe
- The *Applying styles programmatically* recipe

Defining a global style

Page-limited styles are a powerful mechanism to design the various elements on the page consistently. However, what should you do to make the whole application consistent? Do you need to copy such styles to all the pages? Absolutely not, because you can move the definition of styles to the `App.xaml` file to use them in the whole application. You will learn how to do it in this recipe.

As an example, you will create a simple menu page with a few buttons, such as **Dashboard**, **News**, and **Gallery**. To make the design consistent across the whole application, all buttons should have the same appearance specified by the global style.

Getting ready

To step through this recipe, you only need the automatically generated project.

How to do it...

To prepare a simple menu page with a globally-defined style for buttons, you need to perform the following steps:

1. Specify the global style for the `Button` and `ScrollViewer` controls by modifying the content of the `App.xaml` file as follows:

```
<Application (...)>
    <Application.Resources>
        <Style TargetType="Button">
            <Setter Property="Background" Value="LightGray" />
            <Setter Property="Foreground" Value="Black" />
            <Setter Property="BorderBrush" Value="Black" />
            <Setter Property="BorderThickness" Value="1" />
            <Setter Property="Margin" Value="10" />
            <Setter Property="Padding" Value="10" />
            <Setter Property="HorizontalAlignment"
                Value="Stretch" />
        </Style>
        <Style x:Key="ScrMain" TargetType="ScrollViewer">
            <Setter Property="Padding" Value="10" />
            <Setter Property="ScrollViewer.
                VerticalScrollBarVisibility" Value="Auto" />
        </Style>
    </Application.Resources>
</Application>
```

2. Add the necessary controls on the page and apply the `ScrMain` style to the `ScrollViewer` control by modifying the content of the `MainPage.xaml` file as follows:

```
<Page (...)>
    <ScrollViewer Style="{StaticResource ScrMain}">
        <StackPanel>
```

```
            <Button Content="Dashboard" />
            <Button Content="News" />
            <Button Content="Gallery" />
            <Button Content="Movies" />
            <Button Content="Contact" />
        </StackPanel>
    </ScrollViewer>
</Page>
```

How it works...

The example shows a page with five buttons representing menu options, namely
Dashboard, **News**, **Gallery**, **Movies**, and **Contact**, as shown in the following image:

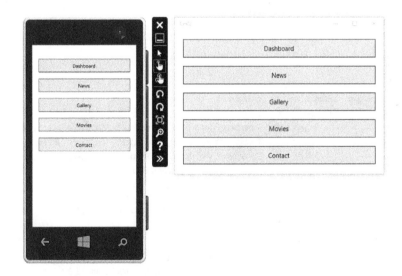

To maintain consistency in the whole application, the common style for all Button controls
is defined in the App.xaml file. Each button has a light gray background, black border, as
well as 10 pixels margin and padding. What is more, the text is presented in black color.

Another style is defined with the ScrMain key and could be applied to ScrollViewer
controls. In the page, it is assigned to the ScrollViewer control by setting a value of the
Style property, as shown in the code.

See also

- The *Defining a page-limited style* recipe
- The *Applying styles programmatically* recipe

Applying styles programmatically

According to the information presented in the two previous recipes, you can use styles to easily adjust the design of your application. However, do you know that you can also apply styles programmatically? Thus, you can dynamically control the appearance of user interface. In this recipe, you will learn how to get data of the style defined in the page resources and apply it to an element with a suitable type.

As an example, you will prepare a page that presents four images. By default, they have a black border with a width of 3 pixels and its opacity set to 30%. After clicking on each image, its opacity should be changed to 100% and the border color should be set to blue. You will solve this problem by defining two styles, namely for active and inactive elements and applying a proper style after tapping on the photo.

Getting ready

To step through this recipe, you will only need the automatically generated project.

How to do it...

To prepare an example of applying styles programmatically, perform the following steps:

1. Specify styles for an active and inactive element (`BorImageActive` and `BorImageInactive`) and add four `Border` controls with `Image` controls to the page. Each of them should be located in a separate cell within the grid. To do so, modify the code of the `MainPage.xaml` file as follows:

```
<Page (...)>
    <Page.Resources>
        <Style x:Key="BorImageInactive" TargetType="Border">
            <Setter Property="BorderBrush" Value="Black" />
            <Setter Property="BorderThickness" Value="3" />
            <Setter Property="Opacity" Value="0.3" />
            <Setter Property="Background" Value="Black" />
```

```xml
                    <Setter Property="VerticalAlignment"
                        Value="Center" />
                    <Setter Property="Margin" Value="10" />
                </Style>
                <Style x:Key="BorImageActive"
                    BasedOn="{StaticResource BorImageInactive}"
                    TargetType="Border">
                    <Setter Property="BorderBrush"
                        Value="RoyalBlue" />
                    <Setter Property="Opacity" Value="1.0" />
                </Style>
                <Style TargetType="Image">
                    <Setter Property="Stretch"
                        Value="UniformToFill" />
                    <Setter Property="HorizontalAlignment"
                        Value="Center" />
                </Style>
            </Page.Resources>
            <Grid Margin="10">
                <Grid.RowDefinitions>
                    <RowDefinition Height="1*" />
                    <RowDefinition Height="1*" />
                </Grid.RowDefinitions>
                <Grid.ColumnDefinitions>
                    <ColumnDefinition Width="1*" />
                    <ColumnDefinition Width="1*" />
                </Grid.ColumnDefinitions>
                <Border
                    Grid.Row="0" Grid.Column="0"
                    Tapped="BorImage_Tapped"
                    Style="{StaticResource BorImageInactive}">
                    <Image Source="/Assets/Gallery1.jpg" />
                </Border> (...)
            </Grid>
        </Page>
```

2. Set a proper style for a `Border` control after clicking on it. You can achieve this goal by adding the `BorImage_Tapped` method, as shown in the following code snippet:

```csharp
private void BorImage_Tapped(object sender,
    TappedRoutedEventArgs e)
{
    Style styleInactive =
        (Style)Resources["BorImageInactive"];
    Style styleActive = (Style)Resources["BorImageActive"];
    Border border = (Border)sender;
    border.Style = border.Style == styleInactive ?
```

```
    styleActive : styleInactive;
}
```

You can define one method for handling an event fired from many controls. In such a case, you can get an object representing the source control using the `sender` parameter.

How it works...

To apply a style in a programmatic way, you need to get an instance of the `Style` class representing a given style, and assign it to the `Style` property of a control. Thus, you are able to update the style while the application is running to dynamically adjust the design of various elements located on the page.

A small comment could be necessary to the way of getting the `Style` instance representing a style. To do so, you can just get a proper entry from the `Resources` dictionary and cast it to `Style`. Of course, while getting an entry from the `Resources` dictionary, you should use the same key as the key of the `Style` element defined in the page resources. The relevant part of code is as follows:

```
Style styleInactive = (Style)Resources["BorImageInactive"];
```

In this recipe, the controls are arranged in a grid. You can find more information about the `Grid` control in the following recipe.

If you run the application and click on some images, you should see a result similar to the following screenshot:

See also

- The *Defining a page-limited style* recipe
- The *Defining a global style* recipe

Arranging controls in a grid

The arrangement of controls in a linear way is not the only possible option. You can also arrange controls in a grid by specifying in which rows and columns each control should be located. What is interesting is that the available solution gives developers a lot of flexibility, such as defining the width of columns and the height of rows. In this recipe, you will learn how to define a grid and arrange controls within it.

As an example, you will design a simple calculator with `TextBlock` for the results and 16 `Button` controls (with **0–9** digits, **+**, **–**, *****, **/**, **=**, and a comma).

Getting ready

To step through this recipe, you only need the automatically generated project.

How to do it...

To create a simple calculator demonstrating arrangement of controls in a grid, you need to perform the following steps:

1. Specify styles for `Button` and `TextBlock` controls. Do this by modifying the content of the `MainPage.xaml` file as follows:

```
<Page (...)>
    <Page.Resources>
        <Style TargetType="Button">
            <Setter Property="HorizontalAlignment"
                    Value="Stretch" />
            <Setter Property="VerticalAlignment"
                    Value="Stretch" />
            <Setter Property="Margin" Value="10" />
            <Setter Property="FontSize" Value="24" />
        </Style>
        <Style x:Key="TxtResult" TargetType="TextBlock">
            <Setter Property="FontSize" Value="60" />
            <Setter Property="HorizontalAlignment"
                    Value="Right" />
            <Setter Property="Margin" Value="10" />
        </Style>
    </Page.Resources>
</Page>
```

2. Add the necessary `Grid`, `TextBlock`, and `Button` controls by modifying the content of the `MainPage.xaml` file as follows:

```
<Page (...)>
    <Page.Resources> (...)
    </Page.Resources>
    <Grid>
        <Grid.RowDefinitions>
            <RowDefinition Height="Auto" />
            <RowDefinition Height="1*" />
            <RowDefinition Height="1*" />
            <RowDefinition Height="1*" />
            <RowDefinition Height="1*" />
        </Grid.RowDefinitions>
    </Grid.RowDefinitions>
```

```
<Grid.ColumnDefinitions>
    <ColumnDefinition Width="1*" />
    <ColumnDefinition Width="1*" />
    <ColumnDefinition Width="1*" />
    <ColumnDefinition Width="1*" />
</Grid.ColumnDefinitions>
<TextBlock
    Grid.Row="0" Grid.Column="0"
    Grid.ColumnSpan="4"
    Style="{StaticResource TxtResult}"
    Text="0" />
<Button Grid.Row="1" Grid.Column="0" Content="7" />
<Button Grid.Row="1" Grid.Column="1" Content="8" />
<Button Grid.Row="1" Grid.Column="2" Content="9" />
<Button Grid.Row="2" Grid.Column="0" Content="4" />
<Button Grid.Row="2" Grid.Column="1" Content="5" />
<Button Grid.Row="2" Grid.Column="2" Content="6" />
<Button Grid.Row="3" Grid.Column="0" Content="1" />
<Button Grid.Row="3" Grid.Column="1" Content="2" />
<Button Grid.Row="3" Grid.Column="2" Content="3" />
<Button Grid.Row="4" Grid.Column="0" Content="," />
<Button Grid.Row="4" Grid.Column="1" Content="0" />
<Button Grid.Row="4" Grid.Column="2" Content="=" />
<Button Grid.Row="1" Grid.Column="3" Content="+" />
<Button Grid.Row="2" Grid.Column="3" Content="-" />
<Button Grid.Row="3" Grid.Column="3" Content="*" />
<Button Grid.Row="4" Grid.Column="3" Content="/" />
</Grid>
</Page>
```

How it works...

The most important part of this code is the definition of a grid. It contains five rows,
represented by RowDefinition elements, as follows:

```
<Grid.RowDefinitions>
    <RowDefinition Height="Auto" />
    <RowDefinition Height="1*" />
    <RowDefinition Height="1*" />
    <RowDefinition Height="1*" />
    <RowDefinition Height="1*" />
</Grid.RowDefinitions>
```

The first row has the height calculated automatically to fit all the controls placed inside (Auto). The height of each of the four following rows is specified as 1*. This means that all these four rows should have the same height.

Of course, you can define the height of particular rows also in other proportions. For example, if height of one row is set as 1* and the other as 3*, the second row's height will be three times bigger than the first one.

Apart from the mentioned methods of specifying height, it is also possible to provide fixed values (such as 100) or type * to indicate that the row should fill the remaining space.

Each grid has not only rows, but also at least one column. You can specify them similarly as you specify rows. A part of the code is as follows:

```
<Grid.ColumnDefinitions>
    <ColumnDefinition Width="1*" />
    <ColumnDefinition Width="1*" />
    <ColumnDefinition Width="1*" />
    <ColumnDefinition Width="1*" />
</Grid.ColumnDefinitions>
```

In this case, the grid has four columns with exactly the same width. Thus, each column takes 25 percent of the total width of the Grid control.

The location of a particular control within a grid is specified by Grid.Row and Grid.Column attached properties, as shown in this example. As the values of these properties, you should enter an index of a row and column, respectively. Of course, such indices are zero-based, so the first row and the first column are represented by zero indices.

Apart from placing controls in particular cells, indicated by a given row and column, it is possible to place them in more than one row and more than one column by using Grid.RowSpan and Grid.ColumnSpan. In the example, the place for presenting the result of the calculations should be located in one row, but in all four columns. Thus, the TextBlock control representing the result is defined as follows:

```
<TextBlock
    Grid.Row="0"
    Grid.Column="0"
    Grid.ColumnSpan="4"
    Style="{StaticResource TxtResult}"
    Text="0" />
```

A final design of the calculator is shown in the following screenshot:

See also

- The *Arranging controls vertically* recipe
- The *Arranging controls horizontally* recipe
- The *Arranging controls in a scrollable view* recipe
- The *Arranging controls in absolute positions* recipe

Arranging controls in absolute positions

In some scenarios, it may be necessary to place controls in absolute positions in a given area. Such a task can be performed using the Canvas control. In this recipe, you will learn how to place a rectangle and an ellipse over the image in a fixed location, specified in pixels from the top-left corner.

Getting ready

To step through this recipe, you only need the automatically generated project.

How to do it...

To create a page presenting how to arrange controls in absolute positions, perform the following steps:

1. Add the Image.jpg file to the Assets directory.
2. Modify the content of the MainPage.xaml file as follows:

```
<Page (...) Background="Black">
    <Canvas>
        <Canvas.Background>
            <ImageBrush
                ImageSource="/Assets/Image.jpg"
                Stretch="UniformToFill" />
        </Canvas.Background>
        <Rectangle
            Canvas.Left="50"
            Canvas.Top="100"
            Fill="DarkGreen"
            Width="150"
            Height="50" />
        <Ellipse
            Canvas.Left="100"
            Canvas.Top="450"
            Width="200"
            Height="150">
            <Ellipse.Fill>
                <LinearGradientBrush>
                    <GradientStop Color="Yellow"
                                  Offset="0.2" />
                    <GradientStop Color="Red"
                                  Offset="0.8" />
                </LinearGradientBrush>
            </Ellipse.Fill>
        </Ellipse>
    </Canvas>
</Page>
```

How it works...

As already mentioned, Canvas allows you to place controls in fixed locations, specified in pixels from the top-left corner. In the example shown in this recipe, the canvas has an image-based background and two controls:

- The dark green rectangle (Rectangle) with dimensions 150 x 50 pixels, located 50 pixels from the left and 100 pixels from the top
- The yellow-red ellipse (Ellipse) with dimensions 200 x 150 pixels, located 100 pixels from the left and 450 pixels from the top

The location of a particular control is specified using Canvas.Left and Canvas.Top.

If you run the application, you should see a result similar to the following:

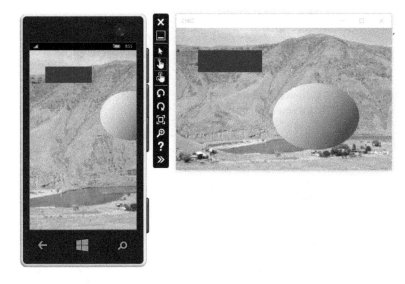

An additional comment regarding a way of defining the fill of the Ellipse control as a gradient is necessary. It can be achieved by using LinearGradientBrush and defining a set of GradientStop elements with the given colors (Color) and offsets (Offset, between 0.0 and 1.0). In the example, the yellow color is used for 20 percent of space, then the color smoothly changes from yellow to red, until it occupies 80 percent of the space. Then, the red color is used.

See also

- The *Arranging controls vertically* recipe
- The *Arranging controls horizontally* recipe
- The *Arranging controls in a scrollable view* recipe
- The *Arranging controls in a grid* recipe

Choosing date and time

When a user of your application enters a particular date or time, such as a birth date or a time when an order should be delivered, it is a good idea to provide a built-in mechanism of choosing the date and time. Such mechanisms allow a user to select them in a comfortable way, without the necessity of entering such information in a textual form. In this recipe, you will learn how to choose a date either from the calendar or a list and how to specify time by choosing a particular hour and minute.

Getting ready

To step through this recipe, you only need the automatically generated project.

How to do it...

To allow a user to choose date or time in a few ways, perform the following steps:

1. To add the `CalendarDatePicker` control to the page, which will allow a user to choose a date from the calendar, modify the content of the `MainPage.xaml` file as follows:

```
<Page (...)>
    <StackPanel Padding="20">
        <CalendarDatePicker
            PlaceholderText="Choose a start date..."
            DateChanged="CalendarDatePicker_DateChanged" />
    </StackPanel>
</Page>
```

2. To handle the event of changing a date in the `CalendarDatePicker` control, modify the code of the `CalendarDatePicker_DateChanged` method in the `MainPage.xaml.cs` file as follows:

```
private void CalendarDatePicker_DateChanged(
    CalendarDatePicker sender,
    CalendarDatePickerDateChangedEventArgs args)
{
    DateTimeOffset? offset = sender.Date;
    if (offset.HasValue)
    {
        DateTime selectedDate = offset.Value.Date;
    }
}
```

3. To add the `DatePicker` control to the page, which will allow a user to select a date by choosing a particular day, month, and year from the list, modify the content of the `MainPage.xaml` file as follows:

```
<Page (...)>
    <StackPanel Padding="20">
        <DatePicker DateChanged="DatePicker_DateChanged" />
    </StackPanel>
</Page>
```

4. To handle the event of changing a date in the `DatePicker` control, modify the code of the `DatePicker_DateChanged` method in the `MainPage.xaml.cs` file as follows:

```
private void DatePicker_DateChanged(
    object sender,
    DatePickerValueChangedEventArgs e)
{
    DateTime selectedDate = e.NewDate.Date;
}
```

5. To add the `TimePicker` control to the page, which will allow a user to select time by choosing a particular hour and minute from the list, modify the content of the `MainPage.xaml` file as follows:

```
<Page (...)>
    <StackPanel Padding="20">
        <TimePicker TimeChanged="TimePicker_TimeChanged" />
    </StackPanel>
</Page>
```

6. To handle the event of changing time in the `TimePicker` control, modify the code of the `TimePicker_TimeChanged` method in the `MainPage.xaml.cs` file as follows:

```
private void TimePicker_TimeChanged(
    object sender,
    TimePickerValueChangedEventArgs e)
{
    TimeSpan selectedTime = e.NewTime;
}
```

How it works...

These code snippets are really simple and self-explanatory. However, some explanation is necessary to show the differences between the `CalendarDatePicker`, `DatePicker`, and `TimePicker` controls.

The first one, `CalendarDatePicker`, presents a textbox by default. When you click on it, a popup with a calendar appears. One can easily select a proper date by clicking on a box representing a particular day. Of course, it is possible to navigate between months. The appearance of this control is as follows:

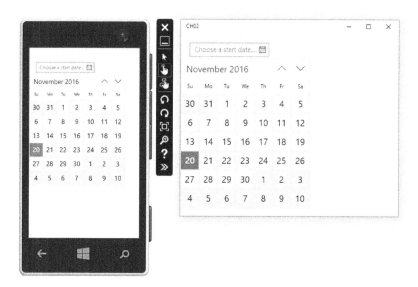

If choosing a date from the calendar is not convenient, you can use the `DatePicker` control. It presents a date that is divided into three parts, namely month, day, and year. After pressing any part, the control expands and the user can select values for a month, day, and year separately. The operation of choosing a particular date is confirmed by pressing a tick icon. Of course, it is also possible to cancel a selection by clicking on the cross icon.

The result is shown in the following image:

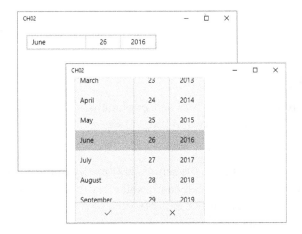

The last control is named `TimePicker`, and it allows a user to choose a given hour and minute. Its operation is very similar to the `DatePicker` control. It presents time divided into three boxes, namely hour, minute, and AM/PM switch. After clicking on the control, it expands and it is possible to select a given time. The result is as follows:

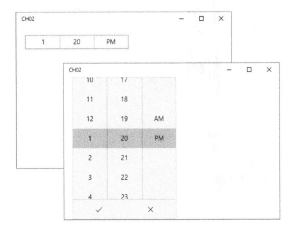

Adding icons to app bars

If you want to allow the user to have quick access to some useful operations, you can equip the page with either the top or bottom app bar. Such bars are collapsed by default, but they can be easily expanded by the user by clicking on them. In this recipe, you will learn how to add icons to both the top and bottom app bars, as well as how to handle the scenario of pressing particular icons.

Getting ready

To step through this recipe, you only need the automatically generated project.

How to do it...

To prepare an example that shows how to add either top or bottom app bar and handle an event of clicking on icons located within an app bar, perform the following steps:

1. To add a bottom app bar with three icons, modify the content of the `MainPage.xaml` file as follows:

```
<Page (...) Background="Black">
    <Grid Padding="20" Background="White">
        <TextBlock
            Text="Exemplary page that contains an app bar
                with a set of icons."
            TextWrapping="Wrap" />
    </Grid>
    <Page.BottomAppBar>
        <AppBar Background="Coral" Foreground="White">
            <StackPanel Orientation="Horizontal">
                <AppBarButton
                    Label="Edit"
                    Foreground="White"
                    Icon="Edit"
                    Click="BtnEdit_Click" />
                <AppBarButton
                    Label="Delete"
                    Foreground="White"
                    Icon="Delete"
                    Click="BtnDelete_Click" />
                <AppBarButton
                    Label="Cancel"
                    Foreground="White"
```

```
                          Icon="Cancel"
                          Click="BtnCancel_Click" />
                   </StackPanel>
               </AppBar>
          </Page.BottomAppBar>
     </Page>
```

2. To handle the event of clicking on an icon, modify the code of a proper method, such as BtnEdit_Click, in the MainPage.xaml.cs file. The automatically generated code of the method is as follows:

```
private void BtnEdit_Click(object sender,
    RoutedEventArgs e) { }
```

3. To replace the bottom app bar with the top app bar, modify the content of the MainPage.xaml file as follows:

```
<Page (...)>
    <Grid (...)>
        <TextBlock
            Text="Exemplary page that contains an app bar
                with a set of icons."
            TextWrapping="Wrap" />
    </Grid>
    <Page.TopAppBar>
        <AppBar Background="RoyalBlue" Foreground="White">
            <StackPanel Orientation="Horizontal">
                <AppBarButton
                    Label="Edit"
                    Foreground="White"
                    Icon="Edit"
                    Click="BtnEdit_Click" />
                <AppBarButton
                    Label="Delete"
                    Foreground="White"
                    Icon="Delete"
                    Click="BtnDelete_Click" />
                <AppBarButton
                    Label="Cancel"
                    Foreground="White"
                    Icon="Cancel"
                    Click="BtnCancel_Click" />
            </StackPanel>
        </AppBar>
    </Page.TopAppBar>
</Page>
```

4. To use both the top app bar and the bottom app bar, both the `TopAppBar` and `BottomAppBar` elements should be set in the `MainPage.xaml` file as follows:

```
<Page (...)>
    <Grid (...)> (...)
    </Grid>
    <Page.BottomAppBar>
        <AppBar Background="Coral" Foreground="White">
            (...)
        </AppBar>
    </Page.BottomAppBar>
    <Page.TopAppBar>
        <AppBar Background="RoyalBlue" Foreground="White">
            (...)
        </AppBar>
    </Page.TopAppBar>
</Page>
```

How it works...

Each app bar is represented by the `AppBar` element, located either in `Page.TopAppBar` or `Page.BottomAppBar`. As shown in the example, it is possible to specify both the color of the app bar (`Background`) and choose the foreground color (`Foreground`). The elements in an app bar are arranged horizontally using the `StackPanel` control. Within it, buttons are placed.

Each button is represented by the `AppBarButton` control and has a given label (`Label`), foreground color (`Foreground`), as well as an icon (`Icon`). You do not need to create your own icons because there is a set of predefined ones that you can easily choose by typing the name of the selected one, such as `Edit` or `Cancel`.

After running the application with app bars, you should get the results shown in the following image. On the left, the top app bar is expanded, while on the right, the bottom one is expanded:

Creating and using a user control

While developing applications, you can use a set of predefined controls, but it is also possible to define your own ones. Such an approach is really beneficial and important. In this recipe, you will learn how to create your own user control (representing a tile with an icon and a title), define its properties, and place it on the page. What is more, you will see how to use the NuGet Package Manager to download additional packages.

Getting ready

To step through this recipe, you only need the automatically generated project.

How to do it...

To install the additional package from the NuGet Package Manager, define an example user control, and place it on the page, you should perform the following steps:

1. Install `PropertyChanged.Fody` using the NuGet Package Manager. To do this, refer to the following steps:
    1. Choose **Manage NuGet Packages...** from the context menu of the project node in the **Solution Explorer** window.
    2. Click on the **Browse** tab in the newly opened window.
    3. Type `PropertyChanged.Fody` in the search box.
    4. Click on the row with **PropertyChanged.Fody**.
    5. Click on the **Install** button, as shown in the following image.
    6. Click on **OK** in the **Preview** window.
    7. Wait until the message **Successfully installed 'PropertyChanged.Fody 1.51.3' to CH02** is presented in the **Output** window:

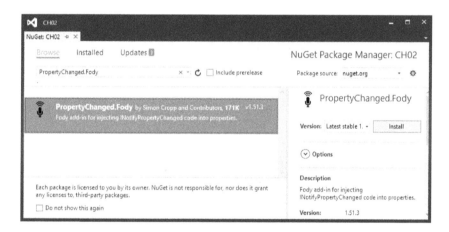

2. Add the `FodyWeavers.xml` file to the project. To do so, refer to this:
    1. Navigate to **Add | New Item...** from the context menu of the project node in the **Solution Explorer** window.
    2. Navigate to **Visual C# | Data** on the left, in the **Add New Item** window. Then, choose **XML File** on the right.
    3. Type `FodyWeavers.xml` as the name of the XML file.
    4. Click on the **Add** button.

3. Modify the content of the `FodyWeavers.xml` file as follows:

```
<?xml version="1.0" encoding="utf-8"?>
<Weavers>
  <PropertyChanged />
</Weavers>
```

4. Add a new user control representing a simple tile. To do so, refer to the following steps:
    1. Navigate to **Add** | **New Item…** from the context menu of the project node in the **Solution Explorer** window.
    2. Navigate to **Visual C#** | **XAML** on the left, in the **Add New Item** window. Then, choose **User Control** on the right.
    3. Type `TileControl.xaml` as the name of the file.
    4. Click on the **Add** button.

5. Design a user control, representing a tile, by modifying the content of the `TileControl.xaml` file as follows:

```xml
<UserControl (...)
    d:DesignHeight="100"
    d:DesignWidth="100">
    <UserControl.Resources>
        <Style x:Key="GrdTile" TargetType="Grid">
            <Setter Property="Padding" Value="5" />
        </Style>
        <Style x:Key="ImgIcon" TargetType="Image">
            <Setter Property="MaxWidth" Value="40" />
            <Setter Property="MaxHeight" Value="40" />
        </Style>
        <Style x:Key="TxtTitle" TargetType="TextBlock">
            <Setter Property="VerticalAlignment"
                    Value="Bottom" />
            <Setter Property="FontSize" Value="12" />
        </Style>
    </UserControl.Resources>
    <Grid
        Style="{StaticResource GrdTile}"
        Background="{Binding TileBackground}">
        <Grid.RowDefinitions>
            <RowDefinition Height="*" />
            <RowDefinition Height="Auto" />
        </Grid.RowDefinitions>
        <Image
            Grid.Row="0"
            Style="{StaticResource ImgIcon}"
            Source="{Binding IconUrl}" />
        <TextBlock
            Grid.Row="1"
            Style="{StaticResource TxtTitle}"
            Text="{Binding Title}"
            Foreground="{Binding TileForeground}" />
    </Grid>
```

```
</UserControl>
```

6. Add the `Favorites.png` and `Settings.png` files to the `Assets` directory. The example `.png` files are available together with the code for this chapter.

7. Define the necessary properties, set the data context, and associate the `ImplementPropertyChanged` attribute with the `TileControl` class. Do this by modifying the `TileControl.xaml.cs` file as follows:

```
using PropertyChanged;
using Windows.UI.Xaml.Controls;
using Windows.UI.Xaml.Media;
namespace CH02
{
    [ImplementPropertyChanged]
    public sealed partial class TileControl : UserControl
    {
        public SolidColorBrush TileBackground { get; set; }
        public SolidColorBrush TileForeground { get; set; }
        public string IconUrl { get; set; }
        public string Title { get; set; }

        public TileControl()
        {
            InitializeComponent();
            DataContext = this;
        }
    }
}
```

8. Place the newly added control (`TileControl`) on the main page and configure it by modifying the content of the `MainPage.xaml` file as follows:

```
<Page (...)>
    <StackPanel HorizontalAlignment="Center">
        <local:TileControl
            TileBackground="#353535"
            TileForeground="White"
            Title="Favorites"
            IconUrl="/Assets/Favorites.png"
            Width="100"
            Height="100"
            Margin="0 0 0 20"
            Tapped="TilFavorites_Tapped" />
        <local:TileControl
            TileBackground="RoyalBlue"
            TileForeground="White"
            Title="Settings"
```

```
                    IconUrl="/Assets/Settings.png"
                    Width="100"
                    Height="100"
                    Tapped="TilSettings_Tapped" />
          </StackPanel>
      </Page>
```

9. Handle the events of clicking on particular tiles by adjusting the body of the `TilFavorites_Tapped` and `TilSettings_Tapped` methods.

How it works...

If you run the application, you should get the result shown in the following screenshot:

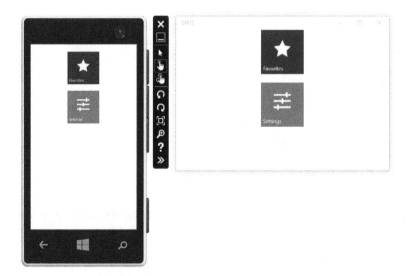

The page contains two tiles: the first represents the **Favorites** option, while the other is related to **Settings**. Each tile has 100 x 100 pixels, a background in a given color, a centered icon, and a caption in the bottom-left corner.

The creation of a user control is a bit more complex topic, which requires additional explanation and comments. First of all, the design of the control is defined in the `.xaml` file, while the associated C# code is located in the `.xaml.cs` file. As you can see, designing a user control is very similar to designing a page. Thus, you can define styles and use a set of controls, including `Grid`, `Image`, and `TextBlock`, as presented in the code that you just saw.

The control can represent various tiles. For this reason, it is crucial to provide a developer with the possibility to adjust its appearance. This can be achieved using a set of properties. Each of them can have different values in the case of each instance of the control. In the example, `TileControl` has four properties, namely representing a brush for background and foreground (`TileBackground` and `TileForeground`, respectively), an address to the icon (`IconUrl`), and a presented text (`Title`), as defined in the `TileControl.xaml.cs` file. The values of such properties are set in the `MainPage.xaml` file for each instance of the control.

However, how can you specify how particular properties affect the appearance of the control? The impact is defined in the `TileControl.xaml` file, where particular properties of `TileControl` are bound to the properties of controls located within `TileControl`:

- `TileBackground`: To set the `Background` property of `Grid`
- `IconUrl`: To set the `Source` property of `Image`
- `Title`: To set the `Text` property of `TextBlock`
- `TileForeground`: To set the `Foreground` property of `TextBlock`

What is more, the data context used for binding is specified in the constructor of the `TileControl` class, within the `TileControl.xaml.cs` file. Here, an instance of `TileControl` is assigned to the `DataContext` property.

 The binding is one of the most important topics of Chapter 3, *MVVM and Data Binding*, where you can find more information about this subject.

The last comment is necessary for the `ImplementPropertyChanged` attribute associated with the `TileControl` class. This attribute is defined within the `PropertyChanged.Fody` package. It allows an automatic notification when the values of properties (defined within the class with this attribute) change. For this reason, it is possible to automatically update each `TileControl` when the values of its properties, such as `Title`, change.

See also

- The *Creating the view model for a page* recipe in Chapter 3, *MVVM and Data Binding*

Presenting a message dialog

There is often a necessity to confirm some operations performed by a user, for example, removing an item or placing an order. There are various ways to do this, such as using an additional message dialog. In this recipe, you will learn how to present a message dialog after pressing the **Delete** button and how to handle the event of choosing an option presented in this dialog.

Getting ready

To step through this recipe, you only need the automatically generated project.

How to do it...

To prepare an example that shows how to present a message dialog and handle the event of choosing an option shown within it, perform the following steps:

1. Add the **Delete** button on the page by modifying the content of the `MainPage.xaml` file as follows:

```
<Page (...)>
    <StackPanel Padding="20">
        <Button
            Content="Delete"
            HorizontalAlignment="Center"
            Click="BtnDelete_Click" />
    </StackPanel>
</Page>
```

2. Present the message dialog after pressing the **Delete** button. Do this by modifying the code of the `BtnDelete_Click` method within the `MainPage.xaml.cs` file as follows:

```
private async void BtnDelete_Click(object sender,
    RoutedEventArgs e)
{
    MessageDialog dialog = new MessageDialog(
        "Are you sure that you want to delete this entry?",
        "Confirmation");
    dialog.Commands.Add(
        new UICommand("Yes", DeleteConfirmed));
    dialog.Commands.Add(new UICommand("No"));
```

```
    await dialog.ShowAsync();
}
```

3. Specify additional operations performed when a user clicks on the **Yes** option in the message dialog by adjusting the code of the `DeleteConfirmed` method, as shown in the following code snippet:

```
private async void DeleteConfirmed(IUICommand command)
{
    await Task.Delay(1000);
    MessageDialog dialog = new MessageDialog(
        "The entry has been removed successfully!",
        "Confirmation");
    dialog.Commands.Add(new UICommand("OK"));
    await dialog.ShowAsync();
}
```

How it works...

Showing a message dialog is performed using the `MessageDialog` class. In its constructor, you can specify both the content and title, as shown in the `BtnDelete_Click` method. You can also define the options presented in the message dialog, using the `Commands` property. In the first message dialog, two options are added, namely **Yes** and **No**. When the user clicks on the **Yes** option, the `DeleteConfirmed` method is called.

The message dialog is presented after calling the `ShowAsync` method. It is worth mentioning that such a method is awaitable, thus the `await` operator is used. What is more, the `async` keyword is applied to the `BtnDelete_Click` method.

 The `await` and `async` keywords support asynchronous programming. You can find more information about it at `https://msdn.microsoft.com /en-us/library/mt674882.aspx`.

The message dialog shown after you click on the **Delete** button is as follows:

In the case of the second message dialog, only one option is added, namely **OK**. There is no additional method specified for handling the event of pressing it. It is important that the presentation of the second message dialog is delayed by one second using the `Delay` static method of the `Task` class.

See also

- The *Localizing content programmatically* recipe

Adjusting design based on the device type

UWP applications can run on many devices, including smartphones, tablets, and desktops. However, such devices contain screens of various sizes. Of course, not all designs will look great on both smartphones and big displays. For this reason, it is sometimes a beneficial approach to create separate designs for various device families.

In this recipe, you will learn how to prepare the same registration form in two versions: the default one suitable for desktops and a special one dedicated to smartphones.

Getting ready

To step through this recipe, you only need the automatically generated project.

How to do it...

To create the registration form with smartphone and desktop-oriented versions, you should perform the following steps:

1. Create a page with the design adjusted to desktops by modifying the content of the `MainPage.xaml` file as follows:

```
<Page (...)
    Background="White">
    <ScrollViewer>
        <Grid>
            <Grid.RowDefinitions>
                <RowDefinition Height="20" />
                <RowDefinition Height="Auto" />
                <RowDefinition Height="40" />
                <RowDefinition Height="Auto" />
                <RowDefinition Height="40" />
                <RowDefinition Height="Auto" />
                <RowDefinition Height="40" />
                <RowDefinition Height="Auto" />
                <RowDefinition Height="40" />
                <RowDefinition Height="Auto" />
                <RowDefinition Height="20" />
            </Grid.RowDefinitions>
            <Grid.ColumnDefinitions>
                <ColumnDefinition Width="20" />
                <ColumnDefinition Width="1*" />
                <ColumnDefinition Width="20" />
                <ColumnDefinition Width="1*" />
                <ColumnDefinition Width="20" />
            </Grid.ColumnDefinitions>
            <TextBlock
                Grid.Row="1"
                Grid.Column="1"
                Grid.ColumnSpan="3"
                FontSize="42"
```

```
                TextWrapping="Wrap">
            <Run Text="Register" />
            <Run Text=" / Please complete the following
                     form to create a new account."
                 FontSize="20"
                 Foreground="Gray" />
        </TextBlock>
        <TextBox
            Grid.Row="3"
            Grid.Column="1"
            PlaceholderText="Type a first name..."
            Header="First name"
            InputScope="PersonalFullName"
            FontSize="20" />
        <TextBox
            Grid.Row="3"
            Grid.Column="3"
            PlaceholderText="Type a first name..."
            Header="Last name"
            InputScope="PersonalFullName"
            FontSize="20" />
        <TextBox
            Grid.Row="5"
            Grid.Column="1"
            PlaceholderText="Type an e-mail address..."
            Header="E-mail address"
            InputScope="EmailNameOrAddress"
            FontSize="20" />
        <TextBox
            Grid.Row="5"
            Grid.Column="3"
            PlaceholderText="Type a phone number..."
            Header="Phone number"
            InputScope="NameOrPhoneNumber"
            FontSize="20" />
        <DatePicker
            Grid.Row="7"
            Grid.Column="1"
            Header="Birth date"
            FontSize="20" />
        <ComboBox
            Grid.Row="7"
            Grid.Column="3"
            PlaceholderText="Choose a country..."
            Header="Country"
            SelectedIndex="0"
            FontSize="20"
            HorizontalAlignment="Stretch">
```

```xml
            <ComboBoxItem Content="Poland" Tag="PL" />
            <ComboBoxItem Content="Germany" Tag="DE" />
            <ComboBoxItem Content="England" Tag="EN" />
        </ComboBox>
        <Button
            Grid.Row="9"
            Grid.Column="3"
            Content="Submit"
            FontSize="22"
            BorderBrush="Gray"
            BorderThickness="2"
            Background="LightGray"
            HorizontalAlignment="Right"
            Padding="30 10" />
    </Grid>
  </ScrollViewer>
</Page>
```

2. To prepare the location of .xaml files for the smartphone-based version, add the DeviceFamily-Mobile folder to the project by navigating to **Add | New Folder** from the context menu of the project node in the **Solution Explorer** window. Once you are there, type the DeviceFamily-Mobile name.

3. Add the MainPage.xaml file to the DeviceFamily-Mobile folder. To do so, refer to the following steps:

    1. Navigate to **Add | New Item...** from the context menu of the DeviceFamily-Mobile node in the **Solution Explorer** window.

    2. Select the **XAML** option under **Visual C#** on the left, in the **Add New Item** window. Then, choose **XAML View** on the right.

    3. Type MainPage.xaml as the name.

    4. Click on the **Add** button.

4. Design the page for smartphones by modifying the content of the MainPage.xaml file (in the DeviceFamily-Mobile folder) as follows:

```xml
<Page (...)
    Background="White">
    <ScrollViewer>
        <StackPanel Padding="20">
            <TextBlock
                Text="Register"
                FontSize="30"
                HorizontalAlignment="Center" />
            <TextBlock
                Text="Please complete the following form to
                    create a new account."
```

```
                    TextWrapping="Wrap"
                    FontSize="18"
                    Margin="0 20" />
            <TextBox
                    PlaceholderText="Type a first name..."
                    Header="First name"
                    InputScope="PersonalFullName"
                    FontSize="18" />
            <TextBox
                    PlaceholderText="Type a first name..."
                    Header="Last name"
                    InputScope="PersonalFullName"
                    FontSize="18"
                    Margin="0 20 0 0" />
            <TextBox
                    PlaceholderText="Type an e-mail address..."
                    Header="E-mail address"
                    InputScope="EmailNameOrAddress"
                    FontSize="18"
                    Margin="0 20 0 0" />
            <TextBox
                    PlaceholderText="Type a phone number..."
                    Header="Phone number"
                    InputScope="NameOrPhoneNumber"
                    FontSize="18"
                    Margin="0 20 0 0" />
            <DatePicker
                    Header="Birth date"
                    FontSize="18"
                    HorizontalAlignment="Stretch"
                    Margin="0 20 0 0" />
            <ComboBox
                    PlaceholderText="Choose a country..."
                    Header="Country"
                    SelectedIndex="0"
                    FontSize="18"
                    Margin="0 20 0 0"
                    HorizontalAlignment="Stretch">
                    <ComboBoxItem Content="Poland" Tag="PL" />
                    <ComboBoxItem Content="Germany" Tag="DE" />
                    <ComboBoxItem Content="England" Tag="EN" />
            </ComboBox>
            <Button
                    Content="Submit"
                    Margin="0 30 0 0"
                    HorizontalAlignment="Stretch"
                    FontSize="18"
                    BorderBrush="Gray"
```

```
                BorderThickness="2"
                Background="LightGray"
                Padding="10" />
        </StackPanel>
    </ScrollViewer>
</Page>
```

How it works...

By preparing two `.xaml` files with the same name (one located in the main directory and the other in `DeviceFamily-Mobile`), it is possible to automatically choose a proper design of the page, depending on a device family. If the application is running on a smartphone, the version of the `MainPage.xaml` file from `DeviceFamily-Mobile` is used. Otherwise, the default `MainPage.xaml` file is applied.

 There are no code-behind files for each device family. The same general `.xaml.cs` file is used for all the versions of the same page.

You can easily see the project in action by running the same application in the smartphone emulator and on the local machine, as shown in the following screenshot:

Of course, you can add separate XAML views for other device families as well. In such a case, you need to create a directory that contains the name of the device family after a dash, for instance, `DeviceFamily-Desktop` or `DeviceFamily-IoT`. When a particular `.xaml` page has its version dedicated to the current device family, it is used automatically.

Localizing content in XAML

In the previous recipes, all the pages are only in English. It means that people who do not know this language may have serious problems using the solution. Fortunately, the localization of your application is really simple, thus it can support multiple languages. You will learn how to do this in this recipe.

Getting ready

To step through this recipe, you only need the automatically generated project.

How to do it...

To create a page with the form of adding a new entry and prepare localized resources (currently only in one language), perform the following steps:

1. Design the page, which should contain a header, textboxes for a title and content, and a button. To do this, adjust the content of the `MainPage.xaml` file as follows:

```
<Page (...)>
    <ScrollViewer>
        <StackPanel Padding="20">
            <TextBlock
                x:Uid="TxtEntryHeader"
                FontSize="26"
                Margin="0 0 0 20" />
            <TextBox
                x:Uid="TxtEntryTitle"
                Margin="0 0 0 20" />
            <TextBox
                x:Uid="TxtEntryContent"
                TextWrapping="Wrap"
                Height="200" />
            <Button
                x:Uid="BtnEntrySubmit"
                HorizontalAlignment="Stretch"
                Padding="10"
                Margin="0 20 0 0" />
        </StackPanel>
    </ScrollViewer>
</Page>
```

2. Add the `Strings` folder within the project by navigating to **Add | New Folder** from the context menu of the project node in the **Solution Explorer** window and typing the `Strings` name.

3. Add the `en-US` folder within the `Strings` folder by navigating to **Add | New Folder** from the context menu of the `Strings` directory in the **Solution Explorer** window and typing the `en-US` name.

4. Add the `Resources.resw` file for localized strings. To do so, refer to this:

   1. Navigate to **Add | New Item...** from the context menu of the `en-US` folder node in the **Solution Explorer** window.

   2. Select the **XAML** option under **Visual C#** on the left, in the **Add New Item** window. Then, choose **Resources File (.resw)** on the right.

   3. Click on the **Add** button.

5. Open the `Resources.resw` file and provide the values, as shown in the following screenshot:

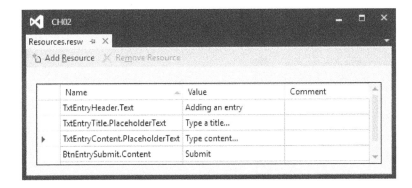

How it works...

As you can see, the XAML code shown in this recipe differs from others, presented earlier. Here, unique identifiers (`x:Uid`) are assigned to some controls, namely `TextBlock`, two `TextBox`, and `Button`. The identifier is used to automatically set the values of properties (such as `Text`, `PlaceholderText`, or `Content`) depending on the current language. Thus, it is unnecessary to set the values of such properties directly in the XAML code.

The localized content is stored in the resource files that have the .resx extension. Such files are located in the subfolders of the Strings folder within the project. The name of the subfolder is the language code, such as en-US or pl-PL. For this reason, to support the English language, the Resources.resw file is added to the Strings\en-US folder.

Within a resource file, there is a set of translations. To automatically assign a localized string to a property of a control with a given unique identifier, the name should be set as [unique-identifier].[property-name], such as the following:

- Use TxtEntryHeader.Text to set a value of the Text property of TxtEntryHeader
- Use TxtEntryTitle.PlaceholderText to set a value of the PlaceholderText property of TxtEntryTitle
- Use BtnEntrySubmit.Content to set a value of the Content property of BtnEntrySubmit

If you run the application, you should get the result shown in the following screenshot. The header text, the placeholder texts, and the button content are automatically set:

See also

- The *Localizing content programmatically* recipe
- The *Forcing the current language* recipe

Localizing content programmatically

Some strings could also be set programmatically from code-behind files. To prepare a localized application, it is also necessary to translate them and present in the current language. In this recipe, you will learn how to use the `ResourceLoader` class to programmatically get localized content.

Getting ready

To step through this recipe, you need the project created in the previous recipe.

How to do it...

To prepare an example that shows how to localize content programmatically, you need to perform the following steps:

1. Handle the event of clicking on the **Submit** button by modifying the `MainPage.xaml` file as follows:

```
<Page (...)>
    <ScrollViewer>
        <StackPanel Padding="20"> (...)
            <Button
                x:Uid="BtnEntrySubmit"
                HorizontalAlignment="Stretch"
                Padding="10"
                Margin="0 20 0 0"
                Click="BtnSubmit_Click" />
        </StackPanel>
    </ScrollViewer>
</Page>
```

2. Present a localized message dialog after clicking on the **Submit** button by modifying the code of the `BtnSubmit_Click` method in the `MainPage.xaml.cs` file as follows:

```
private async void BtnSubmit_Click(object sender,
    RoutedEventArgs e)
{
    ResourceLoader loader = new ResourceLoader();
    MessageDialog dialog = new MessageDialog(
        loader.GetString("EntryAddedMessageContent"),
        loader.GetString("EntryAddedMessageTitle"));
    dialog.Commands.Add(new UICommand(
        loader.GetString("OK")));
    await dialog.ShowAsync();
}
```

3. Add missing resources to `Strings\en-US\Resources.resw`:
   1. **EntryAddedMessageContent** with its value: `The entry has been submitted successfully. Thank you!`.
   2. **EntryAddedMessageTitle** with its value: `Entry added`.
   3. **OK** with its value: `OK`.

How it works...

Access to the localized strings in a programmatic way is possible using the `ResourceLoader` class and its method, named `GetString`. To get a string, you should pass a name of the resource as its parameter. As a result, you will receive a value of the localized string from a proper resource file, depending on the current language used in the application.

After running the application and pressing the **Submit** button, you should get the following result:

See also

- The *Presenting a message dialog* recipe
- The *Localizing content in XAML* recipe
- The *Forcing the current language* recipe

Forcing the current language

By default, the current language is automatically obtained, based on the settings of the operating system. However, sometimes you may need to programmatically force the current language, for instance, to allow a user to use an application in more than one language, which could be switched according to the user's needs. In this recipe, you will learn how to force the current language within the application.

Getting ready

To step through this recipe, you need the project from the previous recipe.

How to do it...

To add translations in another language and force the language to Polish in the application, you should perform the following steps:

1. Translate the content to the Polish language. To do so, refer to the following steps:
    1. Add the pl-PL folder to the Strings folder.
    2. Add the Resources.resw file to the pl-PL folder.
    3. Provide the values in the Resources.resw file, as follows:

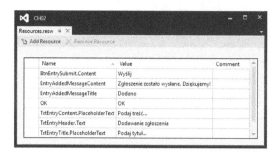

2. Force the current language to Polish by modifying the body of the OnLaunched method in the App.xaml.cs file as follows:

```
protected override void OnLaunched(
    LaunchActivatedEventArgs e)
{
    CultureInfo culture = new CultureInfo("pl-PL");
    ApplicationLanguages.PrimaryLanguageOverride =
        culture.Name;
    CultureInfo.DefaultThreadCurrentCulture = culture;
    CultureInfo.DefaultThreadCurrentUICulture = culture;
    (...)
}
```

How it works...

To force the current language while launching the application, create a new instance of the CultureInfo class passing the language code (pl-PL) in its constructor, as follows:

```
CultureInfo culture = new CultureInfo("pl-PL");
```

Then, set a value of the PrimaryLanguageOverride property:

```
ApplicationLanguages.PrimaryLanguageOverride = culture.Name;
```

At the end, the CultureInfo instance is assigned to the DefaultThreadCurrentCulture and DefaultThreadCurrentUICulture static properties of the CultureInfo class:

```
CultureInfo.DefaultThreadCurrentCulture = culture;
CultureInfo.DefaultThreadCurrentUICulture = culture;
```

As a result, after running the application, you should get the content provided in Polish (pl-PL), as follows (on the right-hand side):

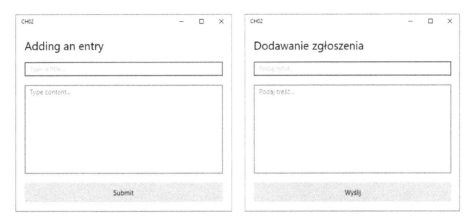

See also

- The *Localizing content in XAML* recipe
- The *Localizing content programmatically* recipe

3
MVVM and Data Binding

In this chapter, we will cover the following recipes:

- Creating the view model for a page
- Introducing bindings and commands
- Binding a value to a textbox
- Binding with a value converter
- Using value converters with parameters
- Showing a progress bar during calculations
- Binding a collection to a list view
- Binding a collection to a grid view
- Binding a collection to a combobox
- Binding a collection to a hub

Introduction

In the previous chapters, you learned how to start developing applications that could be run on various devices, including smartphones and desktops. Then you learned how to design a user interface using a set of predefined and user-defined controls. You also learned how to adjust the design to accommodate various device families.

However, in the case of more complex applications, it is crucial that you organize the project in a suitable way in order to simplify development and introducing further modifications. One of the convenient approaches is the application of the **Model-View-ViewModel** (**MVVM**) design pattern.

This pattern divides the project into three parts, namely model, view, and view model. Each of them performs a specific role and allows you to separate various parts of the project, as shown in the following image:

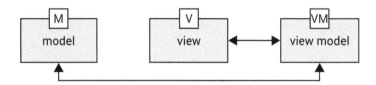

The first part, namely **model**, is related to the business logic of the application. Here you should place, for instance, classes representing entities in the local database, configuration data, or classes that perform various calculations.

The **view** is another part of the project, according to the MVVM design pattern, which represents the user interface. Here, you can locate .xaml files with XAML-based content regarding a page. Of course, this part also contains the code-behind files (.xaml.cs).

The last part of the project is **view model**. It represents the presentation logic for the user interface. As you will see in this chapter, you can create a separate class for each page. The class can contain a set of properties representing values that should be shown in the user interface or which should be set during actions taken by a user, such as after typing a text in a textbox.

While using the MVVM design pattern, it is really easy to apply the **data binding** mechanism. Thus, you can define how data should be presented in the user interface directly in XAML, not within a code-behind file. What is more, the user interface could be automatically updated when the values in an associated view model change. You can also use commands to specify operations that should be performed after a user completes some actions in the user interface, such as clicking on a button.

To take advantage of the data binding mechanism, it is beneficial to learn how to bind particular controls to the properties from the view model. What is more, such an approach allows you to present a collection of items from the view model in the predefined **items controls**, such as ListView, GridView, or ComboBox. Thus, you can just specify the source of the items and a way to render each one of them, and the rest is performed automatically using the data binding mechanism. As you will see, it is a really great feature that can significantly speed up development, shorten code, and make its maintenance easier.

As already mentioned, the data binding mechanism allows you to directly take into account the values from the view model. However, it also allows you to use values after the conversions provided by value converters, either with or without an additional parameter. This topic is also covered in this chapter, together with some examples.

Creating the view model for a page

Let's start by creating the view model for a default page within the automatically generated project. This requires a set of steps, including the installation of the additional package using the NuGet Package Manager, creating suitable directories in the project, and defining some classes. All of these steps are explained in detail in this recipe.

 The content of this recipe also performs a very important role in the subsequent recipes in this chapter. The set of steps allows you to prepare the custom configuration of the MVVM design pattern, which will be used for further examples as well.

Getting ready

To step through this recipe, you need only the automatically generated project.

How to do it...

To create the view model for a default page, perform the following steps:

1. Install `PropertyChanged.Fody` using the NuGet Package Manager. To do so, refer to the following steps:
   1. Choose **Manage NuGet Packages...** from the context menu of the project node in the **Solution Explorer** window.
   2. Click on the **Browse** tab in the newly opened window.
   3. Type `PropertyChanged.Fody` in the search box.
   4. Click on the row with **PropertyChanged.Fody**.
   5. Click on the **Install** button.
   6. Click on **OK** in the **Preview** window.
   7. Wait until the message **Successfully installed 'PropertyChanged.Fody 1.51.3' to CH03** is presented in the **Output** window.
2. Add the `FodyWeavers.xml` file to the project. To do so, refer to this:
   1. Navigate to **Add | New Item...** from the context menu of the project node in the **Solution Explorer** window.
   2. Select the **Data** option under **Visual C#** on the left, in the **Add New Item** window. Then, choose **XML File** on the right.
   3. Type `FodyWeavers.xml` as the name of the XML file.

4. Click on the **Add** button.

3. Modify the content of the `FodyWeavers.xml` file, as follows:

```xml
<?xml version="1.0" encoding="utf-8"?>
<Weavers>
  <PropertyChanged />
</Weavers>
```

4. Add the `ViewModels` folder by navigating to **Add | New Folder** from the context menu of the project node in the **Solution Explorer** window and typing the `ViewModels` name. The `.cs` files with classes representing view models will be stored within the `ViewModels` folder.

5. Add the `MainViewModel` class by navigating to **Add | Class...** from the context menu of the `ViewModels` folder and typing `MainViewModel.cs` as the name in the **Add New Item** window.

6. Define four properties in the view model class, and associate the class with the `ImplementPropertyChanged` attribute by adjusting the code of the `MainViewModel` class in the `MainViewModel.cs` file as follows:

```csharp
[ImplementPropertyChanged]
public class MainViewModel
{
    public string FirstName { get; set; } = "Marcin";
    public string LastName { get; set; } = "Jamro";
    public DateTime BirthDate { get; set; }
        = new DateTime(1988, 11, 9);
    public bool AreRulesAccepted { get; set; } = false;
}
```

Do not forget to add `using` statements for the `PropertyChanged` and `System` namespaces.

7. Add the `Views` folder to the project. The directory will contain `.xaml` and `.xaml.cs` files representing particular pages.

8. Move the `MainPage.xaml` file to the `Views` folder by dragging it to the proper directory in the **Solution Explorer** window.

9. Modify the namespace of the `MainPage` class, add a field representing the view model, and set the data context of the page. To do so, adjust the content of the `MainPage.xaml.cs` file as follows:

```csharp
using CH03.ViewModels;
```

```
using Windows.UI.Xaml.Controls;
namespace CH03.Views
{
    public sealed partial class MainPage : Page
    {
        private MainViewModel _vm = null;

        public MainPage()
        {
            InitializeComponent();
            _vm = new MainViewModel();
            DataContext = _vm;
        }
    }
}
```

Do not forget to adjust the namespace after moving the .xaml and .xaml.cs files manually to the Views folder.

10. Update the namespace of the class specified in the Page element by making a change in the MainPage.xaml file as follows:

```
<Page
    x:Class="CH03.Views.MainPage" (...)> (...)
</Page>
```

11. Add the following using statement to the App.xaml.cs file:

```
using CH03.Views;
```

12. Add the Models directory to the project. Within it, the .cs files with classes representing models will be stored.

13. Add the RelayCommand.cs file to the Models directory. It will contain the code of the RelayCommand class, representing a command that is executed when some operation is performed, such as when the user clicks on a button. Then, adjust the code of the RelayCommand class as follows:

```
public class RelayCommand : ICommand
{
    private Action _action = null;
    public event EventHandler CanExecuteChanged;

    public RelayCommand(Action action)
    {
```

```
        _action = action;
    }

    public bool CanExecute(object parameter)
    {
        return true;
    }

    public void Execute(object parameter)
    {
        _action();
    }
}
```

 Do not forget to add using statements for the System and
System.Windows.Input namespaces.

How it works...

The configuration of the view model for a particular page seems to be quite complicated.
Fortunately, it is not so difficult when you understand the purpose of the following steps.
For this reason, here you will find a detailed description of each step.

As you already know, the project designed according to the MVVM design pattern is
divided into three parts, namely model, view, and view model. For this reason, such
directories (Models, Views, and ViewModels) are added to the project (steps 4, 7, and 12 in
the list you just saw). In each of them, a specified set of files is stored:

- Models: These are .cs files with classes that represent, for example, a model of
  data stored in the database or received from the API
- Views: These are .xaml and .xaml.cs (code-behind) files that represent pages
  and user controls
- ViewModels: These are .cs files with classes that represent the view models for
  particular pages

One of the important tasks is the creation of a class that represents a view model for each
page (step 6). Such a class contains a set of properties, the values of which could be
presented in the user interface in various ways, such as the following:

- A string value shown as text within a textbox or a text block
- A Boolean value that specifies whether a checkbox is set

- A collection of items presented in a list view, a grid view, or a combobox

In the example shown in this recipe, four properties are defined, representing the first and last name (of the `string` type), birth date (`DateTime`), and a value indicating whether the rules are accepted (`bool`). What is more, default values are assigned to all of these properties.

The data binding mechanism allows you to present values from the view model in the user interface and automatically update it when these values change. To do so, it is necessary to notify the mechanism that a value of a particular property has changed. Such a task can be easily solved by associating the view model class with the `ImplementPropertyChanged` attribute from the `PropertyChanged.Fody` package, which can be downloaded using the NuGet Package Manager (step 1). It is worth mentioning that `PropertyChanged.Fody` requires a simple configuration, as shown in steps 2 and 3.

The next group of configuration operations is related to the views within the project. In this case, the files of the automatically generated page (`MainPage.xaml` and `MainPage.xaml.cs`) are moved to the `Views` folder (step 8). Of course, this step is not mandatory, but it is beneficial to store all the views in the same directory, such as `Views`. Then, it is necessary to adjust the content of the `MainPage.xaml.cs` file (step 9) by adding the _vm field, which is an instance of the view model class. A new instance of the `MainViewModel` class is assigned to this field in the constructor. You should not forget to indicate that the view model is used as a data context for the current page, so you can bind controls to the properties from the view model, as presented in the following recipes.

Along with the change of the namespace in which the `MainPage` class is defined (steps 9 and 10), it is also necessary to add the missing `using` statement (regarding `CH03.Views`) in the `App.xaml.cs` file, as mentioned in step 11.

At the end (step 13), the `RelayCommand` class is prepared to support **commands** with the data binding mechanism, as shown in the following recipe. The class implements the `ICommand` interface and allows you to specify an action performed while executing the command. This action is passed as a parameter to the constructor.

 You will see the data binding mechanism in action, together with the presented configuration of the MVVM design pattern, in the following recipes.

There's more…

The previously presented steps are necessary to configure the view model for an automatically generated page. Of course, the process of configuration is much simpler for the next pages. If you want to add another page (for example, `ProductsPage`), only the following steps are required:

1. Add a class representing the view model (`ProductsViewModel`) to the `ViewModels` directory as well as define its properties and associate the class with the `ImplementPropertyChanged` attribute.

2. Adjust the code-behind file of the page (`ProductsPage.xaml.cs`) by doing the following steps:

    1. Define a field representing the view model (_vm).
    2. Assign an instance of the view model class (`ProductsViewModel`) to the _vm field in the constructor.
    3. Indicate that the instance of the view model class is used as a data context of the page by assigning the _vm field to the `DataContext` property.

See also

- The *Introducing bindings and commands* recipe
- The *Binding a value to a textbox* recipe
- The *Binding a collection to a list view* recipe
- The *Binding a collection to a grid view* recipe
- The *Binding a collection to a combobox* recipe
- The *Binding a collection to a hub* recipe

Introducing bindings and commands

When the view model is properly configured for a page, it is necessary to indicate how the values of properties should be shown in the user interface, such as where a particular string value should be presented. Of course, it is possible to use the data binding mechanism not only to bind textual values, but also to support other types, such as colors.

What is more, the data binding mechanism supports **commands**. They allow you to place C# code to handle a particular scenario (such as clicking on a button) in a view model class, not in a code-behind file. In the presented MVVM configuration, the usage of commands requires the `RelayCommand` class, as presented in the previous recipe.

As an example, you will create a simple page with a text block and a button. In the text block, the invitation is shown as **Hello, Guest** or **Hello, Marcin**, depending on whether the user is logged in. The button content (**Log in** or **Log out**) as well as its background (green or red) also changes when the user logs in or logs out.

Getting ready

To step through this recipe, you need the automatically generated project configured according to the MVVM design pattern, as described in the *Creating the view model for a page* recipe.

How to do it...

To prepare an example that shows how to use bindings and commands, you should perform the following steps:

1. Define the necessary properties (`UserName`, `ButtonText`, `ButtonColor`) and the command (`CmdLogInOut`). Also, define a private method (`LogInOut`), which will be called when the `CmdLogInOut` command is executed. To do so, modify the code of the `MainViewModel` class in the `MainViewModel.cs` file, as shown in the following code:

```
[ImplementPropertyChanged]
public class MainViewModel
{
    public const string GUEST_NAME = "Guest";
    public const string USER_NAME = "Marcin";
    public const string BTN_TEXT_LOG_IN = "Log in";
    public const string BTN_TEXT_LOG_OUT = "Log out";
    public const string BTN_COLOR_LOG_IN = "#a1ef92";
    public const string BTN_COLOR_LOG_OUT = "#f17272";

    public string UserName { get; set; } = GUEST_NAME;
    public string ButtonText { get; set; } = BTN_TEXT_LOG_IN;
    public string ButtonColor { get; set; } =
        BTN_COLOR_LOG_IN;
    public ICommand CmdLogInOut { get; set; }
```

```
public MainViewModel()
{
    CmdLogInOut = new RelayCommand(() => LogInOut());
}

private void LogInOut()
{
    if (UserName == GUEST_NAME)
    {
        ButtonColor = BTN_COLOR_LOG_OUT;
        ButtonText = BTN_TEXT_LOG_OUT;
        UserName = USER_NAME;
    }
    else
    {
        ButtonColor = BTN_COLOR_LOG_IN;
        ButtonText = BTN_TEXT_LOG_IN;
        UserName = GUEST_NAME;
    }
}
}
```

 Do not forget to add `using` statements for the `CH03.Models`, `PropertyChanged`, and `System.Windows.Input` namespaces.

2. Bind the properties of the view model class to the properties of the `TextBlock` and `Button` controls. First of all, present a username (a value of the `UserName` property from the view model class) within the text block. Then, specify a proper content (`ButtonText`) and background (`ButtonColor`) of the button. At the end, choose the command executed when a user clicks on the button (`CmdLogInOut`). To perform all of these tasks, modify the XAML code within the `MainPage.xaml` file as follows:

```
<Page (...)>
    <StackPanel
        Background="White"
        Padding="20">
        <TextBlock FontSize="20">
            <Run Text="Hello," />
            <Run Text="{Binding UserName}"
                FontWeight="Bold" />
            <Run Text=":-)" />
        </TextBlock>
        <Button
```

```
                    Content="{Binding ButtonText}"
                    Background="{Binding ButtonColor}"
                    Command="{Binding CmdLogInOut}"
                    Margin="0 20 0 0"
                    Padding="10"
                    FontSize="20"
                    HorizontalAlignment="Stretch" />
        </StackPanel>
    </Page>
```

How it works...

The most complicated part of the code is located in the `MainViewModel` class. Here, you define six constant string values that represent the names of logged-out and logged-in users (`GUEST_NAME` and `USER_NAME`) as well as the content (`BTN_TEXT_LOG_IN` and `BTN_TEXT_LOG_OUT`) and color (`BTN_COLOR_LOG_IN` and `BTN_COLOR_LOG_OUT`) of the button in two states: for the logged-out and logged-in user. By using constant values, the code becomes clearer and simpler for further modifications.

Apart from constant values, three `string` properties are defined (`UserName`, `ButtonText`, and `ButtonColor`) together with their default values. These properties are used by the data binding mechanism to present proper text and color to the user interface.

 Apart from the `{Binding}` markup extension, you can use the `{x:Bind}` markup extension. It is a new but powerful and interesting feature available for developing applications for Windows 10. You can find more information about it at `https://msdn.microsoft.com/windows/uwp/xaml -platform/x-bind-markup-extension`.

Another interesting part of the code is the definition of the `CmdLogInOut` property with a type set to `ICommand`. When you bind to it in the XAML code, the command will be executed when an operation is performed, for example, when a user clicks on a button. To specify which method from the view model class should be executed in such a case, you need to set a value of the `CmdLogInOut` property. It can be done in the constructor of the `MainViewModel` class by assigning a new instance of `RelayCommand` with the lambda expression given as a parameter, as follows:

```
CmdLogInOut = new RelayCommand(() => LogInOut());
```

This statement indicates that the LogInOut method should be called when the command is being executed. For this reason, you should also define the LogInOut private method. In the example, it only verifies whether a user is logged in (by comparing UserName with GUEST_NAME) and updates the string values of properties. By using the data binding mechanism, when the values of the ButtonColor, ButtonText, or UserName properties change, the user interface is updated as well.

While the content of the MainPage.xaml.cs file representing the page is the same as explained in the previous recipe, some more explanation is necessary in the case of the MainPage.xaml file. Here, using the data binding mechanism, you specify the following:

- The value of the UserName property should be presented as a part of the text block. This can be done by binding the UserName property (**binding source**) to the Text property (**binding target**) of Run within the TextBlock control.
- The value of the ButtonText property should be presented as text on the button. This can be done by binding the ButtonText property (binding source) to the Content property (binding target) of the Button control.
- The hexadecimal representation of a color, stored as a string value of the ButtonColor property, should be used as the background color of the button. This can be done by binding ButtonColor (the binding source) to the Background property (the binding target) of the Button control.
- The CmdLogInOut command should be executed when the button is pressed.

After running the application and clicking on the button, you should get one of the following results. The left-hand side of the image represents the scenario before you press the button, while the right-hand side represents what happens after you press the button:

See also

- The *Creating the view model for a page* recipe
- The *Binding a value to a textbox* recipe
- The *Binding a collection to a list view* recipe
- The *Binding a collection to a grid view* recipe
- The *Binding a collection to a combobox* recipe
- The *Binding a collection to a hub* recipe

Binding a value to a textbox

Apart from presenting values from the view model in the user interface, it is also possible to adjust the values of the properties in the view model class based on actions performed by the user in the application. For instance, when a user changes the text entered in the textbox, a value of the associated property from the view model class could be automatically updated as well. Of course, you can also read an entered value, transform it in any way, and show a new value in other elements within the user interface. In this recipe, you will learn how to do all of this.

As an example, you will create a simple page with a textbox and a text block. In the textbox, the user can enter a name that will be automatically set as a value of the property in the view model class. What is more, its lowercase, uppercase, and reversed versions will be presented in a text block. Of course, all of these operations will be performed using the data binding mechanism.

Getting ready

To step through this recipe, you need the automatically generated project configured according to the MVVM design pattern, as described in the *Creating the view model for a page* recipe.

How to do it...

To create an example of two-way binding, perform the following steps:

1. Modify the code of the `MainViewModel` class, in the `MainViewModel.cs` file, to define the necessary properties (`UserName`, `UserNameUpper`, `UserNameLower`, and `UserNameReversed`), as follows:

```
[ImplementPropertyChanged]
public class MainViewModel
{
    public string UserName { get; set; } = "";

    [DependsOn("UserName")]
    public string UserNameUpper
    {
        get { return UserName.ToUpper(); }
    }

    [DependsOn("UserName")]
    public string UserNameLower
    {
        get { return UserName.ToLower(); }
    }

    [DependsOn("UserName")]
    public string UserNameReversed
    {
        get
        {
            string reversed = string.Empty;
            for (int i = UserName.Length - 1; i >= 0; i--)
            {
                reversed += UserName[i];
            }
            return reversed;
        }
    }
}
```

2. Present a username in the textbox, together with an option to update a value of the property when a user changes a string in the textbox. Also, present the values of the following three properties (`UserNameLower`, `UserNameUpper`, and `UserNameReversed`) in the text block. To do so, modify the XAML code within the `MainPage.xaml` file as follows:

```
<Page (...)>
    <StackPanel Padding="20">
        <TextBox
            Text="{Binding UserName, Mode=TwoWay}"
            PlaceholderText="Type a username..."
            FontSize="20" />

        <TextBlock FontSize="18">
            <Run Text="Lower:" />
            <Run Text="{Binding UserNameLower}"
                FontWeight="SemiBold" />
            <LineBreak />
            <Run Text="Upper:" />
            <Run Text="{Binding UserNameUpper}"
                FontWeight="SemiBold" />
            <LineBreak />
            <Run Text="Reversed:" />
            <Run Text="{Binding UserNameReversed}"
                FontWeight="SemiBold" />
        </TextBlock>
    </StackPanel>
</Page>
```

How it works...

Some additional comments are necessary in the case of the view model class. Here, you define the UserName property, whose value will be equal to the text entered in the textbox. What is more, you define three additional properties, namely UserNameUpper, UserNameLower, and UserNameReversed. However, they contain only get accessors. For this reason, it will not be possible to update their values manually. They are calculated automatically based on the UserName property. For instance, the UserNameUpper property just calls the ToUpper method on the UserName property and returns the result. Some more complex operations are performed in the UserNameReversed property, where the for loop is used to reverse the string.

It is worth mentioning that the UserNameUpper, UserNameLower, and UserNameReversed properties are associated with the DependsOn attribute. This attribute indicates that a particular property depends on the other, so its value should be updated when the value of the other property is changed. For this reason, by associating the mentioned properties with the DependsOn attribute (with a name of the related property given as a parameter), uppercase, lowercase, and reversed strings are automatically updated when the value of the UserName property is changed.

Another comment is necessary for the content of the `MainPage.xaml` file. Here, you can find a different type of binding in the case of the `TextBox` control. Its `Text` property is bound to the `UserName` property of the view model class, but the `TwoWay` mode is selected, as follows:

```
<TextBox Text="{Binding UserName, Mode=TwoWay}" (...) />
```

It means that the binding should be performed in two ways. Therefore, it not only presents the value of the `UserName` property in the user interface, but it also automatically updates a value of the property when the user modifies the text entered in the textbox.

 It is worth mentioning that the value of the `UserName` property will be updated when the `TextBox` control loses focus, such as when you click somewhere outside of this control.

After running the application, typing a name, and clicking somewhere outside of the textbox, you should get a result similar to the following:

See also

- The *Creating the view model for a page* recipe
- The *Binding a collection to a list view* recipe
- The *Binding a collection to a grid view* recipe

- The *Binding a collection to a combobox* recipe
- The *Binding a collection to a hub* recipe

Binding with a value converter

In the previous recipes, you learned how to adjust the user interface based on the values of properties defined within the view model class. However, you could ask yourself these simple questions: *What should I do to show or hide some elements using the data binding mechanism? Do I need to define a separate property of the Visibility type for each element with such a feature?* Of course, you could solve this problem in the mentioned way. However, there is a much better approach available if you use **value converters**. They allow you to convert a particular value into another. For instance, you can define a value converter that could convert a Boolean value into the `Visibility` enumeration value. You will learn how to do this in the current recipe.

As an example, you will create a simple toggle mechanism that will hide or show the text block after you click on the button. Of course, the data binding mechanism together with the value converter will be used for this purpose.

Getting ready

To step through this recipe, you need the automatically generated project configured according to the MVVM design pattern, as described in the *Creating the view model for a page* recipe.

How to do it...

To prepare a project with a simple value converter, perform the following steps:

1. Define the `BoolToVisibilityConverter` class, implementing the `IValueConverter` interface, in the `BoolToVisibilityConverter.cs` file in the `Models` directory, as follows:

```
public class BoolToVisibilityConverter : IValueConverter
{
    public object Convert(object value, Type
        targetType, object parameter, string language)
    {
        return (bool)value ? Visibility.Visible :
```

```
          Visibility.Collapsed;
   }

   public object ConvertBack(object value, Type
      targetType, object parameter, string language)
   {
       return (Visibility)value == Visibility.Visible;
   }
}
```

Do not forget to add the necessary `using` statements for the `System`, `Windows.UI.Xaml`, and `Windows.UI.Xaml.Data` namespaces.

2. Modify the code of the `MainViewModel` class in the `MainViewModel.cs` file to define the `IsContentShown` property, the `CmdToggleContent` command, and its supporting method (`ToggleContent`), as follows:

```
[ImplementPropertyChanged]
public class MainViewModel
{
    public bool IsContentShown { get; set; } = true;
    public ICommand CmdToggleContent { get; set; }

    public MainViewModel()
    {
        CmdToggleContent = new RelayCommand(
            () => ToggleContent());
    }

    private void ToggleContent()
    {
        IsContentShown = !IsContentShown;
    }
}
```

Do not forget to add the necessary `using` statements for the `CH03.Models`, `PropertyChanged`, and `System.Windows.Input` namespaces.

3. Set the visibility of the text block based on a value of the `IsContentShown` property using the prepared value converter, by modifying the XAML code in the `MainPage.xaml` file, as shown in the following code snippet:

```xml
<Page (...)
    xmlns:converters="using:CH03.Models">
    <Page.Resources>
        <converters:BoolToVisibilityConverter
            x:Key="BoolToVisibility" />
    </Page.Resources>
    <ScrollViewer Background="White">
        <StackPanel>
            <Button
                Content="Toggle the content"
                Command="{Binding CmdToggleContent}"
                Margin="20"
                Padding="10"
                FontSize="20"
                HorizontalAlignment="Stretch" />
            <TextBlock
                Text="Value converters are a really (...)"
                TextWrapping="Wrap"
                Margin="20 0 20 20"
                FontSize="18"
                Visibility="{Binding IsContentShown,
                    Converter={StaticResource
                        BoolToVisibility}}"/>
        </StackPanel>
    </ScrollViewer>
</Page>
```

How it works...

The value converters are powerful solutions that support the data binding mechanism. They allow you to adjust the presentation of the user interface without the necessity of creating dedicated properties (in the view model class) for each binding, where the value of the property (the binding source) cannot be used directly. However, a way of creating and using a value converter requires a short explanation.

First of all, a value converter is represented by a class (for example, BoolToVisibilityConverter) that implements the IValueConverter interface. Such an interface requires the implementation of two methods, namely Convert and ConvertBack. The first converts a given value (value) to a target value, which is returned by this method. In the body of Convert, you need to cast the value parameter to a suitable type and then perform additional operations to return the right result. In the current example, the value parameter is a Boolean value, such as the value of the IsContentShown property. When the value parameter is equal to true, the Visible enumeration value (from Visibility) is returned. Otherwise, the Collapsed value is used instead.

You can also specify the body of the `ConvertBack` method. In the example, it returns a Boolean value depending on the `Visibility` value passed as a parameter.

While the view model class and the code-behind file do not contain parts that require explanation, some comments are necessary in the case of the `MainPage.xaml` file. At the beginning, a new namespace is added to the `Page` element, as follows:

```
<Page (...) xmlns:converters="using:CH03.Models">
```

Then, you need to define the converter as a resource within the page. Of course, a key should be assigned to it, such as `BoolToVisibility`. A definition of the resource is as follows:

```
<converters:BoolToVisibilityConverter x:Key="BoolToVisibility" />
```

Lastly, some explanation is required for the way in which you can bind some property using the value converter. In the example, you use the `BoolToVisibility` converter while binding the `IsContentShown` property of the view model class to the `Visibility` property of `TextBlock`. To do so, you can use the already known `Binding` element. This element is equipped with an additional parameter, namely `Converter`, indicating a resource representing the value converter. The code is as follows:

```
<TextBlock (...) Visibility="{Binding IsContentShown,
    Converter={StaticResource BoolToVisibility}}"/>
```

After running the application, you should get the result shown in the following image. Clicking on the button either collapses or expands the text block:

See also

- The *Creating the view model for a page* recipe
- The *Using value converters with parameters* recipe
- The *Showing a progress bar during calculations* recipe

Using value converters with parameters

As you saw in the previous recipe, a value converter allows you to convert one value into another, with the same or different type. However, such a solution also makes it possible to take into account a parameter during a conversion. Thus, you can prepare one value converter and parameterize it directly in the XAML code to limit code duplication and improve its quality. You will learn how to do this in this recipe.

As an example, you will create a page with a button and a text block. After consecutive clicks on the button, the color of the text block should be changed to green, red, green, and so on. Of course, the example will use the data binding mechanism with a value converter. This converter takes a parameter with a string representation of two colors for the various states of a Boolean value, such as #db0707|#33b11a. Thus, the first color will be returned when the Boolean value is equal to true. Otherwise, the second color will be used.

Getting ready

To step through this recipe, you need the automatically generated project configured according to the MVVM design pattern, as described in the *Creating the view model for a page* recipe.

How to do it...

To see how to use a value converter with a parameter, perform the following steps:

1. Define the BoolToColorConverter class implementing the IValueConverter interface in the BoolToColorConverter.cs file in the Models directory as follows:

```
public class BoolToColorConverter : IValueConverter
{
    public object Convert(object value, Type
```

```
        targetType, object parameter, string language)
    {
        string colorsString = (string)parameter;
        string[] colors = colorsString.Split(
            new char[] { '|' },
            StringSplitOptions.RemoveEmptyEntries);
        return (bool)value ? colors[0] : colors[1];
    }

    public object ConvertBack(object value, Type
        targetType, object parameter, string language)
    {
        throw new NotImplementedException();
    }
}
```

2. Modify the code of the `MainViewModel` class in the `MainViewModel.cs` file to define the `IsPrimaryColor` property as well as the `CmdChangeColor` command and its supporting method (`ChangeColor`):

```
[ImplementPropertyChanged]
public class MainViewModel
{
    public bool IsPrimaryColor { get; set; } = true;
    public ICommand CmdChangeColor { get; set; }

    public MainViewModel()
    {
        CmdChangeColor = new RelayCommand(
            () => ChangeColor());
    }

    private void ChangeColor()
    {
        IsPrimaryColor = !IsPrimaryColor;
    }
}
```

3. Specify the command executed when the button is pressed. Also, set the foreground color of the text block based on a value of the `IsPrimaryColor` property, using the defined value converter, by modifying the XAML code in the `MainPage.xaml` file, as shown in the following code:

```
<Page (...)
    xmlns:converters="using:CH03.Models">
    <Page.Resources>
        <converters:BoolToColorConverter
```

```
            x:Key="BoolToColor" />
    </Page.Resources>
    <ScrollViewer Background="White">
        <StackPanel>
            <Button
                Content="Change the color"
                Command="{Binding CmdChangeColor}"
                Margin="20"
                Padding="10"
                FontSize="20"
                HorizontalAlignment="Stretch" />
            <TextBlock
                Foreground="{Binding IsPrimaryColor,
                    Converter={StaticResource BoolToColor},
                    ConverterParameter='#db0707|#33b11a'}"
                Text="Value converters are a really (...)"
                TextWrapping="Wrap"
                Margin="20 0 20 20"
                FontSize="18" />
        </StackPanel>
    </ScrollViewer>
</Page>
```

How it works...

Taking a parameter into account, the definition of a value converter is very similar to the basic version, explained in the previous recipe. The class also implements the `IValueConverter` interface, as well as contains the `Convert` and `ConvertBack` methods. However, in this case, you can use one of the methods' parameters, named `parameter`. Its type is defined as `object`, thus you need to cast it to a proper type. In the example, the parameter is cast to `string` and divided by the | character to create an array. Then, its first or second item is returned.

Another comment is necessary for the `.xaml` file, where you use the value converter with a parameter. This may be achieved in the same way as without a parameter, except that the `ConverterParameter` value is provided, as follows:

```
<TextBlock Foreground="{Binding IsPrimaryColor,
    Converter={StaticResource BoolToColor},
    ConverterParameter='#db0707|#33b11a'}" (...) />
```

After running the application, you should get the following result:

See also

- The *Creating the view model for a page* recipe
- The *Binding with a value converter* recipe
- The *Showing a progress bar during calculations* recipe

Showing a progress bar during calculations

While performing some time-consuming calculations or downloading data from the Internet, it is a good idea to present a progress bar showing that a longer operation is currently in progress and the user would need to wait. In this recipe, you will learn how to show the progress bar during calculations and how to hide it when calculations are completed.

Getting ready

To step through this recipe, you need the automatically generated project configured according to the MVVM design pattern, as described in the *Creating the view model for a page* recipe.

How to do it...

To create a page with a progress bar shown during calculations, and hidden automatically when calculations are completed, perform the following steps:

1. Define a `BoolToVisibilityNegatedConverter` class implementing the `IValueConverter` interface in the `BoolToVisibilityNegatedConverter.cs` file in the `Models` directory:

```
public class BoolToVisibilityNegatedConverter :
    IValueConverter
{
    public object Convert(object value, Type targetType,
        object parameter, string language)
    {
        return (bool)value ? Visibility.Collapsed :
            Visibility.Visible;
    }

    public object ConvertBack(object value,
        Type targetType, object parameter, string language)
    {
        return (Visibility)value != Visibility.Visible;
    }
}
```

2. Modify the code of the `MainViewModel` class in the `MainViewModel.cs` file to define the `IsCompleted` property and the `Calculate` awaitable method, as shown in the following part of code:

```
[ImplementPropertyChanged]
public class MainViewModel
{
    public bool IsCompleted { get; set; }

    public async Task Calculate()
    {
        await Task.Delay(5000);
```

```
            IsCompleted = true;
    }
}
```

 Do not forget to add `using` statements for the `PropertyChanged` and `System.Threading.Tasks` namespaces.

3. Call the `Calculate` method (from the view model class) after navigating to the page. Do this by modifying the code in the `MainPage.xaml.cs` file as follows:

```
public sealed partial class MainPage : Page
{ (...)
    protected async override void OnNavigatedTo(
        NavigationEventArgs e)
    {
        base.OnNavigatedTo(e);
        await _vm.Calculate();
    }
}
```

 Do not forget to add the necessary `using` statements for the `CH03.ViewModels`, `Windows.UI.Xaml.Controls`, and `Windows.UI.Xaml.Navigation` namespaces.

4. Add the progress bar and set its visibility based on a value of the `IsCompleted` property. Do this by modifying the XAML code within the `MainPage.xaml` file, as follows:

```
<Page (...)
    xmlns:converters="using:CH03.Models">
    <Page.Resources>
        <converters:BoolToVisibilityNegatedConverter
            x:Key="BoolToVisibilityNegated" />
    </Page.Resources>
    <Grid>
        <ProgressBar
            IsIndeterminate="True"
            VerticalAlignment="Center"
            Visibility="{Binding IsCompleted, Converter=
                {StaticResource BoolToVisibilityNegated}}" />
    </Grid>
</Page>
```

How it works...

The example presented in this recipe uses another value converter that converts a Boolean value into a `Visibility` value, but it assumes that an element should be visible if the Boolean value is equal to `false`. A small comment is necessary for the view model class. It contains the `Calculate` method that waits for five seconds and then sets the value of the `IsCompleted` property to `true`. Of course, in a real scenario, the `Delay` call should be replaced with code that performs time-consuming operations.

After running the application, for the first five seconds you should see the progress bar, as shown in the following image. Later, the progress bar disappears automatically.

See also

- The *Creating the view model for a page* recipe
- The *Binding with a value converter* recipe
- The *Using value converters with parameters* recipe

Binding a collection to a list view

In the previous recipes, you learned how to use the MVVM design pattern and data binding with various controls available out of the box, such as a textbox, a text block, or a progress bar. Apart from these controls, there is another set that presents a list of items, such as a list view, a grid view, or a combobox. Of course, they could also benefit from data binding. In this recipe, you will learn how to use data binding for a list view.

As an example, you will create a page that will present a list of people. Each row will contain a name, current location, and the number of days remaining until the next birthday. After clicking on an item, a message dialog will be shown.

Getting ready

To step through this recipe, you need the automatically generated project configured according to the MVVM design pattern, as described in the *Creating the view model for a page* recipe.

How to do it...

To bind a collection to a list view, in order to present a list of people on the page, perform the following steps:

1. Define the `UserViewModel` class representing the data of a single person in the `UserViewModel.cs` file in the `ViewModels` folder. The class contains four properties (`Name`, `Location`, `BirthDate`, and `DaysToBirthday`), as shown in the following code snippet:

```
[ImplementPropertyChanged]
public class UserViewModel
{
    public string Name { get; set; }
    public string Location { get; set; }
    public DateTime BirthDate { get; set; }

    [DependsOn("BirthDate")]
    public int DaysToBirthday
    {
        get
        {
            DateTime thisYearBirthday =
                new DateTime(DateTime.Now.Year,
                    BirthDate.Month, BirthDate.Day);
            int remainingDays = (int)(thisYearBirthday
                - DateTime.Now.Date).TotalDays;
            if (remainingDays >= 0)
            {
                return remainingDays;
            }
            else
            {
                DateTime nextYearBirthday =
                    new DateTime(DateTime.Now.Year + 1,
                        BirthDate.Month, BirthDate.Day);
                return (int)(nextYearBirthday -
                    DateTime.Now.Date).TotalDays;
            }
```

```
        }
      }
    }
```

2. Define the `Users` property as a list of `UserViewModel` instances. What is more, create the `LoadData` method that will populate the `Users` list with the data of exemplary people. To do so, modify the code of the `MainViewModel` class in the `MainViewModel.cs` file as follows:

```
[ImplementPropertyChanged]
public class MainViewModel
{
    public List<UserViewModel> Users { get; set; }

    public void LoadData()
    {
        Users = new List<UserViewModel>()
        {
            new UserViewModel()
            {
                Name = "Marcin",
                BirthDate = new DateTime(1988, 11, 9),
                Location = "Poland"
            },
            new UserViewModel()
            {
                Name = "Kelly",
                BirthDate = new DateTime(1990, 5, 5),
                Location = "England"
            }, (...)
        };
    }
}
```

Do not forget to add `using` statements for the `PropertyChanged`, `System`, and `System.Collections.Generic` namespaces.

3. Add the list view, set a source of its items to the `Users` property, handle the event of clicking on an item, and specify an item template by modifying the XAML code in the `MainPage.xaml` file:

```
<Page (...)>
    <ListView
        ItemsSource="{Binding Users}"
```

```
        SelectionMode="None"
        IsItemClickEnabled="True"
        ItemClick="ListView_ItemClick">
        <ListView.ItemTemplate>
            <DataTemplate>
                <StackPanel Padding="10">
                    <TextBlock
                        Text="{Binding Name}"
                        FontWeight="SemiBold" />
                    <TextBlock>
                        <Run Text="Current location: " />
                        <Run Text="{Binding Location}" />
                    </TextBlock>
                    <TextBlock>
                        <Run Text="{Binding
                            DaysToBirthday}" />
                        <Run Text="day(s) remaining till
                            birthday!" />
                    </TextBlock>
                </StackPanel>
            </DataTemplate>
        </ListView.ItemTemplate>
    </ListView>
</Page>
```

4. Call the `LoadData` method (from the view model class) after navigating to the page, and show a message dialog after clicking on an item by modifying the code in the `MainPage.xaml.cs` file as follows:

```
public sealed partial class MainPage : Page
{ (...)
    protected override void OnNavigatedTo(
        NavigationEventArgs e)
    {
        base.OnNavigatedTo(e);
        _vm.LoadData();
    }

    private async void ListView_ItemClick(
        object sender, ItemClickEventArgs e)
    {
        UserViewModel user = (UserViewModel)e.ClickedItem;
        MessageDialog dialog = new MessageDialog(
            string.Format("{0} is currently in {1}. The next
            birthday in {2} day(s).", user.Name,
            user.Location, user.DaysToBirthday),
            "Details of the selected user");
        dialog.Commands.Add(new UICommand("Close"));
```

```
            await dialog.ShowAsync();
    }
}
```

 Do not forget to add `using` statements for `System`, `CH03.ViewModels`, `Windows.UI.Popups`, `Windows.UI.Xaml.Controls`, and `Windows.UI.Xaml.Navigation`.

How it works...

Binding a collection of items is a bit different than binding simple data that you have already learned in the previous recipes. In the example, the view model class (`MainViewModel`) contains a list of instances of another class, namely `UserViewModel`, with the data of a single person.

A small comment is necessary regarding the `DaysToBirthday` property, which is defined within it. It contains only the `get` accessor that returns the number of days until the next birthday. If the next birthday is not in the current year (that is, a person has already had a birthday in the current year), the one in the next year is taken into account. What is more, the `DaysToBirthday` property is associated with the `DependsOn` attribute indicating that this property depends on `BirthDate`.

A bit more explanation is necessary for the `MainPage.xaml` file. Here, the `ListView` control is added and the `Users` property of the view model class is bound to the `ItemsSource` property. Apart from setting a source of items, it is required to specify a template of a single item, as `DataTemplate` within `ListView.ItemTemplate`.

Here, each item is presented as `StackPanel` with three `TextBlock` controls. Of course, it is possible to use the data binding mechanism for such controls, as in the case of a name, location, and the number of days until the next birthday. It is worth mentioning that such bindings are performed in the context of a particular item, that is, an instance of the `UserViewModel` class.

In the example, the list box does not support the selection of an item (`SelectionMode` set to `None`). However, it handles the event of clicking on an item (`IsItemClickEnabled` set to `True`). In such a case, the `ListView_ItemClick` method from the code-behind file is called. As you can see in the body of the `ListView_ItemClick` method in the `MainPage.xaml.cs` file, you can easily get an object representing the clicked item using the `ClickedItem` property of the second parameter, named `e`. In the example, when a user clicks on an item, a message dialog is presented.

After running the application, you should get the following result:

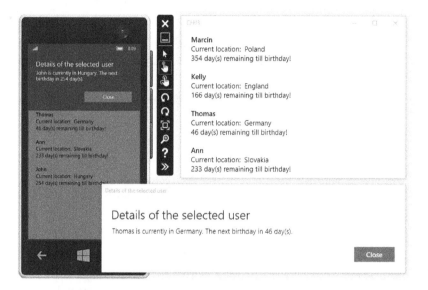

See also

- The *Creating the view model for a page* recipe
- The *Binding a value to a textbox* recipe
- The *Binding a collection to a grid view* recipe
- The *Binding a collection to a combobox* recipe
- The *Binding a collection to a hub* recipe

Binding a collection to a grid view

Presenting items as rows using the list view is not the only way of showing a collection. You can also present items as tiles using the grid view, as shown in this recipe.

As an example, you will prepare a page with a grid view, where tiles will represent the categories of articles. Each tile will contain a name, a counter, and an icon. Of course, the example will use the data binding mechanism.

Getting ready

To step through this recipe, you need the automatically generated project configured according to the MVVM design pattern, as described in the *Creating the view model for a page* recipe.

How to do it...

To bind a collection to a grid view, in order to show a set of tiles on the page, perform the following steps:

1. Add the `Country.png`, `World.png`, `Local.png`, `Culture.png`, `Sport.png`, and `Gov.png` files (representing icons) to the `Assets` directory. Example `.png` files are available together with the code attached to this chapter.

2. Add the `CategoryViewModel` class representing the data of a single category to the `CategoryViewModel.cs` file in the `ViewModels` folder. The class contains four properties (`Id`, `Name`, `Count`, and `IconUrl`), as follows:

```
[ImplementPropertyChanged]
public class CategoryViewModel
{
    public int Id { get; set; }
    public string Name { get; set; }
    public int Count { get; set; }
    public string IconUrl { get; set; }
}
```

3. Define the `Categories` property as an observable collection of `CategoryViewModel` instances. Then, create the `LoadData` method that populates the `Categories` collection with the data of exemplary categories. To do so, modify the code of the `MainViewModel` class in the `MainViewModel.cs` file, as shown in the following code:

```
[ImplementPropertyChanged]
public class MainViewModel
{
    public ObservableCollection<CategoryViewModel> Categories
        { get; set; }

    public void LoadData()
    {
        Categories =
            new ObservableCollection<CategoryViewModel>()
```

```
{
    new CategoryViewModel()
    {
        Id = 1,
        Name = "Country",
        Count = 8,
        IconUrl = "ms-appx:///Assets/Country.png"
    },
    new CategoryViewModel()
    {
        Id = 2,
        Name = "World",
        Count = 12,
        IconUrl = "ms-appx:///Assets/World.png"
    }, (...)
};
}
}
```

 Do not forget to add `using` statements for the `PropertyChanged` and `System.Collections.ObjectModel` namespaces.

4. Call the `LoadData` method (from the view model class) after navigating to the page. Do this by modifying the code in the `MainPage.xaml.cs` file as follows:

```
public sealed partial class MainPage : Page
{ (...)
    protected override void OnNavigatedTo(
        NavigationEventArgs e)
    {
        base.OnNavigatedTo(e);
        _vm.LoadData();
    }
}
```

5. Add the grid view, set the source of its items to the `Categories` property, handle the event of clicking on an item, and specify an item template. Do this by modifying the XAML code in the `MainPage.xaml` file as follows:

```
<Page (...)>
    <GridView
        ItemsSource="{Binding Categories}"
        Padding="10"
        SelectionMode="None">
        <GridView.ItemTemplate>
```

```xml
<DataTemplate>
    <Grid
        Width="135"
        Height="135"
        Background="RoyalBlue"
        Margin="10"
        Padding="10">
        <Grid.RowDefinitions>
            <RowDefinition Height="*" />
            <RowDefinition Height="Auto" />
        </Grid.RowDefinitions>

        <TextBlock
            Grid.Row="1"
            Text="{Binding Name}"
            FontSize="20"
            Foreground="White" />
        <Image
            Grid.Row="0"
            Source="{Binding IconUrl}"
            MaxWidth="32" />
        <Border
            Background="White"
            Width="30"
            Height="30"
            VerticalAlignment="Top"
            HorizontalAlignment="Right">
            <TextBlock
                Text="{Binding Count}"
                Foreground="RoyalBlue"
                HorizontalAlignment="Center"
                VerticalAlignment="Center" />
        </Border>
    </Grid>
</DataTemplate>
            </GridView.ItemTemplate>
        </GridView>
</Page>
```

How it works...

You can present a collection of items in a grid view in a very similar way to a list view.

The implementation of the view model could be even the same as in the case of the list view. However, to make this recipe more interesting, you can find a significant difference in the `MainViewModel` class, where a collection of items is defined as an instance of the `ObservableCollection` class, instead of the `List` class. The `ObservableCollection` class allows to detect situations when any item is added or removed from the collection, thus it is possible to automatically update the user interface in such scenarios. If you use the `List` class, you will need to implement such a behavior on your own.

After running the application and clicking on the **Sport** or **Culture** tile, you should get a result similar to the following:

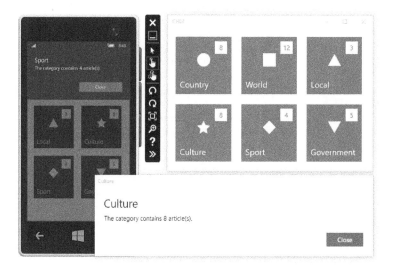

See also

- The *Creating the view model for a page* recipe
- The *Binding a value to a textbox* recipe
- The *Binding a collection to a list view* recipe
- The *Binding a collection to a combobox* recipe
- The *Binding a collection to a hub* recipe

Binding a collection to a combobox

The list view and grid view are not the only controls that allow you to present a collection of items. The other one shows them in a bit different way, as a drop-down list. This control is named combobox. In this recipe, you will learn how to use the data binding mechanism with this control.

As an example, you will create a page with a combobox that will present a list of available languages of the application. Each item will be presented as a flag next to a language name.

Getting ready

To step through this recipe, you need the automatically generated project configured according to the MVVM design pattern, as described in the *Creating the view model for a page* recipe.

How to do it...

To bind a collection to a combobox, in order to present a list of available languages on the page, perform the following steps:

1. Add the `FlagDE.png`, `FlagEN.png`, `FlagFR.png`, `FlatJP.png`, and `FlagPL.png` files (representing flags) to the `Assets` directory. The `.png` files are available together with the code attached to this chapter.

2. Add the `LanguageViewModel` class representing the data of a single language to the `LanguageViewModel.cs` file in the `ViewModels` folder. The class contains three properties (`Code`, `Name`, and `IconUrl`), as follows:

```
[ImplementPropertyChanged]
public class LanguageViewModel
{
    public string Code { get; set; }
    public string Name { get; set; }
    public string IconUrl { get; set; }
}
```

3. Define the `CurrentLanguage` and `Languages` properties. Also, create the `LoadData` method that populates the `Languages` list with the data of five languages and selects a default language. To do so, modify the code of the `MainViewModel` class in the `MainViewModel.cs` file as follows:

```
[ImplementPropertyChanged]
public class MainViewModel
{
    public LanguageViewModel CurrentLanguage { get; set; }
    public List<LanguageViewModel> Languages { get; set; }

    public void LoadData()
    {
        Languages = new List<LanguageViewModel>()
        {
            new LanguageViewModel()
            {
                Code = "DE",
                Name = "German",
                IconUrl = "ms-appx:///Assets/FlagDE.png"
            }, (...)
        };
        CurrentLanguage = Languages[1];
    }
}
```

4. Call the `LoadData` method (from the view model class) after navigating to the page. Do this by modifying the code in the `MainPage.xaml.cs` file as follows:

```
public sealed partial class MainPage : Page
{ (...)
    protected override void OnNavigatedTo(
        NavigationEventArgs e)
    {
        base.OnNavigatedTo(e);
        _vm.LoadData();
    }
}
```

5. Add the combobox, set the source of its items to the `Languages` property, bind the currently selected item to the `CurrentLanguage` property, and specify an item template. Do this by modifying the XAML code in the `MainPage.xaml` file as follows:

```
<Page (...)>
    <StackPanel Padding="20">
```

```xml
<TextBlock
    Text="Language:"
    FontSize="20" />
<ComboBox
    FontSize="18"
    HorizontalAlignment="Stretch"
    Margin="0 10"
    ItemsSource="{Binding Languages}"
    SelectedItem="{Binding CurrentLanguage,
        Mode=TwoWay}">
    <ComboBox.ItemTemplate>
        <DataTemplate>
            <Grid Margin="10">
                <Grid.ColumnDefinitions>
                  <ColumnDefinition Width="Auto" />
                  <ColumnDefinition Width="10" />
                  <ColumnDefinition Width="*" />
                </Grid.ColumnDefinitions>
                <Image
                    Grid.Column="0"
                    Source="{Binding IconUrl}" />
                <TextBlock
                    Grid.Column="2"
                    Foreground="#353535"
                    VerticalAlignment="Center"
                    Text="{Binding Name}" />
            </Grid>
        </DataTemplate>
    </ComboBox.ItemTemplate>
</ComboBox>
    </StackPanel>
</Page>
```

How it works...

You can add items to a combobox in a very similar way as in the case of a list view or a grid view, as already explained in the previous recipes in this chapter. However, the current example also presents how to set the currently selected item and how to obtain an object representing it. This can be achieved by binding the CurrentLanguage property of the view model class to the SelectedItem property of the ComboBox control.

As you can see in the LoadData method in the MainViewModel class, the second item from the Languages collection (the English language) is chosen by default and set as a value of the CurrentLanguage property. When the user changes the selection in the combobox, the value of the CurrentLanguage property is updated accordingly.

After running the application and pressing the combobox, a list of the available languages should expand and you will get a result similar to the following:

See also

- The *Creating the view model for a page* recipe
- The *Binding a value to a textbox* recipe
- The *Binding a collection to a list view* recipe
- The *Binding a collection to a grid view* recipe
- The *Binding a collection to a hub* recipe

Binding a collection to a hub

The last control presented in this chapter is the hub that presents a collection of sections. It can also be supported by the data binding mechanism, as explained in this recipe.

As an example, you will create a page with a scrollable photo gallery. Each photo is presented as a separate hub section with a given header.

Getting ready

To step through this recipe, you need the automatically generated project configured according to the MVVM design pattern, as described in the *Creating the view model for a page* recipe.

How to do it…

To bind a collection to a hub, in order to create a page with a scrollable photo gallery, perform the following steps:

1. Add the `G01.jpg`, `G02.jpg`, `G03.jpg`, and `G04.jpg` files (representing some images in the gallery) to the `Assets` directory.

2. Add the `GalleryItemViewModel` class, which represents the data of a single gallery item, to the `GalleryItemViewModel.cs` file in the `ViewModels` folder. The class contains two properties (`Title` and `ImageUrl`), as follows:

```
[ImplementPropertyChanged]
public class GalleryItemViewModel
{
    public string Title { get; set; }
    public string ImageUrl { get; set; }
}
```

3. Define the `Items` property as a list of `GalleryItemViewModel` instances and create the `LoadData` method that populates the `Items` list with the data of four photos. To do so, modify the code of the `MainViewModel` class in the `MainViewModel.cs` file, as shown in the following code snippet:

```
[ImplementPropertyChanged]
public class MainViewModel
{
    public List<GalleryItemViewModel> Items { get; set; }

    public void LoadData()
    {
        Items = new List<GalleryItemViewModel>()
        {
            new GalleryItemViewModel()
            {
                Title = "Picture Lake",
                ImageUrl = "ms-appx:///Assets/G01.jpg"
            }, (...)
```

```
        };
    }
}
```

4. Add the hub, set its name, and define the section template by modifying the XAML code in the `MainPage.xaml` file as follows:

```xml
<Page (...)>
    <Page.Resources>
        <DataTemplate x:Key="SectionTemplate">
            <Image
                Source="{Binding ImageUrl}"
                Stretch="UniformToFill" />
        </DataTemplate>
    </Page.Resources>
    <Hub
        x:Name="Hub"
        Margin="0 -20 0 10" />
</Page>
```

5. After navigating to the page, call the `LoadData` method (from the view model class) and create a section within the hub for each gallery item. To do so, modify the code in the `MainPage.xaml.cs` file, as shown in the following code snippet:

```csharp
public sealed partial class MainPage : Page
{ (...)
    protected override void OnNavigatedTo(
        NavigationEventArgs e)
    {
        base.OnNavigatedTo(e);
        _vm.LoadData();
        foreach (GalleryItemViewModel item in _vm.Items)
        {
            HubSection section = new HubSection();
            section.Header = item.Title;
            section.ContentTemplate =
                (DataTemplate)Resources["SectionTemplate"];
            section.DataContext = item;
            Hub.Sections.Add(section);
        }
    }
}
```

 Do not forget to add `using` statements for the `CH03.ViewModels`, `Windows.UI.Xaml`, `Windows.UI.Xaml.Controls`, and `Windows.UI.Xaml.Navigation` namespaces.

How it works…

Additional explanation is necessary for the `MainPage.xaml` and `MainPage.xaml.cs` files. In the first one, the data template for each hub section is specified within the page resources. As shown in the code, the section contains just the `Image` control, while the `Source` property is bound to the `ImageUrl` property of the `GalleryItemViewModel` instance representing the given photo. What is more, the name of the `Hub` control is set to `Hub`.

In the example, setting a collection of items is not defined in the `.xaml` file but in the code-behind file. Here, after navigating to the page and loading data, you iterate through all the gallery items. For each one of them, a new hub section is created (as an instance of the `HubSection` class), the header is set to the title of the photo, the data context is set to the current `GalleryItemViewModel` instance, and the content template is set to the data template already defined within the page resources. Then, the newly created section is added to the hub by adding a `HubSection` instance to the collection of sections.

As a result, the page should look similar to the following:

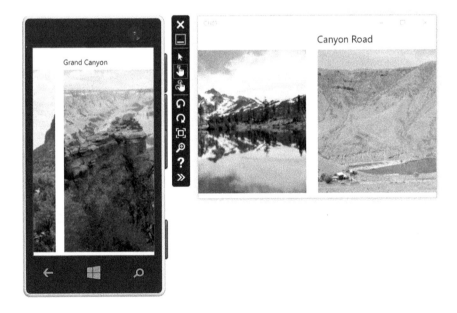

See also

- The *Creating the view model for a page* recipe
- The *Binding a value to a textbox* recipe
- The *Binding a collection to a list view* recipe
- The *Binding a collection to a grid view* recipe
- The *Binding a collection to a combobox* recipe

4

Data Storage

In this chapter, we will cover the following recipes:

- Creating a directory
- Reading a structure of directories
- Creating a file
- Iterating through files
- Renaming a directory
- Renaming a file
- Removing a directory
- Removing a file
- Writing a text file
- Reading a text file
- Writing an XML file
- Reading an XML file
- Writing a JSON file
- Reading a JSON file
- Writing a binary file
- Reading a binary file
- Creating a SQLite database and tables
- Storing data in a SQLite database
- Selecting data from a SQLite database
- Updating data in a SQLite database
- Removing data from a SQLite database

Introduction

A lot of applications use various data, such as posts, photos, or just settings that allow a user to adjust the application to his or her needs. Of course, data can be stored variously, such as in textual and binary files, as well as in databases. Even a text file may contain content defined in various ways, such as in plain text or formatted using **Extensible Markup Language (XML)** or **JavaScript Object Notation (JSON)**. Choosing the proper way of storing data within an application is an important task that could have an impact on the development and maintenance of the project, as well as on the performance of saving or loading data.

At the beginning of this chapter, you will learn how to create, rename, and remove directories, as well as how to manage the files placed within them. In addition, you will see how to obtain the structure of the directories and information about the files located in a particular directory.

In the next part of the chapter, we will analyze scenarios of writing and reading a few kinds of file. You will learn how to use files with plain text as well as with XML- and JSON-formatted content. What is more, there will be a topic on writing data to a binary file using a custom binary format and reading it.

In the last few recipes, you will see how to use a SQLite database in your application. Such a task requires a set of configuration steps, such as downloading a necessary package and creating tables in a database. The scenarios of inserting, selecting, updating, and removing data from particular tables will be shown with examples and descriptions.

Creating a directory

When an application stores data in many files, it is beneficial to organize them in directories. Of course, it is possible to easily create a folder, as you will see in this recipe.

As an example, you will design a simple page with the **Create directories** button. Once you click on it, a set of directories (with subdirectories) will be created. Such a project will be used also in the following recipes to add additional features regarding the management of directories and files. Let's start!

Getting ready

To step through this recipe, you need only the automatically generated project.

How to do it...

To prepare the example that creates a set of directories, together with subdirectories, perform the following steps:

1. Add the **Create directories** button to the page by modifying the `MainPage.xaml` file as follows:

```
<Page (...)>
    <StackPanel>
        <Button
            Content="Create directories"
            HorizontalAlignment="Center"
            VerticalAlignment="Center"
            Click="BtnCreateDirectory_Click" />
    </StackPanel>
</Page>
```

2. Create a set of directories (with subdirectories) after you click on the button. Do this by modifying the content of the `BtnCreateDirectory_Click` method in the `MainPage.xaml.cs` file as follows:

```
private async void BtnCreateDirectory_Click(
    object sender, RoutedEventArgs e)
{
    StorageFolder localFolder =
        ApplicationData.Current.LocalFolder;
    StorageFolder bookFolder =
        await localFolder.CreateFolderAsync("Book",
            CreationCollisionOption.OpenIfExists);
    StorageFolder workFolder =
        await localFolder.CreateFolderAsync("Work",
            CreationCollisionOption.OpenIfExists);
    await bookFolder.CreateFolderAsync("Chapter 1",
        CreationCollisionOption.OpenIfExists);
    await bookFolder.CreateFolderAsync("Chapter 2",
        CreationCollisionOption.OpenIfExists);
    await bookFolder.CreateFolderAsync("Chapter 3",
        CreationCollisionOption.OpenIfExists);
    StorageFolder chapterFolder =
        await bookFolder.CreateFolderAsync("Chapter 4",
            CreationCollisionOption.OpenIfExists);
    await chapterFolder.CreateFolderAsync("Images",
        CreationCollisionOption.OpenIfExists);
    await chapterFolder.CreateFolderAsync("Codes",
        CreationCollisionOption.OpenIfExists);
}
```

How it works...

The most interesting part of the code is located in the `BtnCreateDirectory_Click` method. Here, the following structure of directories is created:

```
- Work
- Book
    - Chapter 1
    - Chapter 2
    - Chapter 3
    - Chapter 4
        - Images
        - Codes
```

First of all, you get an instance of the `StorageFolder` class that represents the root folder in the local application data store. This could be obtained using the `LocalFolder` property, as follows:

```
StorageFolder localFolder = ApplicationData.Current.LocalFolder;
```

To create a directory, you just need to call the `CreateFolderAsync` method on the `StorageFolder` instance, which represents the folder in which the directory should be created. The code is as follows:

```
StorageFolder bookFolder =
    await localFolder.CreateFolderAsync("Book",
        CreationCollisionOption.OpenIfExists);
```

As the first parameter, you pass a name of the new directory (`Book`), while the other parameter specifies how collisions should be resolved. In the example, the `OpenIfExists` value is chosen, so if a directory with the same name already exists, no operations will be performed. Among other possibilities, in such a situation, an exception could be raised (`FailIfExists`), a unique name formed by adding a number could be generated (`GenerateUniqueName`), or the directory could be replaced (`ReplaceExisting`).

As a result of the `CreateFolderAsync` call, an instance of the `StorageFolder` class, representing the newly created directory, is returned.

See also

- The *Reading a structure of directories* recipe
- The *Creating a file* recipe
- The *Iterating through files* recipe

- The *Renaming a directory* recipe
- The *Renaming a file* recipe
- The *Removing a directory* recipe
- The *Removing a file* recipe

Reading a structure of directories

After creating many folders, it may be necessary to get a list of them, together with subdirectories. Fortunately, it is possible to iterate through directories, as you will see in the current recipe.

As an example, you will modify the project from the previous recipe by adding a text block and an **Iterate through directories** button. After pressing it, a textual representation of the structure of directories is generated and presented in the text block.

Getting ready

To step through this recipe, you need the project from the previous recipe.

How to do it...

To create an example that gets a list of directories, as well as iterate through them, perform the following steps:

1. Add the **Iterate through directories** button and the text block to the page by modifying the content of the `MainPage.xaml` file as follows:

```
<Page (...)>
    <StackPanel> (...)
        <Button
            Content="Iterate through directories"
            HorizontalAlignment="Center"
            VerticalAlignment="Center"
            Click="BtnIterateDirectories_Click" />
        <TextBlock
            x:Name="TxtResult"
            TextWrapping="Wrap" />
    </StackPanel>
</Page>
```

2. Present a textual representation of the structure of directories in the text block after you click on the button. Do this by modifying the `MainPage.xaml.cs` file, as shown in the following code snippet:

```
private async void BtnIterateDirectories_Click(
    object sender, RoutedEventArgs e)
{
    StorageFolder localFolder =
        ApplicationData.Current.LocalFolder;
    List<string> paths = await GetPath(localFolder);
    TxtResult.Text = string.Join(Environment.NewLine, paths);
}
```

3. Define the recursive `GetPath` method. It prepares a list of paths to particular directories, where each part is separated by the | character, as follows:

```
private async Task<List<string>> GetPath(
    StorageFolder folder, string path = "")
{
    List<string> paths = new List<string>();
    if (!string.IsNullOrEmpty(path))
    {
        paths.Add(path);
    }

    IReadOnlyList<StorageFolder> subfolders =
        await folder.GetFoldersAsync();
    foreach (StorageFolder subfolder in subfolders)
    {
        string subpath = path;
        if (!string.IsNullOrEmpty(subpath))
        {
            subpath += " | ";
        }

        subpath += subfolder.Name;
        paths.AddRange(await GetPath(subfolder, subpath));
    }
    return paths;
}
```

How it works...

The most important part of the code is located in the `GetPath` recursive method. It takes two parameters, namely an instance of the `StorageFolder` class representing a directory that is currently being analyzed and the current path to this directory (empty by default).

It is possible to get subdirectories within the folder using the `GetFoldersAsync` method. It returns a list of `StorageFolder` instances that will represent particular subdirectories. You can get a name of the folder using the `Name` property.

After running the application and clicking on the **Create directories** and **Iterate through directories** buttons, you should get the following result in the text block:

```
Book
Book | Chapter 1
Book | Chapter 2
Book | Chapter 3
Book | Chapter 4
Book | Chapter 4 | Codes
Book | Chapter 4 | Images
Work
```

See also

- The *Creating a directory* recipe
- The *Creating a file* recipe
- The *Iterating through files* recipe
- The *Renaming a directory* recipe
- The *Renaming a file* recipe
- The *Removing a directory* recipe
- The *Removing a file* recipe

Creating a file

Different kinds of data may be stored in files. Thus, it is crucial to learn how to create an empty file that can be later filled with content. You will learn how to create a file in a given folder in this recipe.

As an example, you will modify the project from the previous recipe by adding a **Create files** button. After pressing it, a set of files will be created.

Getting ready

To step through this recipe, you need the project from the previous recipe.

How to do it...

To prepare an example that creates files, perform the following steps:

1. Add the **Create files** button to the page by modifying the content of the `MainPage.xaml` file as follows:

```
<Page (...)>
    <StackPanel> (...)
        <Button
            Content="Create files"
            HorizontalAlignment="Center"
            VerticalAlignment="Center"
            Click="BtnCreateFile_Click" />
        <TextBlock
            x:Name="TxtResult"
            TextWrapping="Wrap" />
    </StackPanel>
</Page>
```

2. Create files once you click on the button. Do this by modifying the `BtnCreateFile_Click` method in the `MainPage.xaml.cs` file as follows:

```
private async void BtnCreateFile_Click(object sender,
    RoutedEventArgs e)
{
    StorageFolder localFolder =
        ApplicationData.Current.LocalFolder;
    StorageFolder bookFolder =
        await localFolder.GetFolderAsync("Book");
    StorageFile notesFile =
        await bookFolder.CreateFileAsync("Notes.txt",
            CreationCollisionOption.OpenIfExists);
    StorageFile imageFile =
        await bookFolder.CreateFileAsync("Image.png",
            CreationCollisionOption.OpenIfExists);
    StorageFile movieFile =
```

```
await bookFolder.CreateFileAsync("Movie.mp4",
    CreationCollisionOption.OpenIfExists);
}
```

How it works...

Creating a new file is possible using the `CreateFileAsync` method. It should be called on an instance of the `StorageFolder` class, which represents the directory in which the file should be created. The method takes two parameters: the name of the new file and a value indicating how collisions should be resolved.

In the example, if a file with the same name already exists, no operations will be performed (`OpenIfExists`). Among other possibilities, in such a situation, an exception could be raised (`FailIfExists`), a unique name formed by adding a number could be generated (`GenerateUniqueName`), or the file could be replaced (`ReplaceExisting`).

As a result of `CreateFileAsync`, an instance of the `StorageFile` class representing the newly created file is returned.

 It is worth mentioning the similarity of the code regarding creating a new file and a new directory, as shown in the *Creating a directory* recipe.

In the example presented in this recipe, three files will be created in the `Book` folder: `Notes.txt`, `Image.png`, and `Movie.mp4`. Of course, such files will not have any content. Thus, you will need to add suitable content, such as text, an image, or a movie.

See also

- The *Creating a directory* recipe
- The *Reading a structure of directories* recipe
- The *Iterating through files* recipe
- The *Renaming a directory* recipe
- The *Renaming a file* recipe
- The *Removing a directory* recipe
- The *Removing a file* recipe
- The *Writing a text file* recipe
- The *Reading a text file* recipe

- The *Taking an image from a camera* and *Recording a movie from a camera* recipes from Chapter 6, *Multimedia*.

Iterating through files

As with directories, it is also possible to iterate through the files located in a given folder. You will learn how to do this in this recipe.

As an example, the project from the previous recipe will be modified by adding an **Iterate through files** button. Once you click on it, a list of filenames from the Book directory will be presented in the text block.

Getting ready

To step through this recipe, you need a project from the previous recipe.

How to do it...

To create an example that gets a list of files from a given directory, as well as iterate through them, perform the following steps:

1. Add the **Iterate through files** button to the page by modifying the content of the MainPage.xaml file as follows:

```
<Page (...)>
    <StackPanel> (...)
        <Button
            Content="Iterate through files"
            HorizontalAlignment="Center"
            VerticalAlignment="Center"
            Click="BtnIterateFiles_Click" />
        <TextBlock
            x:Name="TxtResult"
            TextWrapping="Wrap" />
    </StackPanel>
</Page>
```

2. Iterate through the files from the Book directory and present a list of all the files from this folder in the text block after you click on the button. Do this by modifying the MainPage.xaml.cs file as follows:

```
private async void BtnIterateFiles_Click(object sender,
    RoutedEventArgs e)
{
    List<string> fileNames = new List<string>();
    StorageFolder bookFolder =
        await ApplicationData.Current.LocalFolder
            .GetFolderAsync("Book");
    foreach (StorageFile file in
        await bookFolder.GetFilesAsync())
    {
        fileNames.Add(file.Name);
    }
    TxtResult.Text = string.Join(Environment.NewLine,
        fileNames);
}
```

How it works...

Getting data of files from the given directory is possible by calling the `GetFilesAsync` method on an instance of the `StorageFolder` class that represents the directory. The method returns a collection of `StorageFile` instances, each representing a single file.

By iterating through this collection, you can easily perform some operations for each file, such as adding its name to the list, as presented in the example:

```
foreach (StorageFile file in await bookFolder.GetFilesAsync())
{
    fileNames.Add(file.Name);
}
```

Then, elements from the list are stored as a string, where each item is placed in a separate line. At the end, the result is presented in the text block, as follows:

```
Image.png
Movie.mp4
Notes.txt
```

There's more ...

The presented code snippet does not handle a scenario where the mentioned folder does not exist. In such a case, `FileNotFoundException` is raised by the following line:

```
StorageFolder bookFolder = await
    ApplicationData.Current.LocalFolder.GetFolderAsync("Incorrect");
```

You will learn how to check whether the folder exists in the following recipe.

See also

- The *Creating a directory* recipe
- The *Reading a structure of directories* recipe
- The *Creating a file* recipe
- The *Renaming a directory* recipe
- The *Renaming a file* recipe
- The *Removing a directory* recipe
- The *Removing a file* recipe

Renaming a directory

Sometimes, it is necessary to rename an existing folder. You can easily do this using the approach presented in this recipe.

As an example, you will modify the project from the previous recipe by adding a **Rename a directory** button. Once you click on it, the Book folder should be renamed New book. You will also check whether the folder already exists and whether the renaming operation is possible. Otherwise, a suitable message will be presented.

Getting ready

To step through this recipe, you need the project from the previous recipe.

How to do it...

To see how to rename a given directory, perform the following steps:

1. Add the **Rename a directory** button to the page by modifying the content of the MainPage.xaml file as follows:

```
<Page (...)>
    <StackPanel> (...)
        <Button
            Content="Rename a directory"
```

```
                    HorizontalAlignment="Center"
                    VerticalAlignment="Center"
                    Click="BtnRenameDirectory_Click" />
            <TextBlock
                x:Name="TxtResult"
                TextWrapping="Wrap" />
        </StackPanel>
    </Page>
```

2. Rename the `Book` directory once you click on the button. Do this by adjusting the code of the `BtnRenameDirectory_Click` method in the `MainPage.xaml.cs` file, as shown in the following code snippet:

```
private async void BtnRenameDirectory_Click(object sender,
    RoutedEventArgs e)
{
    StorageFolder bookFolder =
        (StorageFolder)await ApplicationData.Current
            .LocalFolder.TryGetItemAsync("Book");
    if (bookFolder != null)
    {
        try
        {
            await bookFolder.RenameAsync("New book");
        }
        catch (Exception)
        {
            TxtResult.Text = "Renaming has failed!";
        }
    }
    else
    {
        TxtResult.Text = "The directory does not exist!";
    }
}
```

How it works...

The operation of renaming a directory is really simple. It requires you to only call the `RenameAsync` method on an instance of `StorageFolder`, which represents the directory that should be renamed. Of course, a new name should be passed as a parameter, as shown in the following line of code:

```
await bookFolder.RenameAsync("New book");
```

However, you should also check whether the folder that you wish to rename exists. To do so, call the `TryGetItemAsync` method on an instance of the `StorageFolder` class. It returns either of the following:

- A `null` value if the item does not exist
- An instance of the class implementing the `IStorageItem` interface (such as `StorageFolder`) if the item exists

Thus, to check whether the folder exists, you just need to check whether the result of the `TryGetItemAsync` method is not equal to `null`. Of course, the result should be cast to a proper type, such as `StorageFolder`, as follows:

```
StorageFolder bookFolder = (StorageFolder)await
    ApplicationData.Current.LocalFolder.TryGetItemAsync("Book");
```

What is more, it is beneficial to ensure that the renaming operation is completed successfully. If there are any problems, an exception will be raised that could be handled as presented in the example.

See also

- The *Creating a directory* recipe
- The *Reading a structure of directories* recipe
- The *Creating a file* recipe
- The *Iterating through files* recipe
- The *Renaming a file* recipe
- The *Removing a directory* recipe
- The *Removing a file* recipe

Renaming a file

Just like folders, files could also be easily renamed using the `RenameAsync` method, which is explained in this recipe.

As an example, you will modify the project from the previous recipe by adding a **Rename a file** button. Once you click on it, the `Notes.txt` file (from the `Book` directory) should be renamed `Note.txt`.

Getting ready

To step through this recipe, you need the project from the previous recipe.

How to do it...

To see how to rename a given file, perform the following steps:

1. Add the **Rename a file** button to the page by modifying the content of the `MainPage.xaml` file as follows:

```
<Page (...)>
    <StackPanel> (...)
        <Button
            Content="Rename a file"
            HorizontalAlignment="Center"
            VerticalAlignment="Center"
            Click="BtnRenameFile_Click" />
        <TextBlock
            x:Name="TxtResult"
            TextWrapping="Wrap" />
    </StackPanel>
</Page>
```

2. Rename the `Notes.txt` file from the `Book` directory once you click on the button. Do this by adjusting the body of the `BtnRenameFile_Click` method in the `MainPage.xaml.cs` file as follows:

```
private async void BtnRenameFile_Click(object sender,
    RoutedEventArgs e)
{
    StorageFolder bookFolder =
        (StorageFolder)await ApplicationData.Current
            .LocalFolder.TryGetItemAsync("Book");
    if (bookFolder != null)
    {
        StorageFile notesFile = (StorageFile)await
            bookFolder.TryGetItemAsync("Notes.txt");
        if (notesFile != null)
        {
            try
            {
                await notesFile.RenameAsync("Note.txt");
            }
            catch (Exception)
```

```
                            {
                                TxtResult.Text = "Renaming has failed!";
                            }
                    }
                    else
                    {
                        TxtResult.Text = "The file does not exist!";
                    }
                }
                else
                {
                    TxtResult.Text = "The directory does not exist!";
                }
        }
```

How it works...

The operation of renaming a file is performed in a way that is similar to renaming a folder, described in the previous recipe. In such a case, the RenameAsync method is called on the StorageFile instance, as shown in the following line of code:

```
await notesFile.RenameAsync("Note.txt");
```

Of course, it is beneficial to check whether both the folder and the file exist and also whether the renaming operation is completed without any errors.

What is interesting, you can use the same method, namely TryGetItemAsync, to get an object that would represent either a file (StorageFile) or a directory (StorageFolder). If the item with a given name does not exist, the null value is returned.

See also

- The *Creating a directory* recipe
- The *Reading a structure of directories* recipe
- The *Creating a file* recipe
- The *Iterating through files* recipe
- The *Renaming a directory* recipe
- The *Removing a directory* recipe
- The *Removing a file* recipe

Removing a directory

Apart from creating and renaming a directory, it is also possible to programmatically delete it. You will learn how to do this in the current recipe.

As an example, you will modify the project from the previous recipe by adding a **Delete a directory** button. Once you click on it, the `Book` folder should be removed.

Getting ready

To step through this recipe, you need the project from the previous recipe.

How to do it...

To see how to remove a given directory, perform the following steps:

1. Add the **Delete a directory** button to the page by modifying the content of the `MainPage.xaml` file as follows:

```
<Page (...)>
    <StackPanel> (...)
        <Button
            Content="Delete a directory"
            HorizontalAlignment="Center"
            VerticalAlignment="Center"
            Click="BtnDeleteDirectory_Click" />
        <TextBlock
            x:Name="TxtResult"
            TextWrapping="Wrap" />
    </StackPanel>
</Page>
```

2. Delete the `Book` directory after you click on the button. Do this by adjusting the body of the `BtnDeleteDirectory_Click` method in the `MainPage.xaml.cs` file as follows:

```
private async void BtnDeleteDirectory_Click(object sender,
    RoutedEventArgs e)
{
    StorageFolder bookFolder =
        (StorageFolder)await ApplicationData.Current
            .LocalFolder.TryGetItemAsync("Book");
    if (bookFolder != null)
```

```
        {
            await bookFolder.DeleteAsync();
        }
        else
        {
            TxtResult.Text = "The directory does not exist!";
        }
    }
```

How it works...

The operation of removing a directory is possible by calling the `DeleteAsync` method on the `StorageFolder` instance. This instance represents the folder that should be removed. The suitable line of code is as follows:

```
await bookFolder.DeleteAsync();
```

What is more, you should check whether the folder exists. If it does not, a message could be presented to the user, as shown in the example.

See also

- The *Creating a directory* recipe
- The *Reading a structure of directories* recipe
- The *Creating a file* recipe
- The *Iterating through files* recipe
- The *Renaming a directory* recipe
- The *Renaming a file* recipe
- The *Removing a file* recipe

Removing a file

Just like a folder, a file can also be removed using the `DeleteAsync` method.

As an example, you will modify the project from the previous recipe by adding a **Delete a file** button. Once you press it, the `Notes.txt` file from the `Book` directory will be deleted.

Getting ready

To step through this recipe, you need the project from the previous recipe.

How to do it...

To see how to remove a given file, perform the following steps:

1. Add the **Delete a file** button to the page by modifying the content of the `MainPage.xaml` file as follows:

```
<Page (...)>
    <StackPanel> (...)
        <Button
            Content="Delete a file"
            HorizontalAlignment="Center"
            VerticalAlignment="Center"
            Click="BtnDeleteFile_Click" />
        <TextBlock
            x:Name="TxtResult"
            TextWrapping="Wrap" />
    </StackPanel>
</Page>
```

2. Delete the `Notes.txt` file once you click on the button. Do this by adjusting the body of the `BtnDeleteFile_Click` method in the `MainPage.xaml.cs` file, as shown in the following code snippet:

```
private async void BtnDeleteFile_Click(object sender,
    RoutedEventArgs e)
{
    StorageFolder bookFolder =
        (StorageFolder)await ApplicationData.Current
            .LocalFolder.TryGetItemAsync("Book");
    if (bookFolder != null)
    {
        StorageFile notesFile = (StorageFile)await
            bookFolder.TryGetItemAsync("Notes.txt");
        if (notesFile != null)
        {
            await notesFile.DeleteAsync();
        }
        else
        {
            TxtResult.Text = "The file does not exist!";
```

```
                }
            }
            else
            {
                TxtResult.Text = "The directory does not exist!";
            }
        }
```

How it works...

Removing a file is possible by calling the `DeleteAsync` method on the `StorageFile` instance, which represents the file that should be removed, as follows:

```
await notesFile.DeleteAsync();
```

What is more, it is beneficial to check whether both the folder and the file exist. In case there are any problems, a suitable message should be presented to the user.

See also

- The *Creating a directory* recipe
- The *Reading a structure of directories* recipe
- The *Creating a file* recipe
- The *Iterating through files* recipe
- The *Renaming a directory* recipe
- The *Renaming a file* recipe
- The *Removing a directory* recipe

Writing a text file

When a file is created, you can write content into it. In this recipe, you will learn how to use plain text as the content of an existing file.

As an example, you will create a simple application for saving notes. The page will contain a text block as the header, a textbox for entering content, and the **Save** button. A design of the page is presented in the following image:

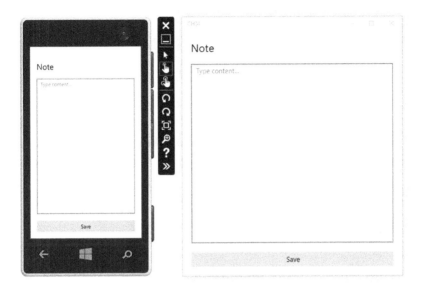

Getting ready

To step through this recipe, you need only the automatically generated project.

How to do it...

To prepare an example that saves notes in a textual file, perform the following steps:

1. Prepare the design of the page by modifying the content of the MainPage.xaml file, as shown in the following code snippet:

```
<Page (...)>
    <Grid Padding="20"> (...)
        <TextBlock
            Grid.Row="0"
            Text="Note"
            FontSize="24" />
        <TextBox
            Grid.Row="2"
            x:Name="TxtNote"
            AcceptsReturn="True"
            PlaceholderText="Type content..." />
        <Button
            Grid.Row="4"
```

```
                    Content="Save"
                    HorizontalAlignment="Stretch"
                    VerticalAlignment="Center"
                    Click="BtnSave_Click" />
        </Grid>
    </Page>
```

2. Save the content to the `Note.txt` file after you click on the button. Do this by adjusting the body of the `BtnSave_Click` method in the `MainPage.xaml.cs` file as follows:

```
private async void BtnSave_Click(object sender,
    RoutedEventArgs e)
{
    StorageFolder folder =
        ApplicationData.Current.LocalFolder;
    StorageFile file =
        await folder.CreateFileAsync("Note.txt",
            CreationCollisionOption.OpenIfExists);
    await FileIO.WriteTextAsync(file, TxtNote.Text);
}
```

How it works...

Writing plain text to a file is very simple due to the availability of the `WriteTextAsync` static method from the `FileIO` class, defined in the `Windows.Storage` namespace. To do so, you just need to call this method and pass two parameters:

- An instance of the `StorageFile` class representing the file where the content should be saved
- The content that should be written to the file

The line of code to do this is shown as follows:

```
await FileIO.WriteTextAsync(file, TxtNote.Text);
```

See also

- The *Reading a text file* recipe
- The *Writing an XML file* recipe
- The *Reading an XML file* recipe

- The *Writing a JSON file* recipe
- The *Reading a JSON file* recipe

Reading a text file

Apart from writing plain text to a file, it is also possible to read its content. In this recipe, you will learn how to do it.

As an example, you will modify the project from the previous recipe to support the operation of reading content of a text file. This modification requires you to add a **Load** button. Once you click on it, the loaded content will be shown in the textbox.

Getting ready

To step through this recipe, you need the project from the previous recipe.

How to do it...

To prepare an example that reads notes from a text file, perform the following steps:

1. Adjust the design of the page by modifying the content of the `MainPage.xaml` file, as shown in the following code snippet:

```
<Page (...)>
    <Grid Padding="20">
        <Grid.RowDefinitions> (...)
            <RowDefinition Height="20" />
            <RowDefinition Height="Auto" />
        </Grid.RowDefinitions> (...)
        <Button
            Grid.Row="6"
            Content="Load"
            HorizontalAlignment="Stretch"
            VerticalAlignment="Center"
            Click="BtnLoad_Click" />
    </Grid>
</Page>
```

2. Load the content from the `Note.txt` file after you click on the button. Perform this step by adjusting the `BtnLoad_Click` method in the `MainPage.xaml.cs` file as follows:

```
private async void BtnLoad_Click(object sender,
    RoutedEventArgs e)
{
    StorageFolder folder =
        ApplicationData.Current.LocalFolder;
    StorageFile file = (StorageFile)await
        folder.TryGetItemAsync("Note.txt");
    if (file == null)
    {
        return;
    }
    TxtNote.Text = await FileIO.ReadTextAsync(file);
}
```

How it works...

Loading text from a file is really simple with the `FileIO` static class. It contains the `ReadTextAsync` method, which takes one parameter, namely an instance of the `StorageFile` class that represents the file whose content should be read. The method returns a `string` value with the content of the file.

The usage is shown in the following line of code:

```
TxtNote.Text = await FileIO.ReadTextAsync(file);
```

See also

- The *Writing a text file* recipe
- The *Writing an XML file* recipe
- The *Reading an XML file* recipe
- The *Writing a JSON file* recipe
- The *Reading a JSON file* recipe

Writing an XML file

The application could use files with various types of content, such as plain text, as presented in the previous recipe. However, you can also use XML for formatting the content, especially when it should be structured. While developing UWP applications, you can use a set of classes to create an XML content, such as `XmlWriter`, `XDocument`, or `XElement`. Then, you can save the XML-formatted content to a file. In this recipe, you will learn how to do it.

As an example, you will create an application for adding data of important events. For each event, both the date and description will be set. The solution will save the data of all the entered events into an XML file. The design of the page is shown as follows:

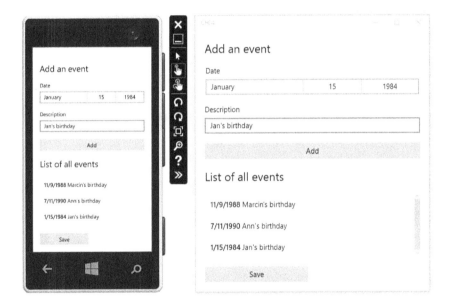

Getting ready

To step through this recipe, you need only the automatically generated project.

How to do it...

To prepare an example that saves data of various events in an XML-formatted file, perform the following steps:

1. Prepare a design of the page by modifying the content of the `MainPage.xaml` file, as shown in the following code snippet:

```
<Page (...)>
    <Grid> (...)
        <TextBlock
            Grid.Row="1" Grid.Column="1"
            Text="Add an event"
            FontSize="24" />
        <StackPanel Grid.Row="3" Grid.Column="1">
            <DatePicker
                Header="Date"
                Date="{Binding Date, Mode=TwoWay}"
                HorizontalAlignment="Stretch"/>
            <TextBox
                Header="Description"
                Text="{Binding Description, Mode=TwoWay}"
                AcceptsReturn="True"
                Margin="0 20 0 0" />
            <Button
                Content="Add"
                HorizontalAlignment="Stretch"
                VerticalAlignment="Center"
                Margin="0 20 0 0"
                Command="{Binding CmdAdd}" />
        </StackPanel>
        <TextBlock
            Grid.Row="5" Grid.Column="1"
            Text="List of all events"
            FontSize="24" />
        <ListView
            Grid.Row="7" Grid.Column="1"
            ItemsSource="{Binding Events}"
            SelectionMode="None">
            <ListView.ItemTemplate>
                <DataTemplate>
                    <TextBlock>
                        <Run Text="{Binding DateFormatted}"
                            FontWeight="SemiBold" />
                        <Run Text="{Binding Description}" />
                    </TextBlock>
                </DataTemplate>
```

```
        </ListView.ItemTemplate>
    </ListView>
    <Grid Grid.Row="9" Grid.Column="1"> (...)
        <Button
            Grid.Column="0"
            Content="Save"
            HorizontalAlignment="Stretch"
            VerticalAlignment="Center"
            Command="{Binding CmdSave}" />
    </Grid>
  </Grid>
</Page>
```

2. Ensure that the `MainPage.xaml` and `MainPage.xaml.cs` files are located in the `Views` directory. Also, make sure that the `MainPage` class is defined in the `CH04.Views` namespace and an instance of the `MainViewModel` class is set as the data context of the page. What is more, you should add the `RelayCommand.cs` file to the `Models` directory, as described in the *Creating the view model for a page* recipe in Chapter 3, *MVVM and Data Binding*.

3. Define the `EventViewModel` class, which represents the data of a single event shown in the user interface, in the `EventViewModel.cs` file in the `ViewModels` directory as follows:

```
public class EventViewModel
{
    public DateTime Date { get; set; }
    public string Description { get; set; }
    public string DateFormatted
    {
        get { return Date.ToString("M/d/yyyy"); }
    }
}
```

4. Define the `MainViewModel` class in the `MainViewModel.cs` file in the `ViewModels` directory. Then, define the property for storing a collection of events (`Events`), the currently selected date (`Date`), the description of an event that is being added (`Description`), and two commands (`CmdAdd` and `CmdSave`), as shown in the following code snippet:

```
public ObservableCollection<EventViewModel> Events
    { get; set; }
public DateTimeOffset Date { get; set; }
    = DateTimeOffset.Now;
public string Description { get; set; }
public ICommand CmdAdd { get; set; }
```

```
public ICommand CmdSave { get; set; }
```

5. Define the constructor of the `MainViewModel` class by modifying the content of the `MainViewModel.cs` file as follows:

```
public MainViewModel()
{
    Events = new ObservableCollection<EventViewModel>();
    CmdAdd = new RelayCommand(() => AddEvent());
    CmdSave = new RelayCommand(async () => await Save());
}
```

6. Define a private method (in the `MainViewModel.cs` file) that is called when a user clicks on the **Add** button as follows:

```
private void AddEvent()
{
    EventViewModel e = new EventViewModel()
    {
        Date = Date.Date,
        Description = Description
    };
    Events.Add(e);
}
```

7. Define a private method (in the `MainViewModel.cs` file) that is called when a user clicks on the **Save** button, as shown in the following part of code:

```
private async Task Save()
{
    StringBuilder builder = new StringBuilder();
    XmlWriterSettings settings = new XmlWriterSettings();
    settings.Indent = true;
    using (XmlWriter writer =
        XmlWriter.Create(builder, settings))
    {
        XDocument doc = new XDocument();
        XElement rootElement = new XElement("events");
        doc.Add(rootElement);
        foreach (EventViewModel e in Events)
        {
            XElement eventElement = new XElement("event",
                new XElement("date",
                    e.Date.ToString("yyyy-MM-dd")),
                new XElement("description",
                    e.Description));
            rootElement.Add(eventElement);
```

```
        }
        doc.Save(writer);
    }

    StorageFolder folder =
        ApplicationData.Current.LocalFolder;
    StorageFile file = await
        folder.CreateFileAsync("Events.xml",
            CreationCollisionOption.OpenIfExists);
    await FileIO.WriteTextAsync(file, builder.ToString());
}
```

How it works...

Creating XML-based content is possible using a set of classes from the `System.Xml` and `System.Xml.Linq` namespaces, as shown in the code in this recipe.

One of the most important roles is performed by the `XmlWriter` class. It contains the `Create` static method that could take two parameters:

- An instance of the `StringBuilder` class, where the XML-formatted result will be stored
- An instance of the `XmlWriterSettings` class, specifying settings, including whether indents should be added to the XML-formatted result to present the well-formatted content

As you see, the `XmlWriter` class implements the `IDisposable` interface. Thus, you can use the `using` statement. Within it, a new instance of the `XDocument` class is created and it represents an XML document. The suitable code is as follows:

```
using (XmlWriter writer = XmlWriter.Create(builder, settings))
{
    XDocument doc = new XDocument(); (...)
}
```

Here, it is worth mentioning the target structure of the XML file with the data of events. In the following part of the code, you need to specify how various data should be formatted using the XML language. The XML-formatted content with data of three events is presented as follows:

```
<?xml version="1.0" encoding="utf-16"?>
<events>
  <event>
    <date>1988-11-09</date>
```

```
            <description>Marcin's birthday</description>
        </event>
        <event>
          <date>1990-07-11</date>
          <description>Ann's birthday</description>
        </event>
        <event>
          <date>1984-01-15</date>
          <description>Jan's birthday</description>
        </event>
    </events>
```

The root element is named `events`. It contains a set of `event` nodes. Each of them contains two elements, namely `date` and `description`. Their values present both the date (in the format `YYYY-MM-DD`) and the description of the event.

To create the XML document with the content mentioned earlier, you should create the `XElement` instance, representing the root element (`events`), and add it to the document, as shown in the following code snippet:

```
XElement rootElement = new XElement("events");
doc.Add(rootElement);
```

When the root node is prepared, you can iterate through the data of all the events. For each of them, a new instance of `XElement`, representing the `event` node, is created. This is done along with the creation of two subnodes, namely `date` and `description`, as follows:

```
foreach (EventViewModel e in Events)
{
    XElement eventElement = new XElement("event",
        new XElement("date",
            e.Date.ToString("yyyy-MM-dd")),
        new XElement("description",
            e.Description));
    rootElement.Add(eventElement);
}
```

At the end, you can save the newly created document by calling the `Save` method, as shown in the following line of code:

```
doc.Save(writer);
```

The XML-formatted content is stored in the `StringBuilder` instance, so you can easily get a `string` value by calling the `ToString` method. The following part of code does not require additional clarification because it is very similar to writing plain text content to a file.

See also

- The *Writing a text file* recipe
- The *Reading a text file* recipe
- The *Reading an XML file* recipe
- The *Writing a JSON file* recipe
- The *Reading a JSON file* recipe

Reading an XML file

Apart from writing XML files, it is also possible to read content from such files. It can be done with the use of similar classes. You will learn how to do it in this recipe.

As an example, you will modify the project from the previous recipe by adding a **Load** button. Once you click on it, the content from the XML file is parsed. Then, the read data of the events are presented in the application.

Getting ready

To step through this recipe, you need the project from the previous recipe.

How to do it...

To modify the example from the preceding recipe to support loading data of various events from an XML-formatted file, perform the following steps:

1. Add the **Load** button to the page by modifying the content of the
   `MainPage.xaml` file as follows:

   ```
   <Page (...)>
       <Grid> (...)
           <Grid Grid.Row="9" Grid.Column="1"> (...)
               <Button
                   Grid.Column="0"
                   Content="Save"
                   HorizontalAlignment="Stretch"
                   Command="{Binding CmdSave}" />
           <Button
               Grid.Column="2"
   ```

```
                       Content="Load"
                       HorizontalAlignment="Stretch"
                       Command="{Binding CmdLoad}" />
              </Grid>
           </Grid>
       </Page>
```

2. Add the `CmdLoad` property, representing the command, to the `MainViewModel` class in the `MainViewModel.cs` file:

```
public ICommand CmdLoad { get; set; }
```

3. Modify the constructor of the `MainViewModel` class in the `MainViewModel.cs` file as follows:

```
public MainViewModel()
{ (...)
    CmdLoad = new RelayCommand(async () => await Load());
}
```

4. Add the `Load` method to the `MainViewModel.cs` file:

```
private async Task Load()
{
    StorageFolder folder =
        ApplicationData.Current.LocalFolder;
    StorageFile file = (StorageFile)await
        folder.TryGetItemAsync("Events.xml");
    if (file == null)
    {
        return;
    }
    string xml = await FileIO.ReadTextAsync(file);

    Events.Clear();
    XDocument doc = XDocument.Parse(xml);
    foreach (XElement eventElement
        in doc.Descendants("event"))
    {
        string dateString =
            eventElement.Element("date").Value;
        string description =
            eventElement.Element("description").Value;
        DateTime date;
        if (DateTime.TryParse(dateString, out date))
        {
            EventViewModel e = new EventViewModel()
```

```
            {
                Date = date,
                Description = description
            };
            Events.Add(e);
        }
    }
}
```

How it works...

A simple approach to loading the data stored in an XML file, shown in the current recipe, starts with reading the content of the text file and storing it in the xml variable. This is parsed by calling the Parse static method from the XDocument class, as follows:

```
XDocument doc = XDocument.Parse(xml);
```

As a result, you get the XDocument instance that represents the whole XML document. Now it is possible to select all the event notes, as follows:

```
doc.Descendants("event")
```

Each node is represented as an XElement instance. You can get a subnode (such as date) by calling the Element method on it, as shown in the following code:

```
string dateString = eventElement.Element("date").Value;
string description = eventElement.Element("description").Value;
```

As you could see, the Value property is used to get the content saved as a value of the node, in the date and description elements.

In the following part of code, you just check whether the provided date is correct. If so, a new instance of the EventViewModel class is created and added to the Events collection. Thus, a new list item is presented in the user interface.

See also

- The *Writing a text file* recipe
- The *Reading a text file* recipe
- The *Writing an XML file* recipe
- The *Writing a JSON file* recipe

• The *Reading a JSON file* recipe

Writing a JSON file

The XML language is a very popular way of storing structured data. It is used not only locally, but also to integrate various solutions over the Internet, such as using the XML-based **SOAP** protocol (**Simple Object Access Protocol**). However, it is not the only way and the JSON format could be used instead. It provides developers with a different structure, which is also lighter, therefore more suitable for sending over mobile networks. In this recipe, you will learn how to write the JSON-formatted content to a file.

It is worth mentioning that serializing an object or a collection of objects into a JSON-encoded string is really simple due to the availability of the `Newtonsoft.Json` library. It provides you with the `SerializeObject` method that returns a string for an object, such as in the following line of code:

```
string json = JsonConvert.SerializeObject(variable);
```

As an example, you will create a simple application that will store data of employees in a JSON file. For each employee, the full name and a list of known languages is stored. The application will also present a list of added employees. An example window, in both smartphone and desktop-based versions, is shown in the following image:

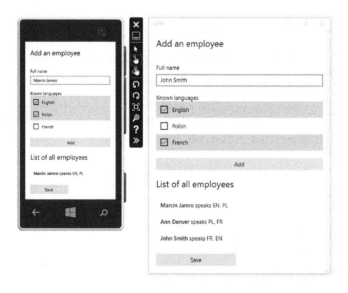

Getting ready

To step through this recipe, you need only the automatically generated project.

How to do it...

To prepare an example that saves data of employees in a JSON-formatted file, perform the following steps:

1. Install the `Newtonsoft.Json` and `PropertyChanged.Fody` libraries using the NuGet Package Manager. Do not forget to add the `FodyWeavers.xml` file, as already explained in the recipe titled *Creating the view model for a page* in `Chapter 3`, *MVVM and Data Binding*.

2. Prepare a design of the page by modifying the content of the `MainPage.xaml` file, as shown in the following code snippet:

```
<Page (...)>
    <ScrollViewer>
        <Grid> (...)
            <TextBlock
                Grid.Row="1" Grid.Column="1"
                Text="Add an employee"
                FontSize="24" />
            <StackPanel Grid.Row="3" Grid.Column="1">
                <TextBox
                    Header="Full name"
                    Text="{Binding FullName, Mode=TwoWay}"
                    AcceptsReturn="True"
                    Margin="0 20 0 0" />
                <ListView
                    Header="Known languages"
                    SelectionMode="Multiple"
                    SelectionChanged=
                        "LsvLanguages_SelectionChanged"
                    Margin="0 20 0 0">
                    <ListViewItem Content="English"
                        Tag="EN" />
                    <ListViewItem Content="Polish"
                        Tag="PL" />
                    <ListViewItem Content="French"
                        Tag="FR" />
                </ListView>
                <Button
                    Content="Add"
```

```
                    HorizontalAlignment="Stretch"
                    VerticalAlignment="Center"
                    Margin="0 20 0 0"
                    Command="{Binding CmdAdd}" />
            </StackPanel>
            <TextBlock
                Grid.Row="5" Grid.Column="1"
                Text="List of all employees"
                FontSize="24" />
            <ListView
                Grid.Row="7" Grid.Column="1"
                ItemsSource="{Binding Employees}"
                SelectionMode="None">
                <ListView.ItemTemplate>
                    <DataTemplate>
                        <TextBlock>
                            <Run Text="{Binding FullName}"
                                FontWeight="SemiBold" />
                            <Run Text="speaks" />
                            <Run Text="{Binding
                                LanguagesFormatted}" />
                        </TextBlock>
                    </DataTemplate>
                </ListView.ItemTemplate>
            </ListView>
            <Grid Grid.Row="9" Grid.Column="1"> (...)
                <Button
                    Grid.Column="0"
                    Content="Save"
                    HorizontalAlignment="Stretch"
                    Command="{Binding CmdSave}" />
            </Grid>
        </Grid>
    </ScrollViewer>
</Page>
```

3. Ensure that the `MainPage.xaml` and `MainPage.xaml.cs` files are located in the `Views` directory, and the `MainPage` class is defined in the `CH04.Views` namespace. What is more, you should add the `RelayCommand.cs` file to the `Models` directory, as described in the *Creating the view model for a page* recipe in Chapter 3, *MVVM and Data Binding*.

4. Set a proper data context for the page and support the selection of many items from the `ListView` control. Do this by modifying the content of the `MainPage.xaml.cs` file as follows:

```
public sealed partial class MainPage : Page
```

```
{
    private MainViewModel _vm = null;

    public MainPage()
    {
        InitializeComponent();
        _vm = new MainViewModel();
        DataContext = _vm;
    }

    private void LsvLanguages_SelectionChanged(
        object sender, SelectionChangedEventArgs e)
    {
        ListView listView = (ListView)sender;
        List<string> languages = new List<string>();
        foreach (ListViewItem item in listView.SelectedItems)
        {
            string language = (string)item.Tag;
            languages.Add(language);
        }
        _vm.Languages = languages;
    }
}
```

5. Define the EmployeeViewModel class, which represents the data of an employee shown in the user interface, in the EmployeeViewModel.cs file in the ViewModels directory, as presented in the following code snippet:

```
[ImplementPropertyChanged]
public class EmployeeViewModel
{
    public string FullName { get; set; }
    public List<string> Languages { get; set; }

    [DependsOn("Language")]
    public string LanguagesFormatted
    {
        get { return string.Join(", ", Languages); }
    }
}
```

6. Define the `MainViewModel` class in the `MainViewModel.cs` file in the `ViewModels` directory. What is more, define the property storing the data of all the employees (`Employees`), representing the currently typed full name and currently selected languages in the form (`FullName` and `Languages`) and two commands (`CmdAdd` and `CmdSave`). Then, adjust the constructor and add two private methods: for adding a new employee (`AddEmployee`) and saving the data of all the employees in the JSON file (`Save`). The necessary modifications are shown in the following code snippet:

```
[ImplementPropertyChanged]
public class MainViewModel
{
    public ObservableCollection<EmployeeViewModel>
        Employees { get; set; }
    public string FullName { get; set; }
    public List<string> Languages { get; set; }
    public ICommand CmdAdd { get; set; }
    public ICommand CmdSave { get; set; }

    public MainViewModel()
    {
        Employees = new
            ObservableCollection<EmployeeViewModel>();
        CmdAdd = new RelayCommand(() => AddEmployee());
        CmdSave = new RelayCommand(
            async () => await Save());
    }

    private void AddEmployee()
    {
        EmployeeViewModel employee =
            new EmployeeViewModel()
        {
            FullName = FullName,
            Languages = Languages
        };
        Employees.Add(employee);
    }

    private async Task Save()
    {
        string json =
            JsonConvert.SerializeObject(Employees);
        StorageFolder folder =
            ApplicationData.Current.LocalFolder;
        StorageFile file = await
```

```
            folder.CreateFileAsync("Employees.json",
                    CreationCollisionOption.OpenIfExists);
            await FileIO.WriteTextAsync(file, json);
        }
    }
```

How it works...

With the usage of the `Newtonsoft.Json` library, serializing an object or a collection of objects to the JSON-formatted string is really simple. You just need to call the `SerializeObject` static method from the `JsonConvert` class, passing an object or a collection of objects that should be serialized as follows:

```
string json = JsonConvert.SerializeObject(Employees);
```

The method returns the JSON-formatted string that could then be stored in a file in the same way as already explained in this chapter. The JSON-encoded content with data of three employees is presented as follows:

```
[
    {
        "full_name": "Marcin Jamro",
        "languages": [
            "EN",
            "PL"
        ]
    },
    {
        "full_name": "Ann Denver",
        "languages": [
            "PL",
            "FR"
        ]
    },
    {
        "full_name": "John Smith",
        "languages": [
            "FR",
            "EN"
        ]
    }
]
```

Another clarification is necessary for handling the selection of multiple items from the list view. First of all, a value of the `SelectionMode` property (of the `ListView` control) should be set to `Multiple`, and the `SelectionChanged` event should be handled.

Within the method handling this event (namely `LsvLanguages_SelectionChanged`), you get a list of the selected items using the `SelectedItems` property, which returns a collection of `ListViewItem` objects.

In the example, a language code is set as a value of the `Tag` property for each `ListViewItem`. Thus, you can easily read it and add it to the collection of supported languages. At the end, a value of the suitable property (`Languages`) is updated in the view model class.

See also

- The *Writing a text file* recipe
- The *Reading a text file* recipe
- The *Writing an XML file* recipe
- The *Reading an XML file* recipe
- The *Reading a JSON file* recipe

Reading a JSON file

Parsing the JSON-formatted content into an object or a collection of objects is significantly simplified using the `Newtonsoft.Json` library, as you will see in this recipe. Thus, you can convert a JSON-formatted string to the target type with just a single line of code, using the `DeserializeObject` method, as shown in the following line:

```
variable = JsonConvert.DeserializeObject<type>(encoded-string)
```

As an example, you will modify the project from the previous recipe by adding a **Load** button. Once you click on it, the content of the `Employees.json` file will be loaded and parsed into a collection of `EmployeeViewModel` instances. Then, the result will be presented in the user interface.

Getting ready

To step through this recipe, you need the project from the previous recipe.

How to do it...

To modify the preceding example to support loading data of employees from a JSON-formatted file, perform the following steps:

1. Add the **Load** button to the page by modifying the content of the `MainPage.xaml` file as follows:

```
<Page (...)>
    <ScrollViewer>
        <Grid> (...)
            <Grid Grid.Row="9" Grid.Column="1"> (...)
                <Button
                    Grid.Column="0"
                    Content="Save"
                    HorizontalAlignment="Stretch"
                    Command="{Binding CmdSave}" />
                <Button
                    Grid.Column="2"
                    Content="Load"
                    HorizontalAlignment="Stretch"
                    Command="{Binding CmdLoad}" />
            </Grid>
        </Grid>
    </ScrollViewer>
</Page>
```

2. Add the `CmdLoad` property, representing the command, to the `MainViewModel` class in the `MainViewModel.cs` file as follows:

```
public ICommand CmdLoad { get; set; }
```

3. Modify the constructor of the `MainViewModel` class in the `MainViewModel.cs` file as follows:

```
public MainViewModel()
{ (...)
    CmdLoad = new RelayCommand(async () => await Load());
}
```

4. Add the `Load` method to the `MainViewModel.cs` file as follows:

```
private async Task Load()
{
    StorageFolder folder =
        ApplicationData.Current.LocalFolder;
    StorageFile file = (StorageFile)await
        folder.TryGetItemAsync("Employees.json");
    if (file == null)
    {
        return;
    }
    string json = await FileIO.ReadTextAsync(file);
    Employees = JsonConvert.DeserializeObject<
        ObservableCollection<EmployeeViewModel>>(json);
}
```

How it works...

Only a small explanation is necessary for the following line:

```
Employees = JsonConvert.DeserializeObject
    <ObservableCollection<EmployeeViewModel>>(json);
```

Here, the JSON-formatted string (the `json` variable) is parsed into an observable collection of `EmployeeViewModel` instances. By using the `Newtonsoft.Json` library, no more operations are necessary.

See also

- The *Writing a text file* recipe
- The *Reading a text file* recipe
- The *Writing an XML file* recipe
- The *Reading an XML file* recipe
- The *Writing a JSON file* recipe

Writing a binary file

In the case of storing huge amounts of data, using XML-formatted or JSON-formatted string values may not be sufficient. For this reason, in this recipe, you will learn how to define you own binary format and store bigger amount of data within binary files.

As an example, you will prepare an application that will simulate the experiment. After you press the **Start experiment** button, the operation of generating a random value will be repeated 100,000 times. For each one of them, a value will be added to the collection of results, together with a period of time in milliseconds that elapsed since the beginning of the experiment. At the end, the minimum, maximum, and average values will be calculated and presented. The window of the application is shown in the following image:

Getting ready

To step through this recipe, you need only the automatically generated project.

How to do it...

To prepare an example that saves data in a custom format within a binary file, perform the following steps:

1. Install the `PropertyChanged.Fody` library using the NuGet Package Manager. Do not forget to add the `FodyWeavers.xml` file, as already explained in the *Creating the view model for a page* recipe in `Chapter 3`, *MVVM and Data Binding*.

2. Prepare the design of the page by modifying the content of the `MainPage.xaml` file, as shown in the following code snippet:

```xml
<Page (...)>
    <StackPanel Padding="20">
        <TextBlock
            Grid.Row="1"
            Grid.Column="1"
            Text="Experiments"
            FontSize="24" />
        <TextBlock Margin="0 20 0 5">
            <Run Text="Minimum:" />
            <Run Text="{Binding Minimum}"
                FontWeight="SemiBold" />
        </TextBlock>
        <TextBlock Margin="0 5">
            <Run Text="Maximum:" />
            <Run Text="{Binding Maximum}"
                FontWeight="SemiBold" />
        </TextBlock>
        <TextBlock Margin="0 5">
            <Run Text="Average:" />
            <Run Text="{Binding Average}"
                FontWeight="SemiBold" />
        </TextBlock>
        <TextBlock Margin="0 5">
            <Run Text="Count:" />
            <Run Text="{Binding Count}"
                FontWeight="SemiBold" />
        </TextBlock>
        <TextBlock Margin="0 5">
            <Run Text="Time [ms]:" />
            <Run Text="{Binding Time}"
                FontWeight="SemiBold" />
        </TextBlock>
        <Button
            Content="Start experiment"
            HorizontalAlignment="Stretch"
            Margin="0 20 0 10"
            Command="{Binding CmdStart}" />
        <Button
            Content="Save results"
            HorizontalAlignment="Stretch"
            Margin="0 10"
            Command="{Binding CmdSave }" />
    </StackPanel>
</Page>
```

3. Ensure that the `MainPage.xaml` and `MainPage.xaml.cs` files are located in the `Views` directory. Also, make sure that the `MainPage` class is defined in the `CH04.Views` namespace and an instance of the `MainViewModel` class is set as the data context of the page. What is more, you should add the `RelayCommand.cs` file to the `Models` directory, as described in the *Creating the view model for a page* recipe in Chapter 3, *MVVM and Data Binding*.

4. Define the `ResultViewModel` class, representing the data of a single result, in the `ResultViewModel.cs` file in the `ViewModels` directory, as shown in the following code snippet:

```
public class ResultViewModel
{
    public int Value { get; set; }
    public int Time { get; set; }
}
```

5. Define the `MainViewModel` class in the `MainViewModel.cs` file, located in the `ViewModels` directory. The class should contain a property that is storing a list of results (`Results`), five properties with values presented in the user interface (`Minimum`, `Maximum`, `Average`, `Count`, and `Time`), and two commands (`CmdStart` and `CmdSave`). The code is as follows:

```
[ImplementPropertyChanged]
public class MainViewModel
{
    public int Minimum { get; set; }
    public int Maximum { get; set; }
    public int Average { get; set; }
    public int Count { get; set; }
    public int Time { get; set; }
    public List<ResultViewModel> Results { get; set; }
    public ICommand CmdStart { get; set; }
    public ICommand CmdSave { get; set; }

    public MainViewModel()
    {
        Results = new List<ResultViewModel>();
        CmdStart = new RelayCommand(() => Start());
        CmdSave = new RelayCommand(
            async () => await Save());
    }
}
```

6. Define the `Start` method, which starts the experiment, in the
   `MainViewModel.cs` file, as shown in the following code snippet:

```
private void Start()
{
    Results.Clear();
    DateTime startTime = DateTime.Now;
    Minimum = int.MaxValue;
    Maximum = int.MinValue;

    Random random = new Random();
    for (int i = 0; i < 100000; i++)
    {
        int value = random.Next();
        int time = (int)(DateTime.Now -
            startTime).TotalMilliseconds;
        ResultViewModel result = new ResultViewModel()
        {
            Value = value,
            Time = time
        };
        Results.Add(result);
    }

    Minimum = Results.Min(r => r.Value);
    Maximum = Results.Max(r => r.Value);
    Average = (int)Results.Average(r => r.Value);
    Count = Results.Count;
    Time = Results.Last().Time;
}
```

7. Define the `Save` method, which saves the results to the binary file, in the
   `MainViewModel.cs` file as follows:

```
private async Task Save()
{
    List<byte> bytes = new List<byte>();
    foreach (ResultViewModel result in Results)
    {
        byte[] timeBytes =
            BitConverter.GetBytes(result.Time);
        byte[] valueBytes =
            BitConverter.GetBytes(result.Value);
        bytes.AddRange(timeBytes);
        bytes.AddRange(valueBytes);
    }
```

```
StorageFolder folder =
    ApplicationData.Current.LocalFolder;
StorageFile file =
    await folder.CreateFileAsync("Results.bin",
        CreationCollisionOption.OpenIfExists);
await FileIO.WriteBytesAsync(file, bytes.ToArray());
}
```

How it works...

To save data in the custom binary format, it is crucial to earlier describe such a format in detail. This is because you should follow the exactly same way of storing particular data while writing and reading the content. In the current example, the format will be very simple, just to introduce you to the topic of preparing binary files.

Each result is stored in 8 bytes:

- 4 bytes for milliseconds that elapsed since the start of the experiment
- 4 bytes for the result

The following results will be stored one after another. Therefore, for example, 10 results will take together only 80 bytes (8 bytes multiplied by 10).

To store data in a binary file, you first prepare a list of the bytes that represent the content, as shown in the following code snippet:

```
List<byte> bytes = new List<byte>();
foreach (ResultViewModel result in Results)
{
    byte[] timeBytes = BitConverter.GetBytes(result.Time);
    byte[] valueBytes = BitConverter.GetBytes(result.Value);
    bytes.AddRange(timeBytes);
    bytes.AddRange(valueBytes);
}
```

Then, the list is converted into an array using the `ToArray` method and saved in the `Results.bin` file using the `WriteBytesAsync` static method from the `FileIO` class, defined in the `Windows.Storage` namespace. The code is as follows:

```
await FileIO.WriteBytesAsync(file, bytes.ToArray());
```

See also

- The *Reading a binary file* recipe

Reading a binary file

The process of reading a binary file is related to the process of its creation, because it is necessary to analyze its content in exactly the same way. In this recipe, you will learn how to read data stored in a binary file.

As an example, you will modify the project from the previous recipe by adding a **Load results** button. After you click on it, data from the `Results.bin` file will be read and added to the collection of results. Also, the minimum, maximum, and average values will be calculated and shown in the user interface, together with a number of results and the time necessary for the previously run and saved experiment.

Getting ready

To step through this recipe, you need the project from the previous recipe.

How to do it...

To modify the preceding example to load experiment data from a binary file, perform the following steps:

1. Add the **Load results** button to the page by modifying the content of the `MainPage.xaml` file as follows:

```
<Page (...)>
    <StackPanel Padding="20"> (...)
        <Button
            Content="Load results"
            HorizontalAlignment="Stretch"
            Margin="0 10"
            Command="{Binding CmdLoad}" />
    </StackPanel>
</Page>
```

2. Add the `CmdLoad` property, representing the command, to the `MainViewModel` class in the `MainViewModel.cs` file as follows:

```
public ICommand CmdLoad { get; set; }
```

3. Modify the constructor of the `MainViewModel` class in the `MainViewModel.cs` file as follows:

```
public MainViewModel()
{ (...)
    CmdLoad = new RelayCommand(async () => await Load());
}
```

4. Add the `Load` method to the `MainViewModel.cs` file:

```
private async Task Load()
{
    Results.Clear();
    StorageFolder folder =
        ApplicationData.Current.LocalFolder;
    StorageFile file = (StorageFile)await
        folder.TryGetItemAsync("Results.bin");
    if (file == null)
    {
        return;
    }
    IBuffer buffer = await FileIO.ReadBufferAsync(file);
    byte[] bytes = buffer.ToArray();
    for (int i = 0; i < bytes.Length; i += sizeof(int) * 2)
    {
        int time = BitConverter.ToInt32(bytes, i);
        int value = BitConverter.ToInt32(bytes,
            i + sizeof(int));
        ResultViewModel result = new ResultViewModel()
        {
            Time = time,
            Value = value
        };
        Results.Add(result);
    }

    Minimum = Results.Min(r => r.Value);
    Maximum = Results.Max(r => r.Value);
    Average = (int)Results.Average(r => r.Value);
    Count = Results.Count;
    Time = Results.Last().Time;
}
```

Do not forget to add the necessary `using` statement for `System.Runtime.InteropServices.WindowsRuntime`. It is required by the `ToArray` extension method.

How it works...

To read the data stored in a binary file, you can start with getting the bytes from this file using the `ReadBufferAsync` static method (from the `FileIO` class) and the `ToArray` method as follows:

```
IBuffer buffer = await FileIO.ReadBufferAsync(file);
byte[] bytes = buffer.ToArray();
```

Then you can just iterate through the bytes of all the results using the `for` loop. It is worth mentioning that each iteration of the loop represents a single result. This is possible if you increase the `i` variable by eight (two values with 4 bytes each) after an iteration.

Within the loop, you use the `BitConverter` class as follows:

- Take 4 bytes starting from the `i` index and save them as an integer value in `time`
- Take 4 bytes starting from the `i+4` index and save them as an integer value in `value`

Such values are then used to set proper values of properties in the `ResultViewModel` instance. It is later added to the collection of results (the `Results` property).

See also

- The *Writing a binary file* recipe

Creating a SQLite database and tables

While storing data in textual and binary files is a convenient solution, using a database gives you significantly more possibilities. Fortunately, it is really easy to use the SQLite database in UWP applications running on various platforms, such as smartphones and desktops. In the current recipe, you will learn how to create a local SQLite database as well as how to create tables when the application is launched for the first time.

The subject of designing databases as well as using queries to select, insert, update, and delete data from particular tables is of course too big and can't be described in detail in this chapter. For this reason, this book will focus on presenting some practical aspects of using databases, so basic knowledge about databases, tables, and queries is necessary.

As an example prepared in this and the following recipes, you will develop a simple application for creating an offline blog, where you can present, add, edit, and delete entries. Each of them will contain a title, content, as well as a category chosen from a drop-down list. To store all of this data, two tables in the database are necessary, namely for data of entries and categories.

The window of the application, created in this recipe, is as follows:

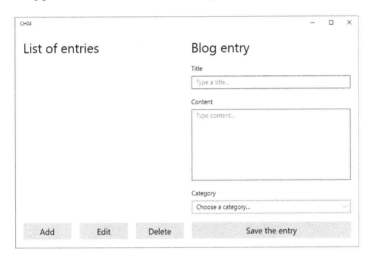

Getting ready

To step through this recipe, you need only the automatically generated project.

How to do it...

To prepare an example that configures a SQLite database and creates two tables within it, perform the following steps:

1. Install the `SQLite for Universal Windows Platform` extension. To do so, navigate to **Tools** | **Extensions and Updates...** from the main menu of the IDE, search for a suitable extension (`SQLite for Universal Windows Platform`), and click on the **Download** button, as shown in the following image. Then, restart the IDE, according to the message.

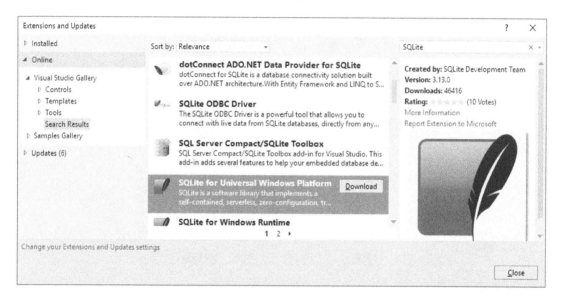

2. Add a reference to the extension. To do so, navigate to **References** | **Add Reference...** from the context menu of the project node in the **Solution Explorer** window. Then navigate to **Universal Windows** | **Extensions** (on the left-hand side), select **SQLite for Universal Windows Platform** (as shown in the following screenshot), and click on **OK**:

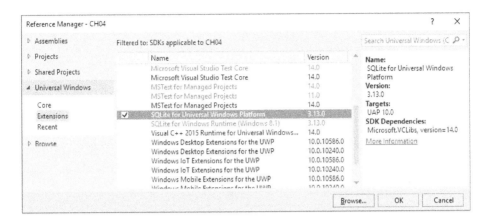

3. Install the **SQLite.Net-PCL** library using the NuGet package manager.

4. Prepare the design of the page by modifying the content of the `MainPage.xaml` file, as shown in the following code snippet (the final `.xaml` file is included in the code attached to this chapter):

```
<Page (...)>
    <Page.Resources> (...) </Page.Resources>
    <Grid> (...)
        <TextBlock
            Grid.Row="1" Grid.Column="1"
            Text="List of entries"
            FontSize="32" />
        <ListView
            Grid.Row="3" Grid.Column="1"
            ItemsSource="{Binding Entries}"
            SelectedItem="{Binding Entry, Mode=TwoWay}">
            <ListView.ItemTemplate>
                <DataTemplate>
                    <StackPanel>
                        <TextBlock
                            Text="{Binding Title}"
                            FontWeight="SemiBold" />
                        <TextBlock
                            Text="{Binding Content}"
                            TextWrapping="Wrap" />
                    </StackPanel>
                </DataTemplate>
            </ListView.ItemTemplate>
        </ListView>
        <Grid Grid.Row="5" Grid.Column="1"> (...)
            <Button
                Grid.Column="0"
```

```
                    Command="{Binding CmdAdd}"
                Content="Add" />
        <Button
            Grid.Column="2"
                Command="{Binding CmdEdit}"
                IsEnabled="{Binding IsEntrySelected}"
            Content="Edit" />
        <Button
            Grid.Column="4"
                Command="{Binding CmdDelete}"
                IsEnabled="{Binding IsEntrySelected}"
            Content="Delete" />
    </Grid>
    <TextBlock
        Grid.Row="1" Grid.Column="3"
        Text="Blog entry"
        FontSize="32" />
    <Grid
        Grid.Row="3" Grid.RowSpan="3" Grid.Column="3">
        <ScrollViewer ScrollViewer.
            VerticalScrollBarVisibility="Auto">
            <StackPanel>
                <TextBox
                    Header="Title"
                    Text="{Binding Title, Mode=TwoWay}"
                    PlaceholderText="Type a title..."/>
                <TextBox
                    Header="Content"
                    Text="{Binding Content, Mode=TwoWay}"
                    PlaceholderText="Type content..."
                    AcceptsReturn="True"
                    Height="200"
                    Margin="0 20 0 0" />
                <ComboBox
                    Header="Category"
                    PlaceholderText="Choose a
                        category..."
                    Margin="0 20 0 0"
                    HorizontalAlignment="Stretch"
                    ItemsSource="{Binding Categories}"
                    SelectedItem="{Binding Category,
                        Mode=TwoWay}"
                    DisplayMemberPath="Name" />
                <Button
                    Margin="0 20 0 0"
                    HorizontalAlignment="Stretch"
                    Content="Save the entry"
                    Command="{Binding CmdSave}" />
```

```
            </StackPanel>
          </ScrollViewer>
        </Grid>
      </Grid>
    </Page>
```

5. Ensure that the `MainPage.xaml` and `MainPage.xaml.cs` files are located in the `Views` directory, and the `MainPage` class is defined in the `CH04.Views` namespace. What is more, you should add the `RelayCommand.cs` file to the `Models` directory, as described in the *Creating the view model for a page* recipe in `Chapter 3`, *MVVM and Data Binding*.

6. Set a proper data context for the page as well as call the method responsible for initializing the database after you navigate to the page. Perform this step by modifying the content of the `MainPage.xaml.cs` file as follows:

```csharp
public sealed partial class MainPage : Page
{
    private MainViewModel _vm = null;

    public MainPage()
    {
        InitializeComponent();
        _vm = new MainViewModel();
        DataContext = _vm;
    }

    protected override void OnNavigatedTo(
        NavigationEventArgs e)
    {
        _vm.InitializeDatabase();
    }
}
```

7. Define the `CategoryViewModel` class representing a category shown in the drop-down list in the user interface in the `CategoryViewModel.cs` file in the `ViewModels` directory:

```csharp
public class CategoryViewModel
{
    public int Id { get; set; }
    public string Name { get; set; }
}
```

8. Define the `EntryViewModel` class representing a single entry shown in the user interface in the `EntryViewModel.cs` file in the `ViewModels` directory:

```
public class EntryViewModel
{
    public int Id { get; set; }
    public string Title { get; set; }
    public string Content { get; set; }
    public CategoryViewModel Category { get; set; }
}
```

9. Define the `Category` class, representing the data of a single category stored in the database in the `Category.cs` file in the `Models` directory:

```
[Table("categories")]
public class Category
{
    [PrimaryKey]
    [AutoIncrement]
    public int Id { get; set; }

    public string Name { get; set; }
}
```

10. Define the `Entry` class representing the data of a single entry stored in the database in the `Entry.cs` file in the `Models` directory:

```
[Table("entries")]
public class Entry
{
    [PrimaryKey]
    [AutoIncrement]
    public int Id { get; set; }

    public int CategoryId { get; set; }
    public string Title { get; set; }
    public string Content { get; set; }
    public DateTime AddedAt { get; set; }
    public DateTime? EditedAt { get; set; }
}
```

11. Define the `MainViewModel` class in the `MainViewModel.cs` file in the `ViewModels` directory as shown in the following code snippet:

```
[ImplementPropertyChanged]
public class MainViewModel
{
```

```csharp
public void InitializeDatabase()
{
    using (SQLiteConnection connection = GetConnection())
    {
        if (connection.GetTableInfo("categories")
            .Count == 0)
        {
            connection.CreateTable<Category>();
            connection.CreateTable<Entry>();
        }
    }
}

private SQLiteConnection GetConnection()
{
    string dbPath = Path.Combine(
        ApplicationData.Current.LocalFolder.Path,
        "db.sqlite");
    return new SQLiteConnection(
        new SQLitePlatformWinRT(), dbPath);
}
}
```

How it works...

The process of adding the SQLite database to the project seems to be quite complex. However, it is not so difficult, as you will find in the following explanation.

First of all, you need to install the SQLite for Universal Windows Platform extension, add a reference to it, and install the SQLite.Net-PCL library using the NuGet package manager. Then, you define a set of classes that represent the data that can be stored in the database, namely Category and Entry. At the end, you just connect to the database and create tables if they do not already exist.

A bit more clarification is necessary to define the Category and Entry classes. Let's take a look at the second one, as follows:

```csharp
[Table("entries")]
public class Entry
{
    [PrimaryKey]
    [AutoIncrement]
    public int Id { get; set; }

    public int CategoryId { get; set; }
```

```
public string Title { get; set; }
public string Content { get; set; }
public DateTime AddedAt { get; set; }
public DateTime? EditedAt { get; set; }
}
```

The class is associated with the `Table` attribute indicating that the class represents a single row stored within a table in the database. The attribute takes the name of the table (`entries`) as a parameter. The class contains a set of properties. Each of them represents a column that will be created in the table. Thus, the `entries` table will allow you to store an entry identifier (`Id`), a category identifier (`CategoryId`), a title (`Title`), content (`Content`), an addition date (`AddedAt`), as well as a nullable last modification date (`EditedAt`).

What is important, the `Id` property is associated with the `PrimaryKey` and `AutoIncrement` attributes. The first attribute indicates that the property represents the primary key of the table, while the other informs that the values in such a column will be automatically incremented while adding the next rows.

Another explanation is beneficial for the `InitializeDatabase` method from the `MainViewModel` class. Here, you call the `GetConnection` private method to get the `SQLiteConnection` object that represents a connection with the database. It is assumed that the database is stored in the `db.sqlite` file in the local folder, as specified in the `dbPath` variable as follows:

```
string dbPath = Path.Combine(
    ApplicationData.Current.LocalFolder.Path, "db.sqlite");
```

After getting the `SQLiteConnection` object, it is possible to check whether the `categories` table exists. You can do it by calling the `GetTableInfo` method and checking whether it returns any results. If not, both the `categories` and `entries` tables are created by calling the `CreateTable` generic method as follows:

```
if (connection.GetTableInfo("categories").Count == 0)
{
    connection.CreateTable<Category>();
    connection.CreateTable<Entry>();
}
```

See also

- The *Storing data in a SQLite database* recipe
- The *Selecting data from a SQLite database* recipe

- The *Updating data in a SQLite database* recipe
- The *Removing data from a SQLite database* recipe

Storing data in a SQLite database

It is quite difficult to imagine an application that uses a database but does not insert anything into it. Thus, it is crucial that you know how to store data in tables in the database. In this recipe, you will learn how to do it.

As an example, you will slightly modify the project from the previous recipe by adding the data of three categories while initializing the database.

Getting ready

To step through this recipe, you need the project from the previous recipe.

How to do it...

To modify the preceding example to add the data of three categories while initializing the database, modify the `InitializeDatabase` method in the `MainViewModel` class in the `MainViewModel.cs` file, as shown in the following code snippet:

```
public void InitializeDatabase()
{
    using (SQLiteConnection connection = GetConnection())
    {
        if (connection.GetTableInfo("categories").Count == 0)
        {
            connection.CreateTable<Category>();
            connection.CreateTable<Entry>();
            Category[] categories =
            {
                new Category() { Name = "Private" },
                new Category() { Name = "Hobby" },
                new Category() { Name = "Sport" }
            };
            connection.InsertAll(categories);
        }
    }
}
```

How it works...

Adding new data to a table in a database is very simple. First, it requires you to create a new instance of a class representing an object that should be stored in the database. Second, you need to call the `Insert` method on the `SQLiteConnection` instance, as shown in the following code snippet:

```
Category category = new Category() { Name = "Life" };
connection.Insert(category);
```

Of course, it is also possible to add a list of objects without calling the `Insert` method multiple times. To do so in the case of data of three categories, an array of `Category` instances is defined and passed as a parameter of the `InsertAll` method, as follows:

```
Category[] categories =
{
    new Category() { Name = "Private" },
    new Category() { Name = "Hobby" },
    new Category() { Name = "Sport" }
};
connection.InsertAll(categories);
```

See also

- The *Creating a SQLite database and tables* recipe
- The *Selecting data from a SQLite database* recipe
- The *Updating data in a SQLite database* recipe
- The *Removing data from a SQLite database* recipe

Selecting data from a SQLite database

As in the case of inserting data into a database, it is quite difficult to imagine any application that uses a database but does not select any data from it. Thus, in this recipe, you will learn how to select data from particular tables in a database using **Language Integrated Query** (**LINQ**). What is interesting is that you do not need to write raw SQL queries on your own, thus it may be a really convenient and simple solution.

As an example, you will modify the project from the previous recipe to load data of all categories and entries after initializing the database. The list of categories will be shown in a drop-down list, while the list of entries in a dedicated place on the left-hand side.

Getting ready

To step through this recipe, you need the project from the previous recipe.

How to do it...

To modify the preceding example to load data of categories and entries after initializing the database, perform the following steps:

1. Load data of categories and entries just after you initialize the database. Do this by modifying the code of the OnNavigatedTo method in the MainPage.xaml.cs file as follows:

```
protected override void OnNavigatedTo(
    NavigationEventArgs e)
{
    _vm.InitializeDatabase();
    _vm.LoadCategories();
    _vm.LoadEntries();
}
```

2. Define the properties that represent the currently selected category (Category) as well as observable collections that store the data of all categories and entries (Categories and Entries). Such properties should be added to the MainViewModel class in the MainViewModel.cs file, as follows:

```
public CategoryViewModel Category { get; set; }
public ObservableCollection<CategoryViewModel> Categories
    { get; set; }
public ObservableCollection<EntryViewModel> Entries
    { get; set; }
```

3. Modify the constructor of the MainViewModel class in the MainViewModel.cs file to assign default values to the Categories and Entries properties as follows:

```
public MainViewModel()
{
    Categories =
        new ObservableCollection<CategoryViewModel>();
    Entries = new ObservableCollection<EntryViewModel>();
}
```

4. Select the data of all the categories, ordered by names (ascending), from the categories table in the database. To do so, add the LoadCategories method to the MainViewModel.cs file as follows:

```
public void LoadCategories()
{
    Categories.Clear();
    using (SQLiteConnection connection = GetConnection())
    {
        List<Category> categoriesDB =
            connection.Table<Category>()
                .OrderBy(c => c.Name).ToList();
        foreach (Category categoryDB in categoriesDB)
        {
            CategoryViewModel category =
                new CategoryViewModel()
            {
                Id = categoryDB.Id,
                Name = categoryDB.Name
            };
            Categories.Add(category);
        }
        Category = Categories[0];
    }
}
```

5. Select the data of all the entries, ordered by identifiers (descending), from the entries table in the database. To do so, add the LoadEntries method to the MainViewModel.cs file, as shown in the following code snippet:

```
public void LoadEntries()
{
    Entries.Clear();
    using (SQLiteConnection connection = GetConnection())
    {
        List<Entry> entriesDB = connection.Table<Entry>()
            .OrderByDescending(e => e.Id).ToList();
        foreach (Entry entryDB in entriesDB)
        {
            EntryViewModel entry = new EntryViewModel()
            {
                Id = entryDB.Id,
                Title = entryDB.Title,
                Content = entryDB.Content,
                Category = Categories.SingleOrDefault(
                    c => c.Id == entryDB.CategoryId)
            };
```

```
        Entries.Add(entry);
    }
  }
}
```

If you cannot see any categories in the drop-down list or any exception is thrown, uninstall the application and run the project again. If you run the application from the previous recipe, the database would have been initialized already. The application will not allow you to reinitialize the database, and therefore, the `categories` table will not contain any rows.

How it works...

You can easily arrange the query by calling a set of methods, such as `OrderBy` and `Where`, on the `TableQuery` instance returned by the `Table` generic method. For instance, let's take a look at the example from the previous code:

```
connection.Table<Category>().OrderBy(c => c.Name).ToList();
```

This expression returns a list of `Category` objects representing all the rows from the `categories` table, ordered by names in the ascending order.

If you want to get a list of entries ordered by their identifiers (descending), you could use the `OrderByDescending` method, as shown as follows:

```
connection.Table<Entry>().OrderByDescending(e => e.Id).ToList();
```

You can also select data according to some additional criteria. For example, you can get data only of entries assigned to the first category:

```
connection.Table<Entry>().Where(e => e.CategoryId == 1).ToList();
```

Of course, you can join the `OrderBy` and `Where` parts in a single query, shown as follows. It will return all the entries added during the last hour, ordered by titles:

```
DateTime minDate = DateTime.Now.AddHours(-1);
connection.Table<Entry>()
    .Where(e => e.AddedAt >= minDate)
    .OrderBy(e => e.Title)
    .ToList();
```

What is more, you can easily get data of a single element, instead of a list of them. For example, let's download a category with an identifier equal to 1, as follows:

```
connection.Get<Category>(1);
```

This is not the only way because you can achieve the same result with this:

```
connection.Table<Category>().SingleOrDefault(c => c.Id == 1);
connection.Table<Category>().FirstOrDefault(c => c.Id == 1);
```

However, what is the difference between the last two statements? The `FirstOrDefault` method will either return the first item from the collection if at least one element is found or `null` if no results are found. The `SingleOrDefault` method will return the item from the collection only if it contains exactly one item. It will return `null` if there are no results, and it will throw an exception if more than one item is found.

See also

- The *Creating a SQLite database and tables* recipe
- The *Storing data in a SQLite database* recipe
- The *Updating data in a SQLite database* recipe
- The *Removing data from a SQLite database* recipe

Updating data in a SQLite database

Apart from inserting data to a table, it is often necessary to update values. Of course, such an operation is also supported in the case of UWP applications using a SQLite database. In this recipe, you will learn how to achieve this goal.

As an example, you will modify the project from the previous recipe by allowing a user to add and edit entries. So, the application will contain almost all the features necessary to become a real offline blog, in which data is stored in the local database.

Getting ready

To step through this recipe, you need the project from the previous recipe.

How to do it...

To modify the preceding example to allow a user to add or edit data of entries, perform the following steps:

1. Modify the code of the `MainViewModel` class, in the `MainViewModel.cs` file, by adding the field with an identifier of the currently edited entry (or 0 if the entry is currently being added, named _entryId). In addition to this, add properties that represent the title and content currently entered in the form (`Title` and `Content`), the currently edited entry (or `null`, named `Entry`), three commands (`CmdSave`, `CmdAdd`, and `CmdEdit`), and the property indicating whether any entry is currently selected (`IsEntrySelected`). The adjusted code is shown as follows:

```
private int _entryId = 0;
public string Title { get; set; }
public string Content { get; set; }
public EntryViewModel Entry { get; set; }
public ICommand CmdSave { get; set; }
public ICommand CmdAdd { get; set; }
public ICommand CmdEdit { get; set; }

[DependsOn("Entries")]
public bool IsEntrySelected
{
    get { return Entry != null; }
}
```

2. Modify the constructor of the `MainViewModel` class, in the `MainViewModel.cs` file, as shown in the following code:

```
public MainViewModel()
{ (...)
    CmdSave = new RelayCommand(() => Save());
    CmdAdd = new RelayCommand(() => LaunchAddMode());
    CmdEdit = new RelayCommand(() => LaunchEditMode());
}
```

3. Add the `LaunchAddMode` private method that switches the current mode of the application to adding a new entry, as follows:

```
private void LaunchAddMode()
{
    _entryId = 0;
    Title = string.Empty;
    Content = string.Empty;
    Category = Categories[0];
}
```

4. Add the `LaunchEditMode` private method, which switches the current mode of the application to editing of the currently selected entry, as follows:

```
private void LaunchEditMode()
{
    _entryId = Entry.Id;
    Title = Entry.Title;
    Content = Entry.Content;
    Category = Entry.Category;
}
```

5. Add the `Save` private method, which updates (or inserts) the entry that is currently being edited (or added), as shown in the following code snippet:

```
private void Save()
{
    using (SQLiteConnection connection = GetConnection())
    {
        Entry entry = null;

        if (_entryId != 0)
        {
            entry = connection.Get<Entry>(_entryId);
            entry.EditedAt = DateTime.Now;
        }
        else
        {
            entry = new Entry();
            entry.AddedAt = DateTime.Now;
        }

        entry.Title = Title;
        entry.Content = Content;
        entry.CategoryId = Category.Id;

        if (_entryId != 0)
        {
            connection.Update(entry);
        }
        else
        {
            connection.Insert(entry);
        }
    }

    LoadEntries();
    LaunchAddMode();
```

}

How it works...

Updating the data stored in a database is very simple. First, you need to get an object that represents a given row from the database. Once you get such an object, modify values of its various properties and call the Update method on the SQLiteConnection instance, passing the modified object as the parameter. As an example, let's take a look at the following code:

```
Entry entry = null;
if (_entryId != 0)
{
    entry = connection.Get<Entry>(_entryId);
    entry.EditedAt = DateTime.Now;
}
else { /* ... */ }

entry.Title = Title;
entry.Content = Content;
entry.CategoryId = Category.Id;

if (_entryId != 0)
{
    connection.Update(entry);
}
else { /* ... */ }
```

First, you get the data of the entry with an identifier equal to _entryId. Then, its last modification date is set to the current date, and its title, content, and category identifier are updated. In the end, the Update method is called and new data are saved.

See also

- The *Creating a SQLite database and tables* recipe
- The *Storing data in a SQLite database* recipe
- The *Selecting data from a SQLite database* recipe
- The *Removing data from a SQLite database* recipe

Removing data from a SQLite database

In the last recipe of the current chapter, you will learn how to remove data from a particular table in the SQLite database.

As an example, you will introduce the last changes in the project from the previous recipe. You will do this by allowing a user to delete the currently selected entry.

Getting ready

To step through this recipe, you need the project from the previous recipe.

How to do it...

To modify the preceding example by introducing the feature of deleting a currently selected entry, perform the following steps:

1. Add the `CmdDelete` property, representing the command, to the `MainViewModel` class in the `MainViewModel.cs` file:

```
public ICommand CmdDelete { get; set; }
```

2. Modify the constructor of the `MainViewModel` class in the `MainViewModel.cs` file as follows:

```
public MainViewModel()
{ (...)
    CmdDelete = new RelayCommand(() => Delete());
}
```

3. Add the `Delete` private method, which removes the currently selected entry, to the `MainViewModel.cs` file as follows:

```
private void Delete()
{
    using (SQLiteConnection connection = GetConnection())
    {
        int entryId = Entry.Id;
        connection.Delete<Entry>(entryId);
    }

    LoadEntries();
```

```
        LaunchAddMode();
    }
```

How it works...

To remove a row with the given primary key you just need to call the `Delete` generic method and follow two steps: indicate the type of object that you want to remove and pass a primary key. As an example, to remove the entry with an identifier equal to the current value of the `entryId` variable, the following line of code can be used:

```
connection.Delete<Entry>(entryId);
```

Of course, it is not the only way of removing a row from the table. You will reach the same result by using the following code:

```
Entry entry = connection.Get<Entry>(_entryId);
connection.Delete(entry);
```

Here, you pass an object, representing a row that should be removed, instead of passing the value of a primary key.

See also

- The *Creating a SQLite database and tables* recipe
- The *Storing data in a SQLite database* recipe
- The *Selecting data from a SQLite database* recipe
- The *Updating data in a SQLite database* recipe

5
Animations and Graphics

In this chapter, we will cover the following recipes:

- Animating the showing of controls
- Using animation to hide controls
- Adding animation to show the collection of items
- Animating the repositioning of items' collection
- Animating the color of an element
- Animating the size of an element
- Animating the position of an element
- Animating the rotation of an element
- Animating the font size of an element
- Drawing shapes programmatically
- Handling the tap touch event
- Handling the pinch touch event
- Handling the rotate touch event
- Handling the pinch and rotate touch events
- Rendering 3D graphics

Introduction

In the previous chapters, you learned how to create UWP applications, add various controls to pages, apply the data binding mechanism, and use data stored in a few ways, such as in a local database. It is the high time that you get to know how to improve the user interface and make it more attractive for a user.

In the beginning, you will see how to animate the showing of a control, such as a text block or a button. With the usage of mechanisms available out of the box, it is really easy to add the effect of *flying* to its target location. What is more, you will see how to add animations to hide a control by changing its opacity in an automatic way.

The showing animation could be even more attractive in the case of controls that present a collection of items. In one of the recipes from this chapter, you will learn how to apply such an effect to each item. You will also see how to add animations while repositioning the items within the collection after you remove an element.

In the following recipes, you will learn how to add basic shapes to the page, such as rectangles, ellipses, polygons, and lines. Of course, such shapes may be added either declaratively in the XAML language or programmatically in the C# language, as you will see in the examples. What is interesting is that various animations, such as color, size, position, or even rotation, could be applied to such controls as well. All of these scenarios are presented and explained in detail.

Apart from animations, you will learn how to handle a few touch events, namely tapping, pinching (zooming), and rotating. You will also learn how to combine the handling of more than one touch event. All such topics are presented in the examples.

Toward the end, the subject of rendering 3D graphics is introduced. You will see how to easily generate a project that uses DirectX, XAML, and C++ language. Various files with code will be briefly described to simplify your first steps into the topic of rendering 3D graphics for applications that could be submitted to the Windows Store.

Animating the showing of controls

By default, controls added to a page are visible just after you open it. However, it is possible to enhance the attractiveness of the user interface by adding simple animations for showing controls while the page is being opened. In this recipe, you will learn how to add the entrance transition to a text block.

Getting ready

To step through this recipe, you need only the automatically generated project.

How to do it...

Apply a transition (`EntranceThemeTransition`) to the text block by modifying the content of the `MainPage.xaml` file, as follows:

```xaml
<Page (...)>
    <Grid>
        <TextBlock Text="Hello! :-)" (...)>
            <TextBlock.Transitions>
                <TransitionCollection>
                    <EntranceThemeTransition />
                </TransitionCollection>
            </TextBlock.Transitions>
        </TextBlock>
    </Grid>
</Page>
```

How it works...

To add an entrance transition for a given control, you just need to specify `EntranceThemeTransition` in a collection of transitions for the control, as follows:

```xaml
<TextBlock.Transitions>
    <TransitionCollection>
        <EntranceThemeTransition />
    </TransitionCollection>
</TextBlock.Transitions>
```

Once you run the application, the control will appear in an animated way, as presented in the following two screenshots:

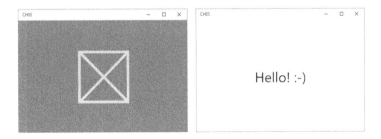

Of course, in the same way, you can use the transition for another type of control, such as `Button`. Then, the XAML code will look like:

```
<Button.Transitions>
    <TransitionCollection>
        <EntranceThemeTransition />
    </TransitionCollection>
</Button.Transitions>
```

There's more...

By default, the entrance animation causes a control to appear from the bottom. However, you can easily choose both horizontal and vertical offsets while defining the transition for a given control. To do so, just set the values of `FromHorizontalOffset` and `FromVerticalOffset`, as presented in the following example:

```
<TextBlock.Transitions>
    <TransitionCollection>
        <EntranceThemeTransition
            FromHorizontalOffset="200"
            FromVerticalOffset="200" />
    </TransitionCollection>
</TextBlock.Transitions>
```

As a result, the text block *flies* from the bottom right corner, as shown in the following screenshots:

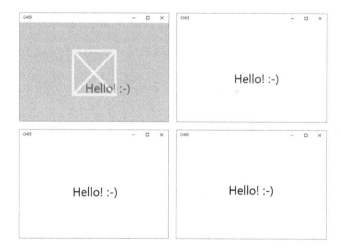

See also

- The *Using animation to hide controls* recipe
- The *Adding animation to show the collection of items* recipe
- The *Animating the repositioning of items' collection* recipe

Using animation to hide controls

Sometimes, it may be necessary to hide some controls on the page, for example, when they are no longer active or important for a user. Of course, you can easily change their visibility, but is it possible to hide a control with an animation? Of course! In this recipe, you will learn how to fade out the text block once you press the button.

Getting ready

To step through this recipe, you need the project from the previous recipe.

How to do it...

To modify the preceding example to fade out the text block after pressing the button, perform the following steps:

1. Define the storyboard with the fade out animation in the page resources and add a button to start the animation. Perform this step by modifying the content of the `MainPage.xaml` file, as shown in the following code snippet:

```
<Page (...)>
    <Page.Resources>
        <Storyboard x:Name="HeaderHide">
            <FadeOutThemeAnimation
                TargetName="TxtHeader"
                Duration="0:0:3" />
        </Storyboard>
    </Page.Resources>
    <StackPanel
        VerticalAlignment="Center"
        HorizontalAlignment="Center">
        <TextBlock
            x:Name="TxtHeader"
```

```
            Text="Hello! :-)"
            FontSize="32">
            <TextBlock.Transitions>
                <TransitionCollection>
                    <EntranceThemeTransition />
                </TransitionCollection>
            </TextBlock.Transitions>
        </TextBlock>
        <Button
            Content="Hide header"
            FontSize="24"
            Margin="0 20 0 0"
            Click="BtnHide_Click" />
    </StackPanel>
</Page>
```

2. Begin the storyboard after you click on the button. Do this by defining the
   BtnHide_Click method in the MainPage class in the MainPage.xaml.cs file as
   follows:

```
private void BtnHide_Click(
    object sender, RoutedEventArgs e)
{
    HeaderHide.Begin();
}
```

How it works...

Adding an animation to hide a control is a bit more difficult than specifying the entrance
transition. In this case, you need to define a storyboard with one animation, namely
FadeOutThemeAnimation. It indicates that, when the storyboard begins, the control will
change its opacity till it is invisible.

The storyboard can be defined as a page resource, as shown in the following code:

```
<Page.Resources>
    <Storyboard x:Name="HeaderHide">
        <FadeOutThemeAnimation
            TargetName="TxtHeader"
            Duration="0:0:3" />
    </Storyboard>
</Page.Resources>
```

Here, you specify the name of the target control (`TxtHeader`) as well as a duration (3 seconds). Once you run the application and click on the **Hide header** button, you will get the result shown in the following screenshots:

There's more...

The same mechanism can be used with other animations, either to hide the element (such as `PopOutThemeAnimation`) or to show it (such as `FadeInThemeAnimation` and `PopInThemeAnimation`). It is recommended to check how other kinds of animations can make your applications even more attractive for users.

See also

- The *Animating the showing of control* recipe
- The *Adding animation to show the collection of items* recipe
- The *Animating the repositioning of items' collection* recipe

Adding animation to show the collection of items

Apart from animating the appearance of controls, such as text blocks or buttons, it is also possible to add some animations to the collection of items. In such a case, each item will be animated, which could create a really interesting effect. In this recipe, you will learn how to add the entrance theme transition for elements within `ItemsControl`.

Getting ready

To step through this recipe, you need only the automatically generated project.

How to do it...

Apply a transition (EntranceThemeTransition) to all the items within ItemsControl by modifying the content of the MainPage.xaml file, as follows:

```
<Page (...)>
    <Grid
        VerticalAlignment="Center"
        HorizontalAlignment="Center">
        <ItemsControl>
            <ItemsControl.ItemContainerTransitions>
                <TransitionCollection>
                    <EntranceThemeTransition
                        IsStaggeringEnabled="True" />
                </TransitionCollection>
            </ItemsControl.ItemContainerTransitions>
            <ItemsControl.Items>
                <TextBlock Text="January 2016" /> (...)
                <TextBlock Text="December 2016" />
            </ItemsControl.Items>
        </ItemsControl>
    </Grid>
</Page>
```

How it works...

To add an animation for each item, you do not need to specify it for each element. You can use the ItemsControl.ItemContainerTransitions property to achieve this goal, as shown in the following code:

```
<ItemsControl.ItemContainerTransitions>
    <TransitionCollection>
        <EntranceThemeTransition IsStaggeringEnabled="True" />
    </TransitionCollection>
</ItemsControl.ItemContainerTransitions>
```

It is important to set the value of `IsStaggeringEnabled` to `True`. Otherwise, you will not see the effect of animating the following items within the control.

After you run the application, you will see the following animation:

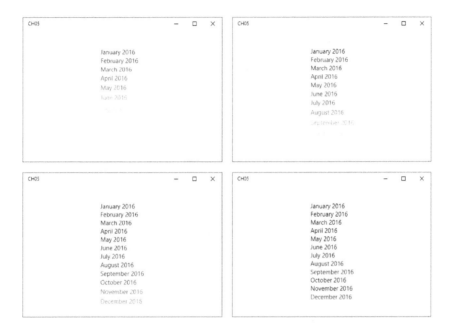

See also

- The *Animating the showing of control* recipe
- The *Using animation to hide controls* recipe
- The *Animating the repositioning of items' collection* recipe

Animating the repositioning of items' collection

Once you remove an item from the collection, it just disappears. However, it is possible to reposition the remaining elements with the animation, as shown in this recipe.

Getting ready

To step through this recipe, you need the project from the previous recipe.

How to do it...

To modify the preceding example to use animation while repositioning elements within ItemsControl when any are removed, perform the following steps:

1. Add a name to ItemsControl and apply RepositionThemeTransition to enable the effect of repositioning items after you remove any of them. Do this by modifying the content of the MainPage.xaml file, as follows:

```
<Page (...)>
    <Grid (...)>
        <ItemsControl x:Name="Months">
            <ItemsControl.ItemContainerTransitions>
                <TransitionCollection>
                    <EntranceThemeTransition
                        IsStaggeringEnabled="True" />
                    <RepositionThemeTransition />
                </TransitionCollection>
            </ItemsControl.ItemContainerTransitions>
            <ItemsControl.Items>
                <TextBlock Text="January 2016" /> (...)
                <TextBlock Text="December 2016" />
            </ItemsControl.Items>
        </ItemsControl>
    </Grid>
</Page>
```

2. Prepare the exemplary scenario of removing an item from the collection every 2 seconds. To do so, modify the code of the MainPage class in the MainPage.xaml.cs file, shown as follows:

```
public sealed partial class MainPage : Page
{
    private DispatcherTimer _timer = null;

    public MainPage()
    {
        InitializeComponent();
        _timer = new DispatcherTimer();
        _timer.Interval = TimeSpan.FromSeconds(2);
        _timer.Tick += Timer_Tick;
```

```
            _timer.Start();
        }

        private void Timer_Tick(object sender, object e)
        {
            if (Months.Items.Count > 0)
            {
                Random random = new Random();
                Months.Items.RemoveAt(random.Next(
                    Months.Items.Count));
            }
        }
    }
}
```

How it works...

Adding the repositioning animation is really simple. To do so, you just need to add another transition (RepositionThemeTransition) to the collection of transitions, as shown in the following code:

```
<ItemsControl.ItemContainerTransitions>
    <TransitionCollection>
        <EntranceThemeTransition IsStaggeringEnabled="True" />
        <RepositionThemeTransition />
    </TransitionCollection>
</ItemsControl.ItemContainerTransitions>
```

That's all! The remaining modifications described in the *How to do it...* section presents the scenario of removing the items to show the solution in action.

However, a small explanation is necessary in the case of the timer. It is represented by the DispatcherTimer class and is configured in the constructor of the MainPage class. The Tick event is fired every 2 seconds (the Interval property) and the Timer_Tick method is called. The timer is started by calling the Start method. Within the Timer_Tick method, you just remove a random item. Of course, no items are removed if the total number of elements is equal to zero.

See also

- The *Animating the showing of control* recipe
- The *Using animation to hide controls* recipe
- The *Adding animation to show the collection of items* recipe

Animating the color of an element

Apart from the already described animations, it is also possible to animate the values of various properties of controls. In this recipe, you will learn how to animate colors.

As an example, you will create a simple page with basic shapes that will form a visualization of three lights–red, yellow, and green–arranged horizontally one next to another. After you click on the drawing, the animation should start and these lights should be switched on (one per second): red, yellow, and green. Of course, the color should be changed from black with the help of animation.

Getting ready

To step through this recipe, you need only the automatically generated project.

How to do it...

To prepare the example that animates the color of ellipses, perform the following steps:

1. Define a storyboard for animating colors of three ellipses, representing lights, by modifying the code of the `MainPage.xaml` file, as follows:

```
<Page (...)>
    <Page.Resources>
        <Storyboard x:Name="LightsStart">
            <ColorAnimation
                Storyboard.TargetName="LightRed"
                Storyboard.TargetProperty=
                    "(Rectangle.Fill).(SolidColorBrush.Color)"
                To="Red"
                Duration="0:0:1" />
            <ColorAnimation
                Storyboard.TargetName="LightYellow"
                Storyboard.TargetProperty=
                    "(Rectangle.Fill).(SolidColorBrush.Color)"
                To="Yellow"
                Duration="0:0:1"
                BeginTime="0:0:1" />
            <ColorAnimation
                Storyboard.TargetName="LightGreen"
                Storyboard.TargetProperty=
                    "(Rectangle.Fill).(SolidColorBrush.Color)"
                To="Green"
```

```
              Duration="0:0:1"
              BeginTime="0:0:2" />
        </Storyboard>
    </Page.Resources> (...)
</Page>
```

2. Add a canvas with a rectangle, three ellipses, and four lines by modifying the content of the `MainPage.xaml` file, as shown in the following code:

```
<Page (...)>
    <Page.Resources> (...) </Page.Resources>
    <Grid Tapped="Grid_Tapped">
        <Canvas>
            <Rectangle
                Canvas.Left="80" Canvas.Top="80"
                Width="360" Height="140"
                Fill="#353535" />
            <Ellipse
                x:Name="LightRed"
                Canvas.Left="100" Canvas.Top="100"
                Width="100" Height="100"
                Fill="Black" />
            <Ellipse
                x:Name="LightYellow"
                Canvas.Left="210" Canvas.Top="100"
                Width="100" Height="100"
                Fill="Black" />
            <Ellipse
                x:Name="LightGreen"
                Canvas.Left="320" Canvas.Top="100"
                Width="100" Height="100"
                Fill="Black" />
            <Line
                Stroke="Black" StrokeThickness="10"
                X1="80" X2="80" Y1="75" Y2="225" />
            <Line
                Stroke="Black" StrokeThickness="10"
                X1="440" X2="440" Y1="75" Y2="225" />
            <Line
                Stroke="Black" StrokeThickness="10"
                X1="80" X2="440" Y1="80" Y2="80" />
            <Line
                Stroke="Black" StrokeThickness="10"
                X1="80" X2="440" Y1="220" Y2="220" />
        </Canvas>
    </Grid>
</Page>
```

3. Begin the storyboard after you click on the button. Do this by defining the Grid_Tapped method in the MainPage class in the MainPage.xaml.cs file, as presented in the following code snippet:

```
private void Grid_Tapped(object sender,
    TappedRoutedEventArgs e)
{
    LightsStart.Begin();
}
```

How it works...

To begin with, let's take a look at the definition of a storyboard. It contains three animations (ColorAnimation) related to changing colors. The last one is as follows:

```
<ColorAnimation
    Storyboard.TargetName="LightGreen"
    Storyboard.TargetProperty=
        "(Rectangle.Fill).(SolidColorBrush.Color)"
    To="Green"
    Duration="0:0:1"
    BeginTime="0:0:2" />
```

The values for the following properties are specified:

- Storyboard.TargetName: The name of the control that should be animated.
- Storyboard.TargetProperty: The name of the property whose value should be animated. In the case of filling color in a rectangle, you need to adjust the value of the Color property of the Fill property of Rectangle. For this reason, here you can find an expression with two parts separated by a dot. The first is (Rectangle.Fill) and indicates the Fill property of Rectangle. The other is (SolidColorBrush.Color) and indicates the Color property of SolidColorBrush, which is a type used for Rectangle.Fill.
- To: The target value to which the animation is performed (Red, Yellow, or Green, depending on the animation).
- Duration: The length of the animation (1 second).
- BeginTime: A delay in starting the animation (zero, 1, or 2 seconds).

Another comment is necessary for the addition of basic shapes, namely a rectangle, an ellipse, and a line. The first one is represented by the Rectangle control, as follows:

```
<Rectangle
```

```
            Canvas.Left="80" Canvas.Top="80"
            Width="360" Height="140"
            Fill="#353535" />
```

Here, you specify a rectangle filled with dark gray color (#353535, `Fill`) with the size equal to 360 x 140 pixels (`Width` and `Height`). You also specify that it is located in the position (80, 80) within the canvas (`Canvas.Left` and `Canvas.Top`).

The second basic shape is an ellipse, represented by the `Ellipse` control:

```
<Ellipse
        x:Name="LightRed"
        Canvas.Left="100" Canvas.Top="100"
        Width="100" Height="100"
        Fill="Black" />
```

The size of the black ellipse (`Fill`) is 100 x 100 pixels (`Width` and `Height`). It is located in the position (100, 100) within the canvas (`Canvas.Left` and `Canvas.Top`). Its name is set to `LightRed` (`x:Name`).

The last shape, shown in this recipe, is a line, represented by the `Line` control:

```
<Line
        Stroke="Black"
        StrokeThickness="10"
        X1="80" X2="80"
        Y1="75" Y2="225" />
```

The black line (`Stroke`), with width set to 10 pixels (`StrokeThickness`), starts at the point (80, 75) (`X1` and `Y1`) and ends at (80, 225) (`X2` and `Y2`) within the canvas.

Once you run the application and tap on the drawing, you will get the following result:

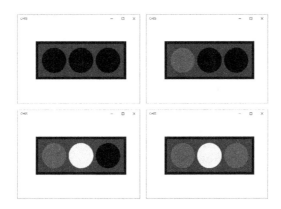

See also

- The *Animating the size of an element* recipe
- The *Animating the position of an element* recipe
- The *Animating the rotation of an element* recipe
- The *Animating the font size of an element* recipe
- The *Drawing shapes programmatically* recipe

Animating the size of an element

As in the case of color, you can also easily animate the size of an element. In this recipe, you will learn how to animate the width and height of a rectangle and how to automatically reverse the animation when it is completed.

Getting ready

To step through this recipe, you need only the automatically generated project.

How to do it...

To prepare the example that animates the size of a rectangle, perform the following steps:

1. Add a rectangle to the page and define a storyboard to resize the rectangle. Do this by modifying the content of the `MainPage.xaml` file, as follows:

```
<Page (...)>
    <Page.Resources>
        <Storyboard x:Name="RectangleResize">
            <DoubleAnimation
                Storyboard.TargetName="RectangleMain"
                Storyboard.TargetProperty="Width"
                To="200"
                Duration="0:0:1"
                AutoReverse="True"
                EnableDependentAnimation="True" />
            <DoubleAnimation
                Storyboard.TargetName="RectangleMain"
                Storyboard.TargetProperty="Height"
                To="100"
```

```
                    Duration="0:0:1"
                    AutoReverse="True"
                    EnableDependentAnimation="True" />
            </Storyboard>
        </Page.Resources>
        <Grid>
            <Canvas>
                <Rectangle
                    x:Name="RectangleMain"
                    Canvas.Left="100" Canvas.Top="100"
                    Width="100" Height="50"
                    Fill="RoyalBlue"
                    Tapped="Rectangle_Tapped" />
            </Canvas>
        </Grid>
    </Page>
```

2. Begin the storyboard once a user taps on the rectangle. Do this by defining the
   `Rectangle_Tapped` method in the `MainPage` class in the `MainPage.xaml.cs`
   file, as shown in the following code:

```
private void Rectangle_Tapped(object sender,
    TappedRoutedEventArgs e)
{
    RectangleResize.Begin();
}
```

How it works...

Adding an animation for the size of an element requires you to define a storyboard. Each
dimension can be modified using `DoubleAnimation`. In the example, two animations are
defined. The first animates width, while the other animates height. The latter is presented in
the following code snippet:

```
<DoubleAnimation
    Storyboard.TargetName="RectangleMain"
    Storyboard.TargetProperty="Height"
    To="100"
    Duration="0:0:1"
    AutoReverse="True"
    EnableDependentAnimation="True" />
```

Some additional clarification is necessary for the `AutoReverse` property. When it is set to `True` (as in the example), the animation is played from the beginning to the end and then automatically from the end to the beginning. Otherwise, the animation is played only from the beginning to the end.

Another property, which should be explained, is `EnableDependentAnimation`. It is related to the subject of **dependent animations**, that is, animations whose improper use could have a negative impact on UI performance. One of the examples is the resizing of elements, which may require recalculating the positions and sizes of many additional controls placed on the page. For this reason, such dependent animations cannot be played without an explicit request from a developer, and this is done by setting the value of the `EnableDependentAnimation` property to `True`.

After you run the application and click on the rectangle, the animation will start and you will get a result similar to the following:

See also

- The *Animating the color of an element* recipe
- The *Animating the position of an element* recipe
- The *Animating the rotation of an element* recipe
- The *Animating the font size of an element* recipe
- The *Drawing shapes programmatically* recipe

Animating the position of an element

You have already learned how to animate the color and size of an element, but what about its position? Could you create some animations regarding the location of an element? Of course! In this recipe, you will get to know how to do it.

Getting ready

To step through this recipe, you need only the automatically generated project.

How to do it...

To prepare the example that animates the square position, perform the following steps:

1. Add a square to the page and define a storyboard for moving the square. Do this by modifying the content of the `MainPage.xaml` file, as follows:

```
<Page (...)>
    <Page.Resources>
        <Storyboard x:Name="RectangleMove">
            <DoubleAnimation
                Storyboard.TargetName="RectangleMain"
                Storyboard.TargetProperty="(Canvas.Left)"
                To="350"
                Duration="0:0:1" />
            <DoubleAnimation
                Storyboard.TargetName="RectangleMain"
                Storyboard.TargetProperty="(Canvas.Top)"
                To="175"
                Duration="0:0:1" />
        </Storyboard>
    </Page.Resources>
    <Grid>
        <Canvas>
            <Rectangle
                x:Name="RectangleMain"
                Canvas.Left="50" Canvas.Top="50"
                Width="100" Height="100"
                Fill="RoyalBlue"
                Tapped="Rectangle_Tapped" />
        </Canvas>
    </Grid>
</Page>
```

2. Begin the storyboard after a user taps on the rectangle. Do this by defining the `Rectangle_Tapped` method in the `MainPage` class in the `MainPage.xaml.cs` file, as follows:

```
private void Rectangle_Tapped(object sender,
    TappedRoutedEventArgs e)
{
    RectangleMove.Begin();
}
```

How it works...

Animating the position of an element is very similar to animating its size. However, in this case, you need to adjust the values of the `Canvas.Left` and `Canvas.Top` attached properties, instead of `Width` and `Height`, as shown in the previous recipe. For this reason, a bit different syntax of the value of `Storyboard.TargetProperty` is necessary, as shown in the following code:

```
<DoubleAnimation
    Storyboard.TargetName="RectangleMain"
    Storyboard.TargetProperty="(Canvas.Left)"
    To="350"
    Duration="0:0:1" />
```

The following part of code does not require any additional explanation. After you run the application and click on the rectangle, the animation will start and you will get the result similar to the following:

See also

- The *Animating the color of an element* recipe
- The *Animating the size of an element* recipe
- The *Animating the rotation of an element* recipe
- The *Animating the font size of an element* recipe
- The *Drawing shapes programmatically* recipe

Animating the rotation of an element

While performing complex calculations or downloading data from the Internet, it is beneficial to present suitable information to the user. Of course, you can use the progress bar or just a text block, but it may be significantly more attractive to use the rotating image. In this recipe, you will learn how to create animation from two files: a background with a circle and a point rotating around the circle. What is more, you will see how to programmatically stop and restart the animation.

Getting ready

To step through this recipe, you need only the automatically generated project.

How to do it...

To prepare the example that animates rotation of an image, to create the effect of the rotating progress bar, perform the following steps:

1. Add the `ProgressBackground.png` and `ProgressForeground.png` files to the `Assets` directory. Here is an example of such files (background on the left and foreground on the right):

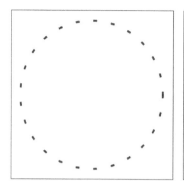 

2. Add such images to the page and define a storyboard for rotating the second image. Do this by modifying the content of the `MainPage.xaml` file, as shown in the following code snippet:

```
<Page (...)>
    <Page.Resources>
        <Storyboard x:Name="ImageRotate">
            <DoubleAnimation
                Storyboard.TargetName="Rotation"
                Storyboard.TargetProperty="Angle"
                From="0" To="360"
                Duration="0:0:2"
                RepeatBehavior="Forever" />
        </Storyboard>
    </Page.Resources>
    <Grid>
        <Image
            Source="/Assets/ProgressBackground.png"
            VerticalAlignment="Center"
            HorizontalAlignment="Center"
            Width="300" />
        <Image
            Source="/Assets/ProgressForeground.png"
            VerticalAlignment="Center"
            HorizontalAlignment="Center"
            Width="300"
            Tapped="Image_Tapped">
            <Image.RenderTransform>
                <RotateTransform
                    x:Name="Rotation"
                    CenterX="150"
                    CenterY="150" />
            </Image.RenderTransform>
        </Image>
```

```
        </Grid>
    </Page>
```

3. Begin or stop the storyboard after you tap on the image (depending on its current state). Do this by adjusting the body of the `Image_Tapped` method and defining the `_isRunning` field in the `MainPage` class in the `MainPage.xaml.cs` file, as follows:

```
private bool _isRunning = false; (...)

private void Image_Tapped(object sender,
    TappedRoutedEventArgs e)
{
    if (_isRunning)
    {
        ImageRotate.Stop();
    }
    else
    {
        ImageRotate.Begin();
    }
    _isRunning = !_isRunning;
}
```

How it works...

The example of the rotating point around a circle uses a set of information that you have already learned while reading this book. However, to make it clearer, this example is described in detail.

Let's start with the arrangement of the user interface. The animation requires that the `ProgressBackground.png` file is placed below the `ProgressForeground.png` file, but exactly in the same location and with the same size. To do so, you can use the `Grid` control with two `Image` elements inside. Each of them has the same width and height as well as vertical and horizontal alignments. Some more explanation is necessary in the case of the second `Image` control, for which the code is shown as follows:

```
<Grid>
    <Image (...) />
    <Image
        Source="/Assets/ProgressForeground.png"
        VerticalAlignment="Center"
        HorizontalAlignment="Center"
        Width="300"
```

```
            Tapped="Image_Tapped">
        <Image.RenderTransform>
            <RotateTransform
                x:Name="Rotation"
                CenterX="150"
                CenterY="150" />
        </Image.RenderTransform>
    </Image>
</Grid>
```

Here, you specify the render transformation with the given center point (150, 150) and name it as Rotation. Now, you just need to animate the Angle property of Rotation, so the following part of the task seems to be quite easy, doesn't it? Let's take a look at the following code with the definition of the storyboard:

```
<Storyboard x:Name="ImageRotate">
    <DoubleAnimation
        Storyboard.TargetName="Rotation"
        Storyboard.TargetProperty="Angle"
        From="0" To="360"
        Duration="0:0:2"
        RepeatBehavior="Forever" />
</Storyboard>
```

As already mentioned, you animate the double value (DoubleAnimation) in regard to an angle (Angle) of the rotation transformation (Rotate) from 0 (From) to 360 (To) degrees. However, in such a configuration, the point will rotate only once around the circle. If you want it to continue rotating when it reaches 360 degrees, you can set the value of RepeatBehavior to Forever. That's all!

In the previous recipes, it was only required to start an animation. To do so, you just needed to call the Begin method on the storyboard object. Of course, you can also manage the state of an animation. For instance, to stop the animation, you can use the Stop method. The stopped animation can be restarted with the Begin method, as shown in the following code:

```
if (_isRunning)
{
    ImageRotate.Stop();
}
else
{
    ImageRotate.Begin();
}
_isRunning = !_isRunning;
```

After you run the application and tap on the image, the animation will start and you will see a result similar to the following:

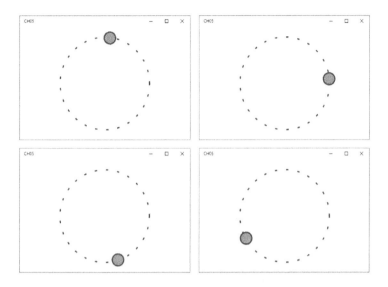

See also

- The *Animating the color of an element* recipe
- The *Animating the size of an element* recipe
- The *Animating the position of an element* recipe
- The *Animating the font size of an element* recipe
- The *Drawing shapes programmatically* recipe

Animating the font size of an element

It is possible to animate the values of various properties, and it is not limited to basic shapes, such as rectangles or ellipses. In this recipe, you will learn how to animate the font size for a text block. Such a solution may be useful to visually inform the user about some important message presented in the user interface.

Getting ready

To step through this recipe, you need only the automatically generated project.

How to do it...

To prepare the example that animates the font size, perform the following steps:

1. Add a text block to the page and define a storyboard for changing its font size. Do this by modifying the content of the `MainPage.xaml` file, as shown in the following code:

```
<Page (...)>
    <Page.Resources>
        <Storyboard x:Name="HeaderChangeSize">
            <DoubleAnimation
                Storyboard.TargetName="TxtHeader"
                Storyboard.TargetProperty="FontSize"
                EnableDependentAnimation="True"
                Duration="0:0:1"
                To="48" />
        </Storyboard>
    </Page.Resources>
    <StackPanel
        VerticalAlignment="Center"
        HorizontalAlignment="Center">
        <TextBlock
            x:Name="TxtHeader"
            Text="Hello! :-)"
            FontSize="32" />
        <Button
            Content="Start animation"
            FontSize="24"
            Margin="0 20 0 0"
            Click="BtnStart_Click" />
    </StackPanel>
</Page>
```

2. Begin the storyboard after you click on the button. Do so by defining the `BtnStart_Click` method in the `MainPage` class in the `MainPage.xaml.cs` file, as follows:

```
private void BtnStart_Click(
    object sender, RoutedEventArgs e)
{
```

```
HeaderChangeSize.Begin();
}
```

How it works...

Animating the font size of a text block is very similar to the scenarios presented in the previous examples. Here, you just need to indicate that the `FontSize` property of the `TxtHeader` element should be animated. Of course, you should not forget to enable dependent animations.

After you run the application and press the button, the animation will start and you will see a result similar to the following:

See also

- The *Animating the color of an element* recipe
- The *Animating the size of an element* recipe
- The *Animating the position of an element* recipe
- The *Animating the rotation of an element* recipe
- The *Animating the font size of an element* recipe
- The *Drawing shapes programmatically* recipe

Drawing shapes programmatically

As you have already seen in this chapter, basic shapes, such as rectangles, ellipses, or lines, can be defined declaratively in the XAML language. However, they can also be created programmatically using the C# language, as you will see in this recipe.

As an example, you will create a simple page with the `Canvas` control, where a rectangle, an ellipse, a polygon, a polyline, and a set of lines will be drawn.

Getting ready

To step through this recipe, you need only the automatically generated project.

How to do it...

To prepare the example that draws a rectangle, an ellipse, a polygon, a polyline, and a set of lines programmatically, perform the following steps:

1. Add a canvas to the page by modifying the `MainPage.xaml` file, as follows:

```
<Page (...)>
    <Grid>
        <Canvas x:Name="Canvas" />
    </Grid>
</Page>
```

2. Prepare a method to draw a green rectangle (of size 100 x 100 pixels with rounded corners) with a dark green border and locate it in the position (50, 50). To do so, define the `DrawRectangle` method in the `MainPage` class in the `MainPage.xaml.cs` file, as shown in the following code snippet:

```
private void DrawRectangle()
{
    Rectangle rectangle = new Rectangle();
    rectangle.Fill = new SolidColorBrush(Colors.GreenYellow);
    rectangle.Width = 100;
    rectangle.Height = 100;
    rectangle.RadiusX = 25;
    rectangle.RadiusY = 25;
    rectangle.SetValue(Canvas.LeftProperty, 50);
    rectangle.SetValue(Canvas.TopProperty, 50);
    rectangle.Stroke = new SolidColorBrush(Colors.DarkGreen);
```

```
        rectangle.StrokeThickness = 5;
        Canvas.Children.Add(rectangle);
}
```

3. Prepare a method to draw a blue ellipse with a dark blue border and locate it in the position (200, 50). Also, its size should be 100 x 100 pixels. To do so, define the `DrawEllipse` method in the `MainPage` class in the `MainPage.xaml.cs` file, as shown in the following code:

```
private void DrawEllipse()
{
    Ellipse ellipse = new Ellipse();
    ellipse.Fill = new SolidColorBrush(Colors.RoyalBlue);
    ellipse.Width = 100;
    ellipse.Height = 100;
    ellipse.SetValue(Canvas.LeftProperty, 200);
    ellipse.SetValue(Canvas.TopProperty, 50);
    ellipse.Stroke = new SolidColorBrush(Colors.DarkBlue);
    ellipse.StrokeThickness = 5;
    Canvas.Children.Add(ellipse);
}
```

4. Prepare a method to draw a polygon representing a red triangle with a dark red border and locate it in the position (350, 50). Its size should be 100 x 100 pixels. To do so, define the `DrawPolygon` method in the `MainPage` class in the `MainPage.xaml.cs` file, as shown in the following part of the code:

```
private void DrawPolygon()
{
    Polygon polygon = new Polygon();
    polygon.Fill = new SolidColorBrush(Colors.IndianRed);
    polygon.Points = new PointCollection()
    {
        new Point(0, 100),
        new Point(100, 100),
        new Point(50, 0)
    };
    polygon.SetValue(Canvas.LeftProperty, 350);
    polygon.SetValue(Canvas.TopProperty, 50);
    polygon.Stroke = new SolidColorBrush(Colors.DarkRed);
    polygon.StrokeThickness = 5;
    Canvas.Children.Add(polygon);
}
```

5. Prepare a method to draw a polyline representing the ^ char in the magenta color with a dark magenta border and locate it in the position (50, 200). Its size should be 100 x 100 pixels. To do so, define the `DrawPolyline` method in the `MainPage` class in the `MainPage.xaml.cs` file, as follows:

```
private void DrawPolyline()
{
    Polyline polyline = new Polyline();
    polyline.Points = new PointCollection()
    {
        new Point(0, 100),
        new Point(50, 0),
        new Point(100, 100)
    };
    polyline.SetValue(Canvas.LeftProperty, 50);
    polyline.SetValue(Canvas.TopProperty, 200);
    polyline.Stroke = new SolidColorBrush(Colors.DarkMagenta);
    polyline.StrokeThickness = 5;
    Canvas.Children.Add(polyline);
}
```

6. Prepare a method to draw a few orange lines and locate them in the position (200, 200). To do so, define the `DrawLines` method in the `MainPage` class in the `MainPage.xaml.cs` file, as follows:

```
private void DrawLines()
{
    for (int x = 0; x < 300; x += 50)
    {
        Line line = new Line();
        line.X1 = x;
        line.X2 = x + 25;
        line.Y1 = 50;
        line.Y2 = 50;
        line.SetValue(Canvas.LeftProperty, 200);
        line.SetValue(Canvas.TopProperty, 200);
        line.Stroke = new SolidColorBrush(Colors.Orange);
        line.StrokeThickness = 5;
        Canvas.Children.Add(line);
    }
}
```

7. Draw a rectangle, an ellipse, a polygon, a polyline, and a set of lines, using the already defined methods, by modifying the constructor of the `MainPage` class in the `MainPage.xaml.cs` file, as shown in the following code:

```
public MainPage()
{
    InitializeComponent();
    DrawRectangle();
    DrawEllipse();
    DrawPolygon();
    DrawPolyline();
    DrawLines();
}
```

How it works...

You can programmatically draw a basic shape on the canvas by creating an instance of the class representing the given shape (such as `Rectangle` or `Ellipse`). Once this is done, you can add it to the collection of children elements of the canvas, as follows:

Canvas.Children.Add(**shape**);

Some additional explanation may be useful for adjusting the design of particular shapes. Let's start with a rectangle, represented by the `Rectangle` class. It contains a set of properties for various parameters that have impact on the design, including:

- `Width` and `Height`: The dimensions of the rectangle
- `Fill`: A brush (such as `SolidColorBrush`) that is used to fill the rectangle
- `RadiusX` and `RadiusY`: The radius of the rounded corners, if necessary
- `Stroke`: A brush (such as `SolidColorBrush`) that is used to draw a border
- `StrokeThickness`: The width of the border

A different approach is used to set the location of the rectangle in the `Canvas` control. It is achieved by setting the values of the attached properties, namely `Canvas.Left` and `Canvas.Top`. You can do so by calling the `SetValue` method on the `Rectangle` instance and passing the following two parameters:

- A property that should be modified (such as `Canvas.LeftProperty`)
- A value that should be set (such as 50)

In the case of the part of code related to drawing an ellipse, no additional explanation is necessary. So let's proceed to the `DrawPolygon` and `DrawPolyline` methods. Here, you need to set the coordinates of the points that form a polygon or a polyline, as shown in the following code:

```
new PointCollection()
```

```
        {
            new Point(0, 100),
            new Point(100, 100),
            new Point(50, 0)
        };
```

To do so, you just define a collection of `Point` instances. You can specify the coordinates by passing them as parameters of the constructor–*x* and *y* coordinates, respectively.

The last basic shape, presented in this recipe, is a line. It is represented by the `Line` class, which contains a set of properties, including `X1`, `X2`, `Y1`, and `Y2`. They specify the location of two points, namely (`X1`, `Y1`) and (`X2`, `Y2`), between which the line will be drawn. What is important is that such properties represent the coordinates relative to the top-left corner of the `Line` control within the canvas.

The part of code for defining a line that should be drawn from the point (225, 250) to (300, 350) in the canvas coordinates, that is, from (25, 50) to (100, 150) in the relative coordinates, is shown as follows:

```
Line line = new Line();
line.X1 = 25;
line.Y1 = 50;
line.X2 = 100;
line.Y2 = 150;
line.SetValue(Canvas.LeftProperty, 200);
line.SetValue(Canvas.TopProperty, 200);
```

Once you run the application, you will see the following result:

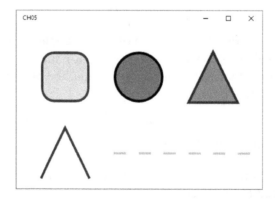

Handling the tap touch event

In the previous recipes, you learned how to handle the event of tapping a control placed on a page. However, in this recipe, you will learn how to get an exact location where the user tapped the canvas, taking into account the multi-touch feature.

As an example, you will create a page with the `Canvas` control. After tapping it, an ellipse should be drawn in such a place. Of course, in the case of multi-touch, more than one shape will be added at the same time.

Getting ready

To step through this recipe, you need only the automatically generated project.

How to do it...

To prepare the example that handles the *tap* touch event and adds an ellipse in each pressed location, perform the following steps:

1. Add a canvas (where the ellipses will be drawn) to the page by modifying the content of the `MainPage.xaml` file, as follows:

```
<Page (...)>
    <Grid>
        <Canvas
            x:Name="Canvas"
            Background="White"
            PointerPressed="Canvas_PointerPressed" />
    </Grid>
</Page>
```

2. Add an ellipse in the exact location pressed by a user and support both *single* and *multi* touch scenarios by modifying the body of the `Canvas_PointerPressed` method, as shown in the following code snippet:

```
private void Canvas_PointerPressed(object sender,
    PointerRoutedEventArgs e)
{
    PointerPoint pressedPoint = e.GetCurrentPoint(Canvas);
    Ellipse ellipse = new Ellipse();
    ellipse.Fill = new SolidColorBrush(Colors.RoyalBlue);
    ellipse.Width = 50;
```

```
ellipse.Height = 50;
ellipse.SetValue(Canvas.LeftProperty,
    pressedPoint.Position.X - 25);
ellipse.SetValue(Canvas.TopProperty,
    pressedPoint.Position.Y - 25);
Canvas.Children.Add(ellipse);
}
```

How it works...

Handling tapping a canvas is possible using the `PointerPressed` event. You should define a method (such as `Canvas_PointerPressed`), which is called when this event is fired. The method takes two parameters, namely `sender` and `e`. The latter one is an instance of the `PointerRoutedEventArgs` class. It has the `GetCurrentPoint` method that returns the coordinates of the pressed point, relative to the given element–the canvas in the current example. The result is an instance of `PointerPoint`, which contains a set of useful properties, including `Position`. It allows you to easily get x and y coordinates of the pressed point.

In the current example, you use such values to specify the location of an ellipse on the canvas. Of course, you need to subtract a half of the ellipse's width (25 pixels) to place the shape in the way, in which a center of the ellipse is exactly in the same position as the pressed point.

After you run the application in the simulator, you can check how it works. You can get a result similar to the following:

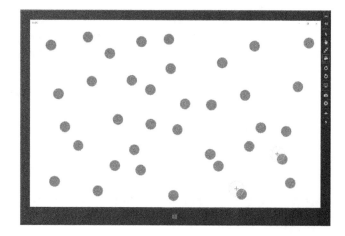

See also

- The *Handling the pinch touch event* recipe
- The *Handling the rotate touch event* recipe
- The *Handling the pinch and rotate touch events* recipe

Handling the pinch touch event

Another interesting touch event is *pinch*, also referred to as *zoom*. While using it, the content could become smaller or bigger. In this recipe, you will learn how to handle this event in the case of an image presented on the page.

Getting ready

To step through this recipe, you need only the automatically generated project.

How to do it...

To prepare the example that handles the *pinch* touch event to scale the image presented on the page, perform the following steps:

1. Add the `Photo.jpg` file to the `Assets` directory.
2. Add an image to the page, support the necessary manipulation modes, and define a scaling transform. Do this by modifying the content of the `MainPage.xaml` file, as follows:

```
<Page (...)>
    <Grid>
        <Image
            Source="/Assets/Photo.jpg"
            ImageOpened="Image_ImageOpened"
            ManipulationMode="Scale,ScaleInertia"
            ManipulationDelta="Image_ManipulationDelta"
            Stretch="UniformToFill">
            <Image.RenderTransform>
                <ScaleTransform
                    x:Name="ImageScaleTransform" />
            </Image.RenderTransform>
        </Image>
```

```
        </Grid>
    </Page>
```

3. Calculate the x and y coordinates of the center point of the image and set them as the values of `CenterX` and `CenterY` properties of the scale transform. Do this by adjusting the code of the `Image_ImageOpened` method, as follows:

```
private void Image_ImageOpened(object sender,
    RoutedEventArgs e)
{
    Image image = (Image)sender;
    ImageScaleTransform.CenterX = image.ActualWidth / 2;
    ImageScaleTransform.CenterY = image.ActualHeight / 2;
}
```

4. Scale the image when the manipulation is discovered. Do this by modifying the body of the `Image_ManipulationDelta` method, as follows:

```
private void Image_ManipulationDelta(object sender,
    ManipulationDeltaRoutedEventArgs e)
{
    ImageScaleTransform.ScaleX /= e.Delta.Scale;
    ImageScaleTransform.ScaleY /= e.Delta.Scale;
}
```

How it works...

To begin with, let's take a look at the `Image` control placed on the page. Here, the manipulation mode is set to handle scaling (`Scale` and `ScaleInertia`), and two events are handled. They are fired after the image is opened (`ImageOpened`) and manipulation is discovered (`ManipulationDelta`). What is more, the scale transformation is defined and named `ImageScaleTransform`. You will later adjust this transformation programmatically after getting information about the manipulation made by the user.

The configuration of the `Image` control is shown in the following code:

```
<Image
    Source="/Assets/Photo.jpg"
    ImageOpened="Image_ImageOpened"
    ManipulationMode="Scale,ScaleInertia"
    ManipulationDelta="Image_ManipulationDelta"
    Stretch="UniformToFill">
    <Image.RenderTransform>
        <ScaleTransform x:Name="ImageScaleTransform" />
```

```
        </Image.RenderTransform>
    </Image>
```

You need to handle the event fired when the image is loaded to calculate the center point of the image. Of course, you need to take into account the actual width and height of the image from the user interface. You can easily do this in the `Image_ImageOpened` method using the `ActualWidth` and `ActualHeight` properties, as follows:

```
Image image = (Image)sender;
ImageScaleTransform.CenterX = image.ActualWidth / 2;
ImageScaleTransform.CenterY = image.ActualHeight / 2;
```

One of the most important parts of the code is related to discovering any suitable manipulations performed by the user. In such a case, you need to get a value indicating how much the image should be made bigger or smaller (`e.Delta.Scale`). Then, you just need to divide the current scale (`ScaleX` and `ScaleY` on `ImageScaleTransform`) by such a value. Of course, an operation of this nature should be performed for both *x* and *y* axes, as presented in the following code:

```
ImageScaleTransform.ScaleX /= e.Delta.Scale;
ImageScaleTransform.ScaleY /= e.Delta.Scale;
```

After you run the application in the simulator, you can launch **Pinch/zoom touch mode** (in the menu on the right) and check how it works. You can get a result similar to this:

See also

- The *Handling the tap touch event* recipe
- The *Handling the rotate touch event* recipe
- The *Handling the pinch and rotate touch events* recipe

Handling the rotate touch event

The last touch event, analyzed in this chapter, is rotation. It is very useful, for example, to rotate the image, as you will see in this recipe.

Getting ready

To step through this recipe, you need only the automatically generated project.

How to do it...

To prepare the example that handles the *rotate* touch event to rotate the image presented on the page, perform the following steps:

1. Add the `Photo.jpg` file to the `Assets` directory.

2. Add an image to the page, support the necessary manipulation modes, and define a rotation transform. Do this by modifying the content of the `MainPage.xaml` file, as follows:

```
<Page (...)>
    <Grid>
        <Image
            Source="/Assets/Photo.jpg"
            ImageOpened="Image_ImageOpened"
            ManipulationMode="Rotate,RotateInertia"
            ManipulationDelta="Image_ManipulationDelta"
            Stretch="UniformToFill">
            <Image.RenderTransform>
                <RotateTransform
                    x:Name="ImageRotateTransform" />
            </Image.RenderTransform>
        </Image>
    </Grid>
</Page>
```

3. Calculate the *x* and *y* coordinates of the center point of the image and set them as the values of the `CenterX` and `CenterY` properties of the rotation transform. Do this by adjusting the code of the `Image_ImageOpened` method, as shown in the following code:

```
private void Image_ImageOpened(object sender,
```

```
        RoutedEventArgs e)
    {
        Image image = (Image)sender;
        ImageRotateTransform.CenterX = image.ActualWidth / 2;
        ImageRotateTransform.CenterY = image.ActualHeight / 2;
    }
```

4. Rotate the image when the manipulation is discovered. Perform this action by modifying the body of the `Image_ManipulationDelta` method, as shown in the following code:

```
    private void Image_ManipulationDelta(object sender,
        ManipulationDeltaRoutedEventArgs e)
    {
        ImageRotateTransform.Angle += e.Delta.Rotation;
    }
```

How it works...

Adding support for rotation is very similar to supporting the *pinch* touch event, as explained in detail in the previous recipe. In this case, you need to specify different manipulation modes (namely `Rotate` and `RotateInertia`) as well as another transformation (`RotateTransform` instead of `ScaleTransform`), as follows:

```
<Image (...)
    ManipulationMode="Rotate,RotateInertia" (...)>
    <Image.RenderTransform>
        <RotateTransform x:Name="ImageRotateTransform" />
    </Image.RenderTransform>
</Image>
```

Similar changes are necessary in the method handling the `ImageOpened` event. Here, you set the coordinates of the point around which the image will be rotated, as follows:

```
    ImageRotateTransform.CenterX = image.ActualWidth / 2;
    ImageRotateTransform.CenterY = image.ActualHeight / 2;
```

Different operations are also required when the manipulation is discovered. In the current scenario, you just need to increase the current angle of rotation by the value obtained from the manipulation mechanism, as shown in the following line of code:

```
    ImageRotateTransform.Angle += e.Delta.Rotation
```

After you run the application in the simulator, you can launch **Rotation touch mode** (in the menu on the right) and check how it works. You can get a result similar to that shown in the following screenshots:

See also

- The *Handling the tap touch event* recipe
- The *Handling the pinch touch event* recipe
- The *Handling the pinch and rotate touch events* recipe

Handling the pinch and rotate touch events

In the two previous recipes, you learned how to handle the *pinch* and *rotate* touch events. However, is it possible to combine them? Of course! You will learn how to scale and rotate the image at the same time in this recipe.

Getting ready

To step through this recipe, you need only the automatically generated project.

How to do it...

To prepare the example that handles both the *pinch* and *rotate* touch events to scale and rotate the image presented on the page, perform the following steps:

1. Add the Photo.jpg file to the Assets directory.

2. Add an image to the page, support the necessary manipulation modes, and define scaling and rotation transforms. Do this by modifying the content of the `MainPage.xaml` file, as follows:

```
<Page (...)>
    <Grid>
        <Image
            Source="/Assets/Photo.jpg"
            ImageOpened="Image_ImageOpened"
            ManipulationMode="Scale, ScaleInertia,
                Rotate, RotateInertia"
            ManipulationDelta="Image_ManipulationDelta"
            Stretch="UniformToFill">
            <Image.RenderTransform>
                <TransformGroup>
                    <ScaleTransform
                        x:Name="ImageScaleTransform" />
                    <RotateTransform
                        x:Name="ImageRotateTransform" />
                </TransformGroup>
            </Image.RenderTransform>
        </Image>
    </Grid>
</Page>
```

3. Calculate the *x* and *y* coordinates of the center point of the image and set them as the values of the `CenterX` and `CenterY` properties of the scaling and rotation transforms. Do this by adjusting the code of the `Image_ImageOpened` method in the `MainPage.xaml.cs` file, as shown in the following code:

```
private void Image_ImageOpened(object sender,
    RoutedEventArgs e)
{
    Image image = (Image)sender;
    ImageRotateTransform.CenterX = image.ActualWidth / 2;
    ImageRotateTransform.CenterY = image.ActualHeight / 2;
    ImageScaleTransform.CenterX = image.ActualWidth / 2;
    ImageScaleTransform.CenterY = image.ActualHeight / 2;
}
```

4. Scale and rotate the image when the manipulation is discovered. Do this by modifying the body of the `Image_ManipulationDelta` method in the `MainPage.xaml.cs` file, as follows:

```
private void Image_ManipulationDelta(object sender,
    ManipulationDeltaRoutedEventArgs e)
```

```
    {
            ImageScaleTransform.ScaleX /= e.Delta.Scale;
            ImageScaleTransform.ScaleY /= e.Delta.Scale;
            ImageRotateTransform.Angle += e.Delta.Rotation;
    }
```

How it works...

Adding support for both *pinch* and *rotate* touch events is really simple. This is because it just combines parts of the code shown in the previous two recipes.

A short explanation is necessary in the case of XAML code. Here, you need to specify both `ScaleTransform` and `RotateTransform` within `TransformGroup`, as follows:

```xml
<Image (...)>
    <Image.RenderTransform>
        <TransformGroup>
            <ScaleTransform x:Name="ImageScaleTransform" />
            <RotateTransform x:Name="ImageRotateTransform" />
        </TransformGroup>
    </Image.RenderTransform>
</Image>
```

Let's run the application in the simulator, launch the proper touch mode, and check how it works. You can get a result similar to what is shown in the following screenshots:

See also

- The *Handling the tap touch event* recipe
- The *Handling the pinch touch event* recipe
- The *Handling the rotate touch event* recipe

Rendering 3D graphics

Apart from drawing various shapes on a two-dimensional canvas using XAML, it is also possible to prepare complex and attractive 3D graphics in applications using the popular and powerful DirectX technology. What is really interesting is that your applications can even combine DirectX-rendered graphics with XAML content.

In this recipe, you will learn how to create a new project that combines DirectX and XAML. Various parts of the automatically generated solution will be described to give you a quick introduction on the topic of developing applications with 3D graphics.

Getting ready

To step through this recipe, you need only the opened IDE.

How to do it...

To create a project that presents 3D graphics, perform the following steps:

1. Create a new project by navigating to **File** | **New** | **Project...** from the main menu.

2. Navigate to **Installed** | **Templates** | **Other Languages** | **Visual C++** | **Windows** and then choose the **Universal** group from the list on the left. Also, select **DirectX 11 and XAML App (Universal Windows)** from the main part of the **New Project** window, as shown in the following screenshot:

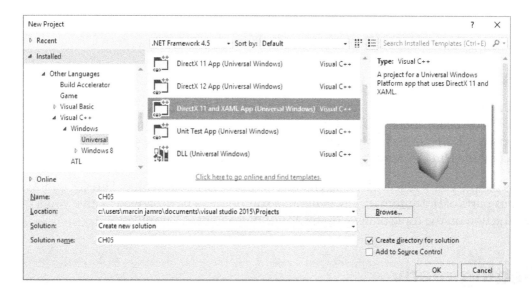

Remember to search for the template in the **Visual C++** group. This example is the only one in the whole book that uses the C++ language, instead of C#.

3. Type a name of the project and solution (**Name** and **Solution name**, respectively) and choose a suitable location. Then click on **OK**.

4. If an additional window with the possibility of choosing a target and minimum supported platform versions appears, choose proper values and click on **OK**. The project will be created automatically.

How it works...

The automatically generated project is a complete example that shows a window with a rotating cube rendered by DirectX. It also presents a text block defined in the XAML language. The result is shown in the following screenshot:

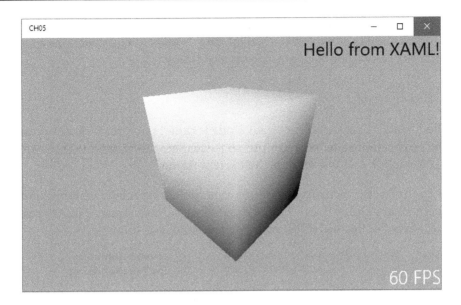

Are you interested to know what is behind this window? What makes it work? If so, it could be interesting for you to analyze the code placed in several files within the solution.

Let's start with the `DirectXPage.xaml` file with the following code:

```
<Page (...)>
    <SwapChainPanel x:Name="swapChainPanel">
        <TextBlock
            Text="Hello from XAML!"
            HorizontalAlignment="Right"
            VerticalAlignment="Top"
            FontSize="30" />
    </SwapChainPanel>
</Page>
```

It represents the main window. The DirectX-rendered content is presented in the `SwapChainPanel` control. What is more, the text block with the **Hello from XAML!** content is shown on the top-right corner of the window. Of course, you can add other controls to the page to combine DirectX-rendered content with XAML-based controls.

`DirectXPage.xaml.h` is a header file in the C++ language for the class regarding the main page. It declares a set of fields and methods, such as to handle user input. For instance, there is a method called when the pointer is pressed (`OnPointerPressed`), moved (`OnPointerMoved`), or released (`OnPointerReleased`). The implementation of such methods, as well as others, is provided in the `DirectXPage.xaml.cpp` file.

Another interesting file is `CH05Main.h`. It is a header file that is related to the process of rendering DirectX-based content on the screen. The `CH05Main` class contains a set of crucial methods, such as `Update` and `Render`, shown as follows:

```
void Update();
bool Render();
```

Both are called in a cyclical way. The `Update` one is called once per frame and can be used to update the application state, for example, to recalculate the values and prepare data for rendering. The `Render` method renders the current frame.

The `CH05Main.h` file also contains some important fields, especially content renderers. In the example, there are two of them. The first renders a sample scene, while the other renders the **Frames Per Second (FPS)** counter. The code is as follows:

```
std::unique_ptr<Sample3DSceneRenderer> m_sceneRenderer;
std::unique_ptr<SampleFpsTextRenderer> m_fpsTextRenderer;
```

The implementation of the `Update` and `Render` methods is available in the `CH05Main.cpp` file. Let's take a look at the first one, where both the content renderers are updated. The code is as follows:

```
void CH05Main::Update()
{
    ProcessInput(); (...)
    m_timer.Tick([&]()
    { (...)
        m_sceneRenderer->Update(m_timer);
        m_fpsTextRenderer->Update(m_timer);
    });
}
```

As already mentioned, the `Render` method renders the current frame. It performs a set of operations, such as resetting the viewport and rendering targets as well as clearing the back buffer and depth stencil view. At the end, the content renderers are used as shown in the following code:

```
bool CH05Main::Render()
{ (...)
    m_sceneRenderer->Render();
    m_fpsTextRenderer->Render(); (...)
}
```

Another group of files is related to content renderers. Let's take a look at the scene renderer, represented by the `Sample3DSceneRenderer` class. Its header file is named `Sample3DSceneRenderer.h` and it declares a set of methods. These methods include `Update` and `Render`, which are called from the `Update` and `Render` methods defined in the `CH05Main` class, as explained earlier.

What is more, the `Sample3DSceneRenderer` class contains a set of fields, such as vertex and index buffers (`m_vertexBuffer` and `m_indexBuffer`), vertex and pixel shaders (`m_vertexShader` and `m_pixelShader`), and the constant buffer (`m_constantBuffer`). The cube geometry is stored as `ModelViewProjectionConstantBuffer` in the `m_constantBufferData` field. The code regarding the mentioned fields is as follows:

```
Microsoft::WRL::ComPtr<ID3D11Buffer> m_vertexBuffer;
Microsoft::WRL::ComPtr<ID3D11Buffer> m_indexBuffer;
Microsoft::WRL::ComPtr<ID3D11VertexShader> m_vertexShader;
Microsoft::WRL::ComPtr<ID3D11PixelShader> m_pixelShader;
Microsoft::WRL::ComPtr<ID3D11Buffer> m_constantBuffer;
ModelViewProjectionConstantBuffer  m_constantBufferData;
```

Let's proceed to the `Sample3DSceneRenderer.cpp` file with the implementation of various methods of the `Sample3DSceneRenderer` class. One of them is named `CreateWindowSizeDependentResources` and initializes the view parameters dependent on a window size. For example, the aspect ratio, **Field of View (FOV)**, as well as projection and view matrices are calculated in this method. The code is as follows:

```
void Sample3DSceneRenderer::CreateWindowSizeDependentResources()
{
    Size outputSize = m_deviceResources->GetOutputSize();
    float aspectRatio = outputSize.Width / outputSize.Height;
    float fovAngleY = 70.0f * XM_PI / 180.0f; (...)
    if (aspectRatio < 1.0f)
    {
        fovAngleY *= 2.0f;
    }
    (...)
    XMMATRIX perspectiveMatrix = XMMatrixPerspectiveFovRH(
        fovAngleY, aspectRatio, 0.01f, 100.0f);
    XMFLOAT4X4 orientation = m_deviceResources
        ->GetOrientationTransform3D();
    XMMATRIX orientationMatrix = XMLoadFloat4x4(&orientation);
    XMStoreFloat4x4(
        &m_constantBufferData.projection,
        XMMatrixTranspose(perspectiveMatrix * orientationMatrix));
    (...)
    static const XMVECTORF32 eye = { 0.0f, 0.7f, 1.5f, 0.0f };
```

```
static const XMVECTORF32 at = { 0.0f, -0.1f, 0.0f, 0.0f };
static const XMVECTORF32 up = { 0.0f, 1.0f, 0.0f, 0.0f };
XMStoreFloat4x4(&m_constantBufferData.view,
    XMMatrixTranspose(XMMatrixLookAtRH(eye, at, up)));
}
```

You can easily modify the location of a camera as well as the point on which the camera is focused. You can do so by modifying the values of eye and at vectors. By default, the camera is located at (0.0, 0.7, 1.5) and is looking at (0.0, -0.1, 0.0).

The CreateDeviceDependentResources method has a name similar to the one described earlier. It allows you to perform operations related to creating resources that are not dependent on a window size. For example, it is used to load shaders, create the constant buffer, load the vertices of the cube (positions and colors), and specify the indices of the vertices that form the triangles to prepare the cube.

The chosen parts of code are shown as follows:

```
void Sample3DSceneRenderer::CreateDeviceDependentResources()
{ (...)
    auto createCubeTask = (createPSTask
        && createVSTask).then([this] () {
        static const VertexPositionColor cubeVertices[] =
        {
          {XMFLOAT3(-0.5f, -0.5f, -0.5f), XMFLOAT3(0.0f, 0.0f, 0.0f)},
          {XMFLOAT3(-0.5f, -0.5f,  0.5f), XMFLOAT3(0.0f, 0.0f, 1.0f)},
          {XMFLOAT3(-0.5f,  0.5f, -0.5f), XMFLOAT3(0.0f, 1.0f, 0.0f)},
          {XMFLOAT3(-0.5f,  0.5f,  0.5f), XMFLOAT3(0.0f, 1.0f, 1.0f)},
          {XMFLOAT3( 0.5f, -0.5f, -0.5f), XMFLOAT3(1.0f, 0.0f, 0.0f)},
          {XMFLOAT3( 0.5f, -0.5f,  0.5f), XMFLOAT3(1.0f, 0.0f, 1.0f)},
          {XMFLOAT3( 0.5f,  0.5f, -0.5f), XMFLOAT3(1.0f, 1.0f, 0.0f)},
          {XMFLOAT3( 0.5f,  0.5f,  0.5f), XMFLOAT3(1.0f, 1.0f, 1.0f)},
        }; (...)
        static const unsigned short cubeIndices [] =
        {
            0,2,1, // -x
            1,2,3,
            4,5,6, // +x
            5,7,6,
            0,1,5, // -y
            0,5,4,
            2,6,7, // +y
            2,7,3,
            0,4,6, // -z
            0,6,2,
            1,3,7, // +z
```

```
           1,7,5,
        };
        m_indexCount = ARRAYSIZE(cubeIndices); (...)
    }); (...)
    createCubeTask.then([this] () {
        m_loadingComplete = true;
    });
}
```

If you want to see the impact of your changes on this exemplary project, let's modify a color of any vertex. The color is defined in the `cubeVertices` array, as the second `XMFLOAT3` value within each `VertexPositionColor` object. For instance, to modify the color of the second vertex from blue to red, you need to change `XMFLOAT3(0.0f, 0.0f, 1.0f)` with `XMFLOAT3(1.0f, 0.0f, 0.0f)`.

Another method is `Update`, which rotates the cube in each frame, as shown in the following code:

```
void Sample3DSceneRenderer::Update(DX::StepTimer const& timer)
{
    if (!m_tracking)
    {
        float radiansPerSecond =
            XMConvertToRadians(m_degreesPerSecond);
        double totalRotation = timer.GetTotalSeconds()
            * radiansPerSecond;
        float radians = static_cast<float>(
            fmod(totalRotation, XM_2PI));
        Rotate(radians);
    }
}
```

You can make rotation faster or slower by modifying the code in the `Update` method. You can change it by increasing the value of the `radians` variable more or less rapidly.

The `Rotate` method updates the model matrix based on the current value of the rotation in radians. The code is shown in the following code snippet:

```
void Sample3DSceneRenderer::Rotate(float radians)
{
    XMStoreFloat4x4(&m_constantBufferData.model,
        XMMatrixTranspose(XMMatrixRotationY(radians)));
}
```

The last method, explained here, is `Render`. It uses vertex and pixel shaders, loaded earlier, to render the current frame. To do so, it performs a set of operations, such as preparing a constant buffer, choosing a proper primitive topology, attaching the vertex and pixel shaders, sending the constant buffer, and drawing the objects by calling the `DrawIndexed` method.

Of course, the automatically generated project presents one possible way of implementation, but it is not the only one. Depending on the project's specificity, another approach may be more suitable.

There's more...

The topic of rendering 3D graphics is really complex, but certainly interesting and challenging. For this reason, it may be beneficial for you to learn more about it.

If you want to get to know how to prepare a simple 3D game for the Windows Phone 8 platform, with parts created also in 2D graphics, using DirectX, DirectXTK, and C++, as well as XAML and C#, you can take a look at *Windows Phone 8 Game Development, Marcin Jamro, Packt Publishing Ltd,* 2013.

6
Multimedia

In this chapter, the following recipes will be covered:

- Playing a movie clip
- Playing an audio file
- Presenting a collection of photos
- Preparing a photo album with captions
- Modifying an image
- Converting an image into grayscale
- Recoloring an image
- Choosing a file to open
- Choosing a file to save
- Taking an image from a camera
- Recording a movie from a camera
- Scanning a QR code
- Synthesizing speech
- Recognizing speech

Introduction

Do you know that modern smartphones provide their users with performance that can be compared to the performance of desktops that were available on the market some time ago? It is really amazing that such small devices have huge potential, which allows developers to prepare various multimedia applications. For this reason, you can enhance your projects, even for smartphones and tablets, with high-quality photos, movies, images from the camera, or speech recognition features!

In this chapter, you will find a set of recipes regarding developing applications with various multimedia content.

To begin with, you will see how to play a movie clip and listen to an audio file, as well as present a collection of photos directly in the application. Then, the subject of modifying images is taken into account, with examples of how to flip an image or convert it into a grayscale photo. What is more, pickers are shown as a way of choosing a file that should be opened or a location where a file should be saved.

The next set of recipes presents how to capture media, including taking an image or recording a movie from a camera. All of these topics are shown in real scenarios. While thinking about recording movies, you may also wonder how to add the ability to scan QR codes to your application. Of course, such a topic is also presented in the book, using the additional package that significantly simplifies development.

The last two recipes are related to speech synthesis and recognition mechanisms. Thus, your applications could *speak* to the user or *listen to* him or her. Such features may be really useful and allow you to develop applications that could be operated by voice.

Playing a movie clip

Developing an application that presents a movie is really easy due to the availability of a dedicated control with a set of useful methods, as you will see in this recipe.

Getting ready

To step through this recipe, you need only the automatically generated project.

How to do it...

Place the `Movie.mp4` file in the `Assets` directory and add the `MediaElement` control to the page by modifying the content of the `MainPage.xaml` file as follows:

```
<Page (...)>
    <Grid>
        <MediaElement
            Source="/Assets/Movie.mp4"
            Stretch="UniformToFill"
            AutoPlay="True"
            AreTransportControlsEnabled="True"
```

```
            VerticalAlignment="Center"
            HorizontalAlignment="Center" />
    </Grid>
</Page>
```

How it works...

MediaElement is a very useful control that allows media content to be played within UWP applications. Of course, it can be used to play both movies and audio. The control is configured by setting the values of various properties, such as the following:

- Source: The source of the movie that should be played. The control supports either local movies (such as the Movie.mp4 file from the Assets directory, as in the example) or clips from the Internet.
- Stretch: A way of presenting the movie, namely Fill, None, Uniform, and UniformToFill. It is interpreted in the same way as explained in the *Adding an image* recipe in Chapter 2, *Designing a User Interface*. In the example, the movie always occupies the whole Grid control, keeping a constant width/height ratio. When the whole image cannot be shown, only a part is presented, according to the values of the VerticalAlignment and HorizontalAlignment properties.
- AutoPlay: A value indicating whether the media content should be played automatically. In the example, the movie is started as soon as it is loaded.
- AreTransportControlsEnabled: A value indicating whether a set of controls should be presented. Such controls, for instance, start playing or change the volume.
- IsFullWindow: A value indicating whether the movie should be presented in the full-screen mode.
- IsLooping: A value indicating whether the media content should be automatically restarted when it is completed.
- IsMuted: A value indicating whether the movie should be muted.
- Volume: A value of the volume.

When you start the application, the movie should be played automatically. By default, it is not running in full-screen mode, but you can easily launch it by clicking on an option presented within the additional controls in the player.

There's more...

As already mentioned, the `MediaElement` control supports not only clips located in the `Assets` directory, but also content available on the Internet. You can easily configure the control to play such a movie by setting the `Source` property to a URL, as follows:

```
<MediaElement Source="http://jamro.biz/movie.mp4" (...) />
```

Of course, you can also set the source programmatically, as follows:

```
MovieElement.Source = new Uri("http://jamro.biz/movie.mp4");
```

It is also possible to programmatically start, stop, or pause the movie, as shown in the following recipe, titled *Playing an audio file*.

See also

- The *Playing an audio file* recipe
- The *Recording a movie from a camera* recipe

Playing an audio file

In a similar way to the case of movies, your applications can also play audio files. Such content may be really useful, for example, in the case of long descriptions that may be cumbersome for users to read. By using audio recordings, they can easily listen to them in earphones while walking or going to work by bus. Playing audio files is very simple due to availability of the `MediaElement` control, as you will see in this recipe.

As an example, you will create a simple page with the **Play audio** button. After clicking on it, the audio recording should be started or stopped, depending on its current state.

Getting ready

To step through this recipe, you need only the automatically generated project.

How to do it...

To prepare an example that plays an audio file, perform the following steps:

1. Add the `Audio.mp3` file to the `Assets` directory.

2. Add the hidden `MediaElement` control and the **Play audio** button to the page by modifying the content of the `MainPage.xaml` file, as follows:

```
<Page (...)>
    <Grid>
        <MediaElement
            x:Name="Audio"
            Source="/Assets/Audio.mp3"
            AutoPlay="False"
            Visibility="Collapsed" />
        <Button
            x:Name="BtnPlay"
            Content="Play audio" (...)
            Click="BtnPlay_Click" />
    </Grid>
</Page>
```

3. Once a user clicks on the button, play or pause the audio recording, as well as adjust the text presented on the button, depending on the current state. To do so, modify the body of the `BtnPlay_Click` method in the `MainPage` class in the `MainPage.xaml.cs` file, as shown in the following code:

```
private void BtnPlay_Click(object sender,
    RoutedEventArgs e)
{
    if (Audio.CurrentState == MediaElementState.Playing)
    {
        BtnPlay.Content = "Continue";
        Audio.Pause();
    }
    else
    {
        BtnPlay.Content = "Pause";
        Audio.Play();
    }
}
```

How it works...

Playing audio files is very similar to movies. The same control is used for this purpose, but–of course–some of its properties are not applicable when playing audio.

In the example, the `MediaElement` control is hidden for a user by setting the value of the `Visibility` property to `Collapsed`. Thus, there will be no visible control, but the audio can be heard by a user. Of course, it is also possible to show the control, together with transport controls, to allow a user to manually start or pause the recording.

As you can see in the code-behind file, you can easily manage the current state of playing by calling a set of methods, such as `Play`, `Pause`, or `Stop`.

See also

- The *Playing a movie clip* recipe
- The *Synthesizing speech* recipe
- The *Recognizing speech* recipe

Presenting a collection of photos

High-quality images are certainly a popular kind of content in multimedia applications, so it is obvious that this topic will be also taken into account in the current chapter. In this recipe, you will learn how to present a collection of photos.

As an example, you will create a simple photo gallery where each photo is presented on a separate *slide*, which could be changed by sliding a finger.

Getting ready

To step through this recipe, you only need the automatically generated project.

How to do it...

Place the 01.jpg, 02.jpg, 03.jpg, and 04.jpg files in the Assets directory. Then, add the FlipView control to the page and specify images by modifying the content of the MainPage.xaml file, as follows:

```
<Page (...)>
    <Page.Resources>
        <Style TargetType="Image">
            <Setter Property="Stretch" Value="UniformToFill" />
            <Setter Property="VerticalAlignment"
                Value="Center" />
            <Setter Property="HorizontalAlignment"
                Value="Center" />
        </Style>
    </Page.Resources>
    <Grid>
        <FlipView>
            <Image Source="/Assets/01.jpg" />
            <Image Source="/Assets/02.jpg" />
            <Image Source="/Assets/03.jpg" />
            <Image Source="/Assets/04.jpg" />
        </FlipView>
    </Grid>
</Page>
```

How it works...

Using the FlipView control is an easy way to create a photo gallery, where each element (Image control in the example) is presented on a separate *slide*. The FlipView control supports switching such *slides* using either touch gestures, clicking on < and > indicators, or even using the keyboard.

After running the application, you will get a result similar to the following one:

There's more...

By default, items presented in the FlipView control are *flipped* horizontally. However, you can easily change this behavior to support the vertical scenario, as follows:

```
<FlipView>
    <FlipView.ItemsPanel>
        <ItemsPanelTemplate>
            <VirtualizingStackPanel Orientation="Vertical" />
        </ItemsPanelTemplate>
    </FlipView.ItemsPanel>
    <Image Source="/Assets/01.jpg" /> (...)
    <Image Source="/Assets/04.jpg" />
</FlipView>
```

See also

- The *Preparing a photo album with captions* recipe
- The *Modifying an image* recipe
- The *Converting an image into grayscale* recipe
- The *Recoloring an image* recipe
- The *Taking an image from a camera* recipe

Preparing a photo album with captions

The `FlipView` control allows you not only to present images defined declaratively in XAML, but also to use the data binding mechanism, as well as enhance the appearance using item templates. In this recipe, you will learn how to prepare an improved version of a photo album with captions.

Getting ready

To step through this recipe, you only need the automatically generated project.

How to do it...

To prepare the improved version of the photo album, where each picture is enhanced with a caption, perform the following steps:

1. Install the `PropertyChanged.Fody` library using the NuGet Package Manager. Do not forget to add the `FodyWeavers.xml` file, as already explained in the *Creating the view model for a page* recipe in Chapter 3, *MVVM and Data Binding*.

2. Add the `01.jpg`, `02.jpg`, `03.jpg`, and `04.jpg` files to the `Assets` directory.

3. Define the `PhotoViewModel` class, representing the data of a single photo shown in the user interface, in the `PhotoViewModel.cs` file in the `ViewModels` directory, as shown in the following code snippet:

```
[ImplementPropertyChanged]
public class PhotoViewModel
{
    public string Url { get; set; }
    public string Caption { get; set; }
}
```

4. Define the `MainViewModel` class, with the `Photos` property, in the `MainViewModel.cs` file in the `ViewModels` directory, as follows:

```
[ImplementPropertyChanged]
public class MainViewModel
{
    public List<PhotoViewModel> Photos { get; set; }
}
```

5. Ensure that the `MainPage.xaml` and `MainPage.xaml.cs` files are located in the `Views` directory, and that the `MainPage` class is defined in the `CH06.Views` namespace. Then, set a proper data context for the page (the `MainViewModel` instance) as explained in the *Creating the view model for a page* recipe in `Chapter 3`, *MVVM and Data Binding*.

6. After navigating to the page, specify the data of the photos that should be shown in the user interface. To do so, override the `OnNavigatedTo` method in the `MainPage.xaml.cs` file, as follows:

```
protected override void OnNavigatedTo(
    NavigationEventArgs e)
{
    _vm.Photos = new List<PhotoViewModel>()
    {
        new PhotoViewModel() { Url = "/Assets/01.jpg",
            Caption = "Picture Lake" }, (...)
        new PhotoViewModel() { Url = "/Assets/04.jpg",
            Caption = "Zion National Park" }
    };
}
```

7. Add the `FlipView` control to the page and specify an item template with an image and a caption by modifying the content of the `MainPage.xaml` file, as shown in the following code snippet:

```
<Page (...)>
    <Grid>
        <FlipView ItemsSource="{Binding Photos}">
            <FlipView.ItemTemplate>
                <DataTemplate>
                    <Grid>
                        <Image
                            Source="{Binding Url}"
                            Stretch="UniformToFill"
                            VerticalAlignment="Center"
                            HorizontalAlignment="Center" />
                        <Border
                            VerticalAlignment="Bottom"
                            Padding="20"
                            Background="Black"
                            Opacity="0.7">
                            <TextBlock
                                Text="{Binding Caption}"
                                FontSize="20"
                                MaxLines="1"
                                TextTrimming=
```

```
                            "CharacterEllipsis"
                        Foreground="White" />
                </Border>
            </Grid>
        </DataTemplate>
      </FlipView.ItemTemplate>
    </FlipView>
  </Grid>
</Page>
```

How it works...

Just a small explanation of the `FlipView` control is necessary. First of all, it is a control that presents a collection of items, thus the `ItemsSource` property is used with the data binding mechanism. An appearance of a particular *slide* shown in the `FlipView` control is specified as an item template.

After running the application, you will get a result similar to the following one:

See also

- The *Presenting a collection of photos* recipe
- The *Modifying an image* recipe
- The *Converting an image into grayscale* recipe
- The *Recoloring an image* recipe

- The *Taking an image from a camera* recipe

Modifying an image

An application may not only present images, but also modify them, such as by rotating, flipping, adjusting contrast, or by adding some additional shapes to it. Such features can be used to allow a user to adjust the photo after taking it using a camera or to create some special effects. Such a task is significantly simplified by the `WriteableBitmapEx` library (h ttps://github.com/teichgraf/WriteableBitmapEx/), which can be downloaded using the NuGet Package Manager, as you will see in this recipe.

As an example, you will create a simple application that loads the `Image.jpg` file from the `Assets` directory and performs a set of modifications, namely adjusting contrast and brightness, vertical flipping, as well as drawing two rectangles. At the end, the modified version will be presented in the user interface.

Getting ready

To step through this recipe, you only need the automatically generated project.

How to do it...

To prepare an example that modifies the image by adjusting contrast and brightness, vertical flipping, and adding two rectangles, perform the following steps:

1. Install the `WriteableBitmapEx` library using the NuGet Package Manager.
2. Add the `Image.jpg` file to the `Assets` directory.
3. Place the `Image` control showing the modified photo on the page by adjusting the content of the `MainPage.xaml` file, as follows:

```
<Page (...)>
    <Grid>
        <Image
            x:Name="Photo"
            Stretch="UniformToFill"
            VerticalAlignment="Center"
            HorizontalAlignment="Center" />
    </Grid>
</Page>
```

4. Modify the photo by adjusting its contrast, brightness, and vertical flipping, as well as adding two rectangles, after navigating to the page. To do so, override the `OnNavigatedTo` method in `MainPage.xaml.cs`, as follows:

```
protected async override void OnNavigatedTo(
    NavigationEventArgs e)
{
    WriteableBitmap bitmap = await BitmapFactory.New(1, 1)
        .FromContent(new Uri("ms-appx:///Assets/Image.jpg"));
    bitmap = bitmap.AdjustContrast(50.0);
    bitmap = bitmap.AdjustBrightness(50);
    bitmap = bitmap.Flip(
        WriteableBitmapExtensions.FlipMode.Vertical);
    bitmap.FillRectangle(10, 10, 30, 30, Colors.DarkBlue);
    bitmap.FillRectangle(bitmap.PixelWidth - 30,
        bitmap.PixelHeight - 30, bitmap.PixelWidth - 10,
        bitmap.PixelHeight - 10, Colors.RoyalBlue);
    Photo.Source = bitmap;
}
```

Do not forget to add necessary `using` statements, such as for the `Windows.UI.Xaml.Media.Imaging` namespace.

How it works...

The `WriteableBitmapEx` library contains a set of features that allow the manipulation of images. In this recipe, only a limited subset of them is shown and described.

Let's take a look at the following instructions executed after navigating to the page. First of all, the `Image.jpg` file from the `Assets` directory is loaded using the following line:

```
WriteableBitmap bitmap = await BitmapFactory.New(1, 1).
    FromContent(new Uri("ms-appx:///Assets/Image.jpg"));
```

Then, you can call various methods on the `WriteableBitmap` instance to perform operations on the loaded image. The following things are possible:

- Adjust the contrast by calling the `AdjustContrast` method and passing a level in the range [-255.0, 255.0]
- Adjust the brightness by calling the `AdjustBrightness` method and passing a level in the range [-255, 255]

- Adjust the gamma by calling the `AdjustGamma` method and passing a suitable gamma value
- Flip by calling the `Flip` method and passing a parameter indicating whether the image should be flipped vertically or horizontally
- Crop by calling the `Crop` method and passing a rectangle indicating the crop region or coordinates of the top-left corner of such a rectangle together with width and height
- Rotate by 90-degree steps by calling the `Rotate` method and passing a rotation angle in degrees
- Rotate by any angle by calling the `RotateFree` method, passing a rotation angle in degrees, and a value indicating whether the canvas size should be adjusted (`true`) or cropped (`false`)
- Resize by calling the `Resize` method and passing the desired width and height, as well as a value indicating the interpolation method

Apart from the preceding features, the `WriteableBitmapEx` library allows drawing various shapes directly on the image, such as the following:

- A non-filled rectangle by calling the `DrawRectangle` method and passing coordinates of the top-left and bottom-right corners, as well as the color of the border
- A filled rectangle by calling the `FillRectangle` method and passing the coordinates of the top-left and bottom-right corners, as well as a fill color
- A non-filled ellipse by calling the `DrawEllipse` method and passing the coordinates of the top-left and bottom-right corners of the bounding rectangle, as well as a color of the border
- A filled ellipse by calling the `FillEllipse` method and passing the coordinates of the top-left and bottom-right corners of the bounding rectangle, as well as a fill color
- A line by calling the `DrawLine` method and passing the coordinates of the start and end points, as well as the color of the line
- An anti-aliased line with a given thickness by calling the `DrawLineAa` method and passing the coordinates of the start and end points, as well as the color of the line, and the width of the line (optionally)
- A non-filled triangle by calling the `DrawTriangle` method and passing the coordinates of three points, as well as the color of the border
- A filled triangle by calling the `FillTriangle` method and passing the coordinates of three points, as well as a fill color

Some of the preceding methods are used in the example. After running the application, you could see a result similar to the following:

See also

- The *Presenting a collection of photos* recipe
- The *Preparing a photo album with captions* recipe
- The *Converting an image into grayscale* recipe
- The *Recoloring an image* recipe
- The *Taking an image from a camera* recipe

Converting an image into grayscale

The previously mentioned `WriteableBitmapEx` library contains a set of great built-in features. Some of them have been already described, but in this recipe you will learn how to easily convert an image into grayscale mode.

Getting ready

To step through this recipe, you only need the automatically generated project.

How to do it...

To prepare the example that loads an image and converts it into grayscale, perform the following steps:

1. Install the `WriteableBitmapEx` library using the NuGet Package Manager.
2. Add the `Image.jpg` file to the `Assets` directory.
3. Place the `Image` control where the grayscale photo will be shown on the page by adjusting the content of the `MainPage.xaml` file, as follows:

```
<Page (...)>
    <Grid>
        <Image
            x:Name="Photo"
            Stretch="UniformToFill"
            VerticalAlignment="Center"
            HorizontalAlignment="Center" />
    </Grid>
</Page>
```

4. Recolor the photo to grayscale after navigating to the page by overriding the `OnNavigatedTo` method in the `MainPage.xaml.cs` file, as follows:

```
protected async override void OnNavigatedTo(
    NavigationEventArgs e)
{
    Uri uri = new Uri("ms-appx:///Assets/Image.jpg");
    WriteableBitmap bitmap =
        await BitmapFactory.New(1, 1).FromContent(uri);
    Photo.Source = bitmap.Gray();
}
```

How it works...

The conversion into grayscale is possible using the `Gray` extension method that is called on an instance of the `WriteableBitmap` class. After calling it, the grayscaled image is returned. In the example, the result is presented in the `Image` control, as shown in the following screenshot:

See also

- The *Presenting a collection of photos* recipe
- The *Preparing a photo album with captions* recipe
- The *Modifying an image* recipe
- The *Recoloring an image* recipe
- The *Taking an image from a camera* recipe

Recoloring an image

Sometimes it is necessary to perform modifications on the image based on the values of particular pixels. Of course, this is possible, and you will learn how to do it in this recipe.

As an example, you will create an application that recolors all light parts of the image to black by analyzing the values of the following pixels. If the R (red), G (green), and B (blue) values are in the range [175, 255], the pixel is recolored to black.

Getting ready

To step through this recipe, you only need the automatically generated project.

How to do it...

To prepare an example that loads an image and recolors light parts of it, perform the following steps:

1. Install the `WriteableBitmapEx` library using the NuGet Package Manager.

2. Add the `Image.jpg` file to the `Assets` directory.

3. Place the `Image` control where the modified photo will be shown on the page by adjusting the content of the `MainPage.xaml` file, as follows:

```
<Page (...)>
    <Grid>
        <Image
            x:Name="Photo"
            Stretch="UniformToFill"
            VerticalAlignment="Center"
            HorizontalAlignment="Center" />
    </Grid>
</Page>
```

4. After navigating to the page, recolor the light parts of the image to black. To do so, override the `OnNavigatedTo` method in the `MainPage.xaml.cs` file, as shown in the following code:

```
protected async override void OnNavigatedTo(
    NavigationEventArgs e)
{
    Uri uri = new Uri("ms-appx:///Assets/Image.jpg");
    WriteableBitmap bitmap =
        await BitmapFactory.New(1, 1).FromContent(uri);
    StorageFile file = await StorageFile.
        GetFileFromApplicationUriAsync(uri);
    using (IRandomAccessStream inputStream =
        await file.OpenAsync(FileAccessMode.Read))
    {
        BitmapDecoder decoder = await
            BitmapDecoder.CreateAsync(inputStream);
        PixelDataProvider provider =
            await decoder.GetPixelDataAsync(
                BitmapPixelFormat.Bgra8,
                BitmapAlphaMode.Straight,
                new BitmapTransform()
                {
                    ScaledWidth = (uint)bitmap.PixelWidth,
                    ScaledHeight = (uint)bitmap.PixelHeight
                },
```

```
                    ExifOrientationMode.IgnoreExifOrientation,
                    ColorManagementMode.DoNotColorManage);
        byte[] pixels = provider.DetachPixelData();
        for (int i = 0; i < pixels.Length; i += 4)
        {
            byte b = pixels[i];
            byte g = pixels[i + 1];
            byte r = pixels[i + 2];
            if (r >= 175 && r <= 255
                    && g >= 175 && g <= 255
                    && b >= 175 && b <= 255)
            {
                pixels[i] = 0;
                pixels[i + 1] = 0;
                pixels[i + 2] = 0;
            }
        }

        using (Stream outputStream =
            bitmap.PixelBuffer.AsStream())
        {
            await outputStream.WriteAsync(pixels, 0,
                pixels.Length);
        }
    }
    Photo.Source = bitmap;
}
```

 Do not forget to add the necessary using statements, such as for System, System.Runtime.InteropServices.WindowsRuntime, Windows.Graphics.Imaging, Windows.Storage, Windows.Storage.Streams, and Windows.UI.Xaml.Media.Imaging.

How it works...

Analyzing the R, G, and B values of particular pixels and recoloring some of them is performed in the OnNavigatedTo method. The instructions seem to be quite complicated, so a detailed explanation is provided here.

At the beginning, the WriteableBitmap instance, representing the Image.jpg file from the Assets directory, is created using the following code:

```
Uri uri = new Uri("ms-appx:///Assets/Image.jpg");
WriteableBitmap bitmap =
    await BitmapFactory.New(1, 1).FromContent(uri);
```

Then, you get the `StorageFile` instance representing the image file, as follows:

```
StorageFile file =
    await StorageFile.GetFileFromApplicationUriAsync(uri);
```

The following code opens the image file for reading and gets its stream:

```
using (IRandomAccessStream inputStream =
    await file.OpenAsync(FileAccessMode.Read))
{
    (...)
}
```

Such a stream is used to create the `BitmapDecoder` instance, which is necessary to get the `PixelDataProvider` instance, which in turn is required to get a byte array with the data of the pixels of the image, as shown in the following code:

```
BitmapDecoder decoder = await
    BitmapDecoder.CreateAsync(inputStream);
PixelDataProvider provider = await decoder.GetPixelDataAsync(
    BitmapPixelFormat.Bgra8,
    BitmapAlphaMode.Straight,
    new BitmapTransform()
    {
        ScaledWidth = (uint)bitmap.PixelWidth,
        ScaledHeight = (uint)bitmap.PixelHeight
    },
    ExifOrientationMode.IgnoreExifOrientation,
    ColorManagementMode.DoNotColorManage);
byte[] pixels = provider.DetachPixelData();
```

It is worth mentioning a few parameters passed to the `GetPixelDataAsync` method. The first parameter indicates the pixel format. In this case, bytes of a particular pixel are stored in this order: blue (B), green (G), red (R), alpha channel (A). All of them take values in the range [0, 255]. The following parameters indicate alpha mode, transform, a way of handling orientation information stored in **Exchangeable Image File Format** (**EXIF**) data, and the color management mode. At the end, a byte array is returned by calling the `DetachPixelData` method.

Now, the most interesting part of code begins, because here you can read the data of particular pixels, as well as modify them! In the current example, you read the blue, green, and red values of each pixel, just by using proper indices from the `pixels` array. Then, you check whether all the color values (R, G, and B) of a given pixel are in the range [175, 255]. If so, the color is modified to black, which means that values of R, G, and B should be set to 0. Let's take a look at the following code snippet:

```
for (int i = 0; i < pixels.Length; i += 4)
{
    byte b = pixels[i];
    byte g = pixels[i + 1];
    byte r = pixels[i + 2];
    if (r >= 175 && r <= 255
            && g >= 175 && g <= 255
            && b >= 175 && b <= 255)
    {
        pixels[i] = 0;
        pixels[i + 1] = 0;
        pixels[i + 2] = 0;
    }
}
```

At the end, the modified values of pixels are written within the pixel buffer, as shown in the following code:

```
using (Stream outputStream = bitmap.PixelBuffer.AsStream())
{
    await outputStream.WriteAsync(pixels, 0, pixels.Length);
}
```

The last operation is presentation of the modified bitmap in the user interface by setting the value of the `Source` property of the `Image` control.

After running the application, you could get a result similar to the following:

There's more...

The presented way of modifying the values of particular pixels is not the only possible one. The WriteableBitmapEx library provides developers with additional methods, namely GetPixel and SetPixel. The first allows you to get the color of a given pixel, identified by its *x* and *y* coordinates. The other method (named SetPixel) is used to update the color of a pixel.

Let's take a look at the simple example:

```
for (int y = 10; y <= 20; y++)
{
    for (int x = 10; x <= 20; x++)
    {
        Color pixel = bitmap.GetPixel(x, y);
        bitmap.SetPixel(x, y, Colors.Red);
    }
}
```

The code draws a red rectangle with its top-left corner at (10, 10) and its bottom-right corner located at (20, 20). What is more, the current colors of all the pixels with *x* and *y* coordinates in the range [10, 20] are obtained. However, they are not used.

Of course, you can use the GetPixel and SetPixel methods to recolor the whole image, but it is not an efficient solution. A significantly faster approach has been presented and described in the recipe.

See also

- The *Presenting a collection of photos* recipe
- The *Preparing a photo album with captions* recipe
- The *Modifying an image* recipe
- The *Converting an image into grayscale* recipe
- The *Taking an image from a camera* recipe

Choosing a file to open

In the previous examples, you have used files whose paths are defined directly in the code, either XAML or C#. However, sometimes it may be necessary to provide a user with the option of choosing a file to open. Of course, the suitable mechanism is available for UWP applications, as you will see in this recipe.

As an example, you will create a page with the **Choose a file** button. After clicking on it, the file picker will be presented, where a user can choose a particular file, restricting the options to .jpg files. When the operation is confirmed, the image is loaded and presented in the user interface.

Getting ready

To step through this recipe, you only need the automatically generated project.

How to do it...

To prepare an example that allows to present an image chosen by the user, perform the following steps:

1. Add the Image control (where the chosen photo will be shown) and the button to the page by adjusting the content of the MainPage.xaml file, as follows:

```
<Page (...)>
    <Grid>
        <Image
            x:Name="Photo"
            Stretch="UniformToFill"
            VerticalAlignment="Center"
            HorizontalAlignment="Center" />
        <Button
            Content="Choose a file" (...)
            Click="BtnChoose_Click" />
    </Grid>
</Page>
```

2. After clicking on the button, open the file picker that only supports .jpg files and present the image on the page. To do so, define the `BtnChoose_Click` method in the `MainPage.xaml.cs` file, as follows:

```
private async void BtnChoose_Click(object sender,
    RoutedEventArgs e)
{
    FileOpenPicker picker = new FileOpenPicker();
    picker.FileTypeFilter.Add(".jpg");
    StorageFile file = await picker.PickSingleFileAsync();
    if (file != null)
    {
        FileRandomAccessStream stream =
            (FileRandomAccessStream) await
                file.OpenAsync(FileAccessMode.Read);
        BitmapImage image = new BitmapImage();
        image.SetSource(stream);
        Photo.Source = image;
    }
}
```

How it works...

Using a file picker is really simple, due to the availability of the `FileOpenPicker` class. You just need to create its instance and call the awaitable `PickSingleFileAsync` method, which returns an instance of `StorageFile` representing the chosen file.

Of course, the file picker has some additional features, such as filtering presented files. In the example you just saw, only .jpg files can be selected (`FileTypeFilter`). You can also choose a suggested starting location (`SuggestedStartLocation`).

> `FileOpenPicker` also supports selecting multiple files. To do so, you should call the `PickMultipleFilesAsync` method, which returns a collection of `StorageFile` instances.

After running the application on a smartphone or a desktop, you will see two different ways of selecting a file, as shown in the following screenshot:

 You can read more about accessing files from various locations at:
https://msdn.microsoft.com/en-us/windows/uwp/files/file-access
-permissions

See also

- The *Choosing a file to save* recipe

Choosing a file to save

Similarly to choosing a file to open, it is also possible to show a file picker for selecting a target location where content should be saved. You will learn how to support such a feature in this recipe.

As an example, you will create a page with the **Choose a file** button. After clicking on it, a file picker will be presented. When a text file is chosen, the name of the current day will be saved within it.

Getting ready

To step through this recipe, you only need the automatically generated project.

How to do it...

To prepare an example that saves a textual content in the file specified by the user, perform the following steps:

1. Add the **Choose a file** button to the page by adjusting the content of the `MainPage.xaml` file, as follows:

```
<Page (...)>
    <Grid Background="White">
        <Button
            Content="Choose a file" (...)
            Click="BtnChoose_Click" />
    </Grid>
</Page>
```

2. After clicking on the button, open the file picker that supports only `.txt` files, and save the name of the current weekday in the selected file. To do so, define the `BtnChoose_Click` method in the `MainPage.xaml.cs` file, as shown in the following code:

```
private async void BtnChoose_Click(object sender,
    RoutedEventArgs e)
{
    FileSavePicker picker = new FileSavePicker();
    picker.SuggestedStartLocation =
        PickerLocationId.DocumentsLibrary;
    picker.SuggestedFileName = "Notes";
    picker.FileTypeChoices.Add("Text file",
        new List<string>() { ".txt" });
    StorageFile file = await picker.PickSaveFileAsync();
    if (file != null)
    {
        string content = string.Format("Today is {0}.",
            DateTime.Now.DayOfWeek);
        await FileIO.WriteTextAsync(file, content);
    }
}
```

How it works...

Usage of the `FileSavePicker` class is similar to `FileOpenPicker`, described in the previous recipe. Of course, you can specify some different properties, such as the suggested filename (`SuggestedFileName`) or possible file types (`FileTypeChoices`).

See also

- The *Choosing a file to open* recipe

Taking an image from a camera

A lot of people use smartphones to take high-quality photos. Of course, they can be taken not only using a built-in application, but also with additional ones. In this recipe, you will learn how to add such a feature to your application.

As an example, you will prepare a page with a **Take a picture!** button. After clicking on it, the process of taking a photo from a camera will be started, using the built-in user interface. When a photo is taken, it will be saved to the `Album` directory and presented on the page.

Getting ready

To step through this recipe, you only need the automatically generated project.

How to do it...

To prepare an example that allows a user to take an image from the camera, using the built-in user interface, and save it as `.jpg` file, perform the following steps:

1. Enable the **Webcam** capability by double-clicking on the `Package.appxmanifest` file in the **Solution Explorer** window, choosing the **Capabilities** tab, and selecting the **Webcam** checkbox.
2. Add the `Image` control, where the taken photo will be shown, and the button that will activate the process of taking an image from a camera, to the page. To do so, adjust the content of the `MainPage.xaml` file, as follows:

```
<Page (...)>
```

```
<Grid Background="White">
    <Image
        x:Name="Photo"
        Stretch="UniformToFill"
        VerticalAlignment="Center"
        HorizontalAlignment="Center" />
    <Button
        Content="Take a picture!"
        Click="BtnTake_Click" (...) />
    </Grid>
</Page>
```

3. After clicking on the button, start the process of taking a photo from the camera. When a photo is taken by a user, present it on the page. To do so, define the BtnTake_Click method in the MainPage.xaml.cs file:

```
private async void BtnTake_Click(object sender,
    RoutedEventArgs e)
{
    CameraCaptureUI capture = new CameraCaptureUI();
    capture.PhotoSettings.Format =
        CameraCaptureUIPhotoFormat.Jpeg;
    StorageFile file = await
        capture.CaptureFileAsync(CameraCaptureUIMode.Photo);
    if (file != null)
    {
        StorageFolder folder = await
            ApplicationData.Current.LocalFolder.
                CreateFolderAsync("Album",
                    CreationCollisionOption.OpenIfExists);
        string fileName = DateTime.Now.Ticks + ".jpg";
        await file.CopyAsync(folder, fileName,
            NameCollisionOption.ReplaceExisting);
        await file.DeleteAsync();

        file = await folder.GetFileAsync(fileName);
        FileRandomAccessStream stream =
            (FileRandomAccessStream)await
                file.OpenAsync(FileAccessMode.Read);
        BitmapImage image = new BitmapImage();
        image.SetSource(stream);
        Photo.Source = image;
    }
}
```

Do not forget to add the necessary `using` statements, such as for `Windows.Media.Capture`.

How it works...

To launch the process of taking an image from a camera, you need just a few simple lines of code, as follows:

```
CameraCaptureUI capture = new CameraCaptureUI();
capture.PhotoSettings.Format = CameraCaptureUIPhotoFormat.Jpeg;
StorageFile file = await
    capture.CaptureFileAsync(CameraCaptureUIMode.Photo);
```

At the beginning, you create a new instance of the `CameraCaptureUI` class, and select `Jpeg` as the format of photos. Then, you call the awaitable `CaptureFileAsync` method with a proper mode, namely `Photo`. The method will return the result, which will be one of the following:

- An instance of `StorageFile` representing a file with the taken photo
- `null` when a user cancels the process

When the photo is taken, its target filename is generated using ticks representing the current date and time, together with the `.jpg` extension. The photo is stored in the `Album` directory by copying the current file to the proper location. Of course, the current file is then removed. The remaining part of code just sets the file as a source for the `Image` control, so its preview can be presented in the user interface.

It is worth mentioning stages of the process, as you can see in the following screenshot:

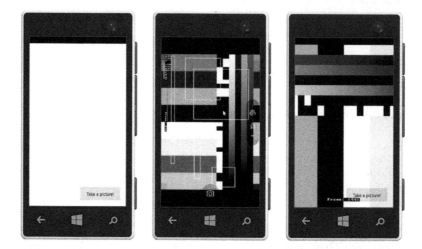

Just after running the application, the white screen with the **Take a picture!** button is shown (the first screenshot). After clicking on it, the built-in screen for taking a picture is presented (the second screenshot). After pressing the camera icon, the photo is taken and the user can confirm or reject the photo. As soon as the user confirms such an operation, the main page is shown with the taken image in the background (the third screenshot). Of course, it is possible to click on the **Take a picture!** button again to take another photo.

See also

- The *Recording a movie from a camera* recipe
- The *Scanning a QR code* recipe

Recording a movie from a camera

Similarly to taking a photo from a camera, it is possible to record a movie and save it on a device. Due to the availability of the `CameraCaptureUI` class, the same as was used in the previous recipe, you can add the movie recording feature to your application in a really easy way. You will learn how to do it while reading this recipe.

As an example, you will create a page with the **Record a movie!** button. After clicking on it, the process of recording a movie will be started. When the movie is ready, it will be saved to the `Movies` directory and played on the page using the `MediaElement` control.

Getting ready

To step through this recipe, you only need the automatically generated project.

How to do it...

To prepare an example that allows a user to record a movie from the camera, using the built-in user interface, and save it as `.mp4` file, perform the following steps:

1. Enable the **Webcam** and **Microphone** capabilities by double-clicking on the `Package.appxmanifest` file in the **Solution Explorer** window, choosing the **Capabilities** tab, and checking the **Webcam** and **Microphone** checkboxes.

2. Add the `MediaElement` control, where the recorded movie will be shown, as well as the button that will activate the process of recording a video from a camera, to the page. To do so, adjust the content of the `MainPage.xaml` file, as shown in the following code:

```
<Page (...)>
    <Grid Background="White">
        <MediaElement
            x:Name="Video"
            AutoPlay="True"
            Stretch="UniformToFill"
            VerticalAlignment="Center"
            HorizontalAlignment="Center" />
        <Button
            Content="Record a movie!"
            Click="BtnRecord_Click" (...) />
    </Grid>
</Page>
```

3. After clicking on the button, start the process of recording a movie from a camera. When the recording is completed by a user, present the movie on the page. To do so, define the `BtnRecord_Click` method in the `MainPage.xaml.cs` file as follows:

```
private async void BtnRecord_Click(object sender,
    RoutedEventArgs e)
```

```
{
    CameraCaptureUI capture = new CameraCaptureUI();
    capture.VideoSettings.Format =
        CameraCaptureUIVideoFormat.Mp4;
    StorageFile file = await capture.CaptureFileAsync(
        CameraCaptureUIMode.Video);
    if (file != null)
    {
        StorageFolder folder = await
            ApplicationData.Current.LocalFolder.
                CreateFolderAsync("Movies",
                    CreationCollisionOption.OpenIfExists);
        string fileName = DateTime.Now.Ticks + ".mp4";
        await file.CopyAsync(folder, fileName,
            NameCollisionOption.ReplaceExisting);
        await file.DeleteAsync();

        file = await folder.GetFileAsync(fileName);
        IRandomAccessStream stream = await
            file.OpenAsync(FileAccessMode.Read);
        Video.SetSource(stream, file.ContentType);
    }
}
```

How it works...

Launching the process of recording a movie does not require a detailed explanation, because it is really similar to taking a picture with a camera, which is the subject of the previous recipe. In the current scenario, you use exactly the same class, namely `CameraCaptureUI`, but the video format is chosen (`Mp4`) and another capture mode is selected (`Video`) while calling the `CaptureFileAsync` method.

When the application is started, the white page with the **Record a movie!** button is presented to the user (the first of the following screenshots). After clicking on the button, the default screen for recording a movie is shown and the user can start recording by pressing the camera icon at the bottom (the second screenshot). After clicking on it again, the recording is stopped. When the user confirms the movie, he or she automatically comes back to the main page, where the movie is played (the third screenshot). Of course, it is also possible to click on the **Record a movie!** button again to record another movie:

  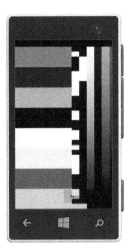

You can read more about various features regarding taking photos and capturing videos in applications at:
`https://msdn.microsoft.com/en-us/windows/uwp/audio-video-camer` `a/capture-photos-and-video-with-cameracaptureui`

See also

- The *Playing a movie clip* recipe
- The *Taking an image from a camera* recipe
- The *Scanning a QR code* recipe

Scanning a QR code

Do you use QR codes as a fast way of accessing websites? If so, it is really good news that you can add a QR code scanning feature directly in your application. In this recipe, you will learn how to do it using the additional library.

As an example, you will create a simple application that will launch the QR scanner. When the result is found, a new page will be opened and the result will be presented in the text block.

Getting ready

To step through this recipe, you only need the automatically generated project.

How to do it...

To prepare an example that makes it possible to scan QR codes using a camera and the additional library, perform the following steps:

1. Enable the **Webcam** capability by double-clicking on the `Package.appxmanifest` file in the **Solution Explorer** window, choosing the **Capabilities** tab, and checking the **Webcam** checkbox.

2. Install the `ZXing.Net.Mobile` library using the NuGet Package Manager.

3. Add a button to the page. Once a user clicks on it, the process of scanning a QR code should be started. To do so, adjust the content of the `MainPage.xaml` file, as follows:

```
<Page (...)>
    <Grid (...)>
        <Button
            Content="Scan code"
            Click="Button_Click" (...) />
    </Grid>
</Page>
```

4. After clicking on the button, start the process of scanning a QR code with the `ZXing.Net.Mobile` library. When a result is found, navigate to another page (`ResultPage` that will be created later), passing the result as a parameter. To do so, define the `Button_Click` method in the `MainPage.xaml.cs` file, as follows:

```
private async void Button_Click(object sender,
    RoutedEventArgs e)
{
    MobileBarcodeScanningOptions options =
        new MobileBarcodeScanningOptions();
    options.PossibleFormats = new List<BarcodeFormat>()
        { BarcodeFormat.QR_CODE };
    MobileBarcodeScanner scanner =
        new MobileBarcodeScanner();
    Result result = await scanner.Scan(options);
    if (result != null)
    {
        Frame.Navigate(typeof(ResultPage), result.Text);
```

```
            }
        }
```

5. Add the new page (named `ResultPage`) to the project.

6. Place the text block, presenting the result, on the newly added page. To do so, adjust the content of the `ResultPage.xaml` file as follows:

```
<Page (...)>
    <Grid>
        <TextBlock x:Name="Code" (...) />
    </Grid>
</Page>
```

7. After navigating to the newly added page, present the result in the text block. To do so, override the `OnNavigatedTo` method in the `ResultPage.xaml.cs` file, as shown in the following code snippet:

```
protected override void OnNavigatedTo(
    NavigationEventArgs e)
{
    string result = (string)e.Parameter;
    Code.Text = result;
}
```

How it works...

Let's start by presenting some QR codes, as follows:

If you scan them, you will get the following results (from the left):

*   Marcin
*   `http://jamro.biz`
*   The example text that is stored in the QR code. Can you read it using any QR reader?

As you can see, QR codes can store various data, not only very simple, such as names or website addresses, but also longer text.

However, how can you understand the content stored in the QR code? It looks just like a set of black and white points without any human-understandable content, doesn't it? Fortunately, you do not need to decode it on your own, because this task is performed by the ZXing.Net.Mobile library (https://github.com/Redth/ZXing.Net.Mobile). It significantly simplifies the development of applications with support for scanning QR codes, because only a few lines of code are necessary to achieve the goal!

Let's take a look at the following code:

```
MobileBarcodeScanningOptions options =
    new MobileBarcodeScanningOptions();
options.PossibleFormats = new List<BarcodeFormat>()
        { BarcodeFormat.QR_CODE };
MobileBarcodeScanner scanner = new MobileBarcodeScanner();
Result result = await scanner.Scan(options);
```

 Do not forget to add the necessary using statements for the ZXing and ZXing.Mobile namespaces.

At the beginning, you specify the supported format of codes (only QR codes in the example) as options of the scanning process (the options variable). Then, you create a new instance of the MobileBarcodeScanner class. To start the process, just call the Scan method, passing options as a parameter. If a QR code is recognized successfully, the Result instance is returned. It contains a set of useful properties, such as Text with the decoded content.

See also

- The *Taking an image from a camera* recipe
- The *Recording a movie from a camera* recipe

Synthesizing speech

Is it possible for an application to *speak* to a user? Of course! The speech synthesis mechanism, also referred as **Text To Speech** (**TTS**), is available for developers, and you will learn how to use it in this recipe.

As an example, you will create an application that says *Hello, dear reader! How are you?* when a user is navigated to the main page.

Getting ready

To step through this recipe, you only need the automatically generated project.

How to do it...

To synthesize the text `Hello, dear reader! How are you?` after navigating to the page, override the `OnNavigatedTo` method in the `MainPage.xaml.cs` file, as follows:

```
protected async override void OnNavigatedTo(NavigationEventArgs e)
{
    SpeechSynthesizer synthesizer = new SpeechSynthesizer();
    SpeechSynthesisStream stream = await
        synthesizer.SynthesizeTextToStreamAsync(
            "Hello, dear reader! How are you?");
    MediaElement audio = new MediaElement();
    audio.SetSource(stream, stream.ContentType);
    audio.Play();
}
```

How it works...

To convert the text to an audio stream, you just need to call the `SynthesizeTextToStreamAsync` method on the `SpeechSynthesizer` instance, passing text as a parameter. Then, such a stream can be played using the `MediaElement` control, as shown in the preceding code.

It is worth mentioning that you can also use **Speech Synthesis Markup Language** (**SSML**) while synthesizing text. An example is shown at: `https://msdn.microsoft.com/pl-pl/library/windows.media.speechsynthesis.aspx`

See also

- The *Recognizing speech* recipe

Recognizing speech

In the previous recipe, you learned how to enable an application to *speak to* a user. However, that is not all, because your application can even *listen to* a user! In this recipe, you will learn how to recognize speech and perform various actions, depending on the result of recognition.

As an example, you will create an application that recognizes a few names of colors, namely red, yellow, white, blue, and green. The recognition should start after tapping on the screen. When the recognition is completed successfully, the color presented on the page should be changed to the correct one.

Getting ready

To step through this recipe, you only need the automatically generated project.

How to do it...

To prepare an example that makes it possible to change the color presented on the page after recognizing the color name by the built-in speech recognition mechanism, perform the following steps:

1. Enable the **Microphone** capability by double-clicking on the `Package.appxmanifest` file in the **Solution Explorer** window, choosing the **Capabilities** tab, and checking the **Microphone** checkbox.

2. Add a grid to the page and handle the `Tapped` event. In such a case, the process of recognizing speech should be started and, depending on the result, the background color of the grid should be set. To do so, adjust the content of the `MainPage.xaml` file, as follows:

```
<Page (...)>
    <Grid
        x:Name="GrdMain"
        Tapped="GrdMain_Tapped"
        Background="White" />
</Page>
```

3. Define a speech recognizer as a private field (`_recognizer`) in the `MainPage` class in the `MainPage.xaml.cs` file, as follows:

```
private SpeechRecognizer _recognizer = null;
```

4. Configure the mechanism of speech recognition after navigating to the page. The defined list of names of five colors should be used while recognizing, namely red, yellow, white, blue, and green. To do so, override the `OnNavigatedTo` method in the `MainPage.xaml.cs` file, as follows:

```
protected async override void OnNavigatedTo(
    NavigationEventArgs e)
{
    _recognizer = new SpeechRecognizer();
    List<string> phrases = new List<string>()
        { "red", "yellow", "white", "blue", "green" };
    SpeechRecognitionListConstraint listConstraint =
        new SpeechRecognitionListConstraint(phrases);
    _recognizer.Constraints.Add(listConstraint);
    await _recognizer.CompileConstraintsAsync();
}
```

5. Prepare an auxiliary method for converting a color name into the `Color` instance. To do so, define the `GetColor` private method in the `MainPage` class in the `MainPage.xaml.cs` file, as follows:

```
private Color GetColor(string color)
{
    switch (color)
    {
        case "red": return Colors.Red;
        case "yellow": return Colors.Yellow;
        case "white": return Colors.White;
        case "blue": return Colors.Blue;
```

```
            case "green": return Colors.Green;
            default: return Colors.Black;
        }
    }
```

6. After tapping on the grid, start the speech recognition process. If the result is obtained successfully, adjust the background color of the grid. To do so, define the `GrdMain_Tapped` method in the `MainPage.xaml.cs` file, as shown in the following code snippet:

```
private async void GrdMain_Tapped(object sender,
    TappedRoutedEventArgs e)
{
    SpeechRecognitionResult result =
        await _recognizer.RecognizeWithUIAsync();
    if (result.Status ==
        SpeechRecognitionResultStatus.Success)
    {
        GrdMain.Background =
            new SolidColorBrush(GetColor(result.Text));
    }
}
```

How it works...

The topic of speech recognition is a bit more complex than speech synthesis. However, due to the availability of built-in mechanisms, you can add support for speech recognition to your applications in quite a simple way.

To begin with, let's take a look at the initialization of the speech recognition mechanism, which is performed after navigating to the page, as follows:

```
_recognizer = new SpeechRecognizer();
List<string> phrases = new List<string>()
    { "red", "yellow", "white", "blue", "green" };
SpeechRecognitionListConstraint listConstraint =
    new SpeechRecognitionListConstraint(phrases);
_recognizer.Constraints.Add(listConstraint);
await _recognizer.CompileConstraintsAsync();
```

The most interesting part of the code is related to defining and compiling constraints. In the current example, the list constraint is used. It defines a set of phrases that could be recognized by the speech recognition mechanism. As you can see, a list with names of five colors is defined and passed as a parameter to the constructor of the `SpeechRecognitionListConstraint` class. Its instance is added to the list of constraints in the `SpeechRecognizer` instance. At the end, the `CompileConstraintsAsync` method is called.

 You can read more about various grammars, namely predefined, programmatic list, **Speech Recognition Grammar Specification (SRGS)**, and voice commands at:
`https://msdn.microsoft.com/en-us/windows/uwp/input-and-devices/speech-recognition`

Another comment is related to the process of starting the recognition, as well as obtaining the result. Such tasks are performed in the `GrdMain_Tapped` method, as follows:

```
SpeechRecognitionResult result =
    await _recognizer.RecognizeWithUIAsync();
if (result.Status == SpeechRecognitionResultStatus.Success)
{
    GrdMain.Background =
        new SolidColorBrush(GetColor(result.Text));
}
```

To start the recognition, you just need to call the `RecognizeWithUIAsync` method on the `SpeechRecognizer` instance. It returns an instance of `SpeechRecognitionResult` that contains a set of useful properties, such as a value indicating a status (`Status`) and a recognized text (`Text`).

After running the application, tapping on the screen, and saying `green`, `yellow`, or `red`, you should see one of the following results:

See also

- The *Synthesizing speech* recipe

7
Built-in Sensors

In this chapter, the following recipes will be covered:

- Detecting motion using an accelerometer
- Reading data from a compass
- Obtaining the orientation of a device
- Reading data from a light sensor
- Launching vibrations
- Reading NFC tags
- Obtaining the current GPS location
- Disabling switching off the screen

Introduction

While developing applications for devices with the Windows 10 operating system, you can use various built-in sensors. The obtained values can be then used to control the application or to adjust its design in order to enhance user experience. Of course, you should think about the availability of such sensors because various devices differ from each other and could be equipped with a different set of built-in sensors.

Fortunately, the ways of obtaining results from different sensors are really similar to each other, from a developer's perspective. Thus, the most important task is to learn what kinds of data you can read from particular sensors, as well as what tasks you can perform using them. For this reason, in the current chapter, you will see the usage of particular sensors in real-world scenarios to simplify understanding and to prepare some basic applications that can be later extended by more advanced features.

You will learn how to get values of G-force along x, y, and z axes using the accelerometer, a heading of magnetic north using the compass, the current orientation of a device, as well as a current value of ambient light using the light sensor. What is more, you will see how to control the vibration of a phone, as well as use **Near-Field Communication** (**NFC**) tags. Then, the topic of reading the current GPS location is taken into account. At the end, you will see how to disable switching off the screen when the application is not used by a user for a long period of time.

Detecting motion using an accelerometer

There are several applications and games that can be controlled by tilting a device. For example, such a mechanism can be used to steer a car or to control a ball that should be located in some specific place on a board. Have you even seen such a solution? Have you wondered how it is possible and whether it is difficult to implement?

If so, this recipe will answer such questions, because here you will learn how to use an accelerometer to read G-force values along the x, y, and z axes. Such values will be used to steer a ball that can freely move on the board, of course, restricted by screen bounds. What is more, the ball should behave quite naturally, that is, it should move faster when the tilting is greater. To implement such a solution, a simple mathematical model has been implemented to calculate the next location of the ball. It takes into account not only the previous location, but also the previous horizontal and vertical speeds, as well as the current readings obtained from the accelerometer. Let's start!

Getting ready

To step through this recipe, you only need the automatically generated project.

How to do it...

To prepare an example that presents steering a ball using an accelerometer, perform the following steps:

1. Add `Canvas` (representing a board) and `Ellipse` (representing a ball) to the page by modifying the content of the `MainPage.xaml` file, as follows:

```
<Page (...) Loaded="Page_Loaded">
    <Canvas x:Name="Board">
        <Ellipse
```

```
        x:Name="Ball"
        Width="50"
        Height="50"
        Fill="RoyalBlue" />
    </Canvas>
</Page>
```

2. Add three private fields, one representing an accelerometer sensor (_accelerometer) and the other two representing the current horizontal and vertical speeds of the ball (_speedX and _speedY, respectively) to the MainPage class by adding the following lines of code to the MainPage.xaml.cs file:

```
private Accelerometer _accelerometer;
private double _speedX = 0.0f;
private double _speedY = 0.0f;
```

3. Modify the constructor of the MainPage class to configure the accelerometer sensor to obtain values and to call the Accelerometer_ReadingChanged method when a reading is available. You can do so by modifying the code in the MainPage.xaml.cs file, as shown in the following code snippet:

```
public MainPage()
{
    InitializeComponent();
    _accelerometer = Accelerometer.GetDefault();
    if (_accelerometer != null)
    {
        _accelerometer.ReportInterval = Math.Max(
            16, _accelerometer.MinimumReportInterval);
        _accelerometer.ReadingChanged +=
            Accelerometer_ReadingChanged;
    }
}
```

4. Add the Accelerometer_ReadingChanged method (in the MainPage.xaml.cs file) to get current G-force values along the *x*, *y*, and *z* axes, and call the method to update the ball location, as follows:

```
private async void Accelerometer_ReadingChanged(
    Accelerometer sender,
    AccelerometerReadingChangedEventArgs args)
{
    double x = args.Reading.AccelerationX;
    double y = args.Reading.AccelerationY;
    double z = args.Reading.AccelerationZ;
    await Dispatcher.RunAsync(
```

```
          CoreDispatcherPriority.Normal,
          () => UpdateBallLocation(x, y));
}
```

5. Set the initial location of the ball to the center point on the board by adding the Page_Loaded method (in the MainPage.xaml.cs file), as shown in the following code snippet:

```
private void Page_Loaded(object sender, RoutedEventArgs e)
{
    double x = (Board.ActualWidth / 2) - 25;
    double y = (Board.ActualHeight / 2) - 25;
    Ball.SetValue(Canvas.LeftProperty, x);
    Ball.SetValue(Canvas.TopProperty, y);
}
```

6. Adjust the current location of the ball according to the horizontal and vertical speed values, the previous location, and the current reading from the accelerometer. To do so, define the UpdateBallLocation method in the MainPage.xaml.cs file, as presented in the following code snippet:

```
private void UpdateBallLocation(
    double accelerometerX, double accelerometerY)
{
    _speedX += accelerometerX / 3.0;
    _speedY -= accelerometerY / 3.0;

    double x = (double)Ball.GetValue(Canvas.LeftProperty);
    double y = (double)Ball.GetValue(Canvas.TopProperty);
    x += _speedX;
    y += _speedY;

    if (x > Board.ActualWidth - 50)
    {
        x = Board.ActualWidth - 50;
        _speedX = 0.0;
    }
    else if (x < 0)
    {
        x = 0;
        _speedX = 0.0;
    }

    if (y > Board.ActualHeight - 50)
    {
        y = Board.ActualHeight - 50;
        _speedY = 0.0;
```

```
    }
    else if (y < 0)
    {
        y = 0;
        _speedY = 0.0;
    }

    Ball.SetValue(Canvas.LeftProperty, x);
    Ball.SetValue(Canvas.TopProperty, y);
}
```

How it works...

First of all, let's take a look at the XAML code used to prepare the design of a page. It contains the Canvas element that fills the whole page. On the canvas, only one element is placed, namely a blue ellipse. Its location will be calculated and updated every time some new readings are obtained from the accelerometer.

Another comment is necessary for the configuration of an accelerometer sensor. At the beginning, you get an instance of the Accelerometer class that represents the default accelerometer available in the device. You can do it by calling the GetDefault static method, as follows:

```
_accelerometer = Accelerometer.GetDefault();
```

Then you check whether such a mechanism is available in the device by comparing the returned value with null. If the accelerometer is available, you can proceed to setting a report interval, taking into account the minimum interval supported by the device. In the next line, you specify a method that is called when a new reading is available. In such a case, the ReadingChanged event is fired. The code is as follows:

```
_accelerometer.ReportInterval = Math.Max(
    16, accelerometer.MinimumReportInterval);
_accelerometer.ReadingChanged += Accelerometer_ReadingChanged;
```

Now, let's take a look at the Accelerometer_ReadingChanged method. Within it, you can easily get the G-force values along the *x*, *y*, and *z* axes using the Reading property of the AccelerometerReadingChangedEventArgs instance, as well as its AccelerationX, AccelerationY, and AccelerationZ properties, as follows:

```
double x = args.Reading.AccelerationX;
double y = args.Reading.AccelerationY;
double z = args.Reading.AccelerationZ;
```

The first two are used for further calculations using the `UpdateBallLocation` method, which is called on the UI thread using `Dispatcher`.

Do not forget to use `Dispatcher` to run the code initiated from a non-UI thread on a UI thread. It is necessary in the case of updating the location of the ball after obtaining new results from an accelerometer sensor because such an operation is performed on a non-UI thread.

The most complicated code is available in the `UpdateBallLocation` method. At the beginning, the current values of horizontal and vertical speed (`_speedX` and `_speedY`) are updated using the current readings from the accelerometer, as follows:

```
_speedX += accelerometerX / 3.0;
_speedY -= accelerometerY / 3.0;
```

Then the current location of the ball on the board is obtained, as follows:

```
double x = (double)Ball.GetValue(Canvas.LeftProperty);
double y = (double)Ball.GetValue(Canvas.TopProperty);
```

In the following code, the new location of the ball (x, y) is calculated. First, the horizontal and vertical speeds are taken into account:

```
x += _speedX;
y += _speedY;
```

In the following step, you check whether the ball is still located within the board. Otherwise, it is snapped to the border and a suitable speed factor is reset. At the end, a new location of the `Ellipse` control is set, as presented in the following lines:

```
Ball.SetValue(Canvas.LeftProperty, x);
Ball.SetValue(Canvas.TopProperty, y);
```

When the code is ready, you should run the application to see how it works. Of course, the most convenient approach is to launch it on a real device, equipped with the accelerometer sensor and connected to the development machine, to check how it works.

Remember that if a device does not support an accelerometer sensor, you will not see any movement of the ball while moving the device.

What is interesting is that the application can also be run on an emulator. In such a case, you should choose any emulator from the list next to the green triangle and press *F5* (to run with debugging) or *Ctrl+F5* (without debugging). Then you should open additional tools for the emulator by clicking on the arrows located next to the emulator. In the **Additional Tools** window, you should choose the **Accelerometer** tab and the **Portrait Flat** orientation and move the image of the phone to simulate the rotation of a real device, as shown in the following screenshot:

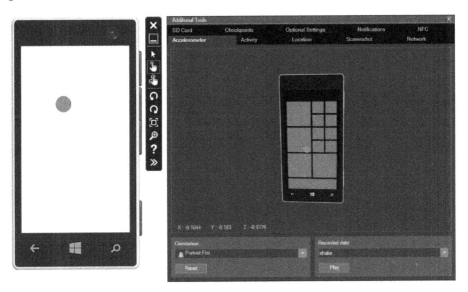

See also

- The *Reading data from a compass* recipe
- The *Obtaining the orientation of a device* recipe
- The *Reading data from a light sensor* recipe
- The *Reading NFC tags* recipe
- The *Arranging controls in absolute positions* recipe in Chapter 2, *Designing a User Interface*

Reading data from a compass

The accelerometer is not the only sensor that can be used by UWP applications. The second one that is presented in this chapter is a compass. It allows you to get a heading relative to the magnetic north or geographic true north, if available. Of course, such a heading is returned in degrees. You will learn how to obtain values from a compass sensor in this recipe.

As an example, you will create an application that presents a compass rose that rotates according to the current heading relative to the magnetic north.

Getting ready

To step through this recipe, you only need the automatically generated project.

How to do it...

To prepare an example of rotating a compass rose according to data obtained from the compass sensor, perform the following steps:

1. Add the `CompassBackground.png` and `CompassIndicator.png` files to the `Assets` directory. These `.png` files are available together with the code attached to this chapter.

2. Add two `Image` controls, representing compass background and indicator, to the page by modifying the content of the `MainPage.xaml` file, as follows:

```
<Page (...)>
    <Grid Padding="20">
        <Image Source="/Assets/CompassBackground.png" />
        <Image
            Source="/Assets/CompassIndicator.png"
            ImageOpened="Image_ImageOpened">
            <Image.RenderTransform>
                <RotateTransform x:Name="Rotation" />
            </Image.RenderTransform>
        </Image>
    </Grid>
</Page>
```

3. Add a private field representing a compass sensor by adding the following line of code to the `MainPage.xaml.cs` file:

```
private Compass _compass;
```

4. Modify the constructor of the `MainPage` class to configure the compass sensor. You can do so by modifying the code in the `MainPage.xaml.cs` file, as shown in the following code:

```
public MainPage()
{
    InitializeComponent();
    _compass = Compass.GetDefault();
    if (_compass != null)
    {
        _compass.ReportInterval = Math.Max(
            16, _compass.MinimumReportInterval);
        _compass.ReadingChanged += Compass_ReadingChanged;
    }
}
```

5. Add the `Compass_ReadingChanged` method (in the `MainPage.xaml.cs` file) to get the current heading of the magnetic north when the compass reading is available, and update the rotation of the indicator, as follows:

```
private async void Compass_ReadingChanged(
    Compass sender, CompassReadingChangedEventArgs args)
{
    double degrees = args.Reading.HeadingMagneticNorth;
    await Dispatcher.RunAsync(
        CoreDispatcherPriority.Normal,
        () => Rotation.Angle = degrees);
}
```

6. Set the center of the rotation when the indicator image is loaded by adding the `Image_ImageOpened` method in the `MainPage.xaml.cs` file, as follows:

```
private void Image_ImageOpened(object sender,
    RoutedEventArgs e)
{
    Image image = (Image)sender;
    Rotation.CenterX = image.ActualWidth / 2;
    Rotation.CenterY = image.ActualHeight / 2;
}
```

How it works...

First, let's take a look at the XAML code used to design a page. It uses two Image controls placed within Grid. Both images should have exactly the same size. The first should present the non-rotating background of the compass while the other, its rotating indicator. Both images (the checkered background indicates transparent areas) are shown in the following screenshot (background on the left, indicator on the right):

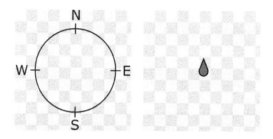

As you could see in the XAML code, the background is static while the indicator is rotated using RotationTransform. Its center *x* and *y* coordinates (CenterX and CenterY, respectively) will be calculated after loading the image. The rotation angle (Angle) will be set after obtaining the reading from the compass sensor.

The way of configuring the compass and reading data from it is almost the same as in the case of the accelerometer. Thus, it should not require any additional clarifications, except for a way of getting the heading relative to the magnetic north. It is possible using the HeadingMagneticNorth property. If you want to obtain the heading relative to the geographic true north, you can use the HeadingTrueNorth property. However, you should ensure that such a value is available by checking whether it is not equal to null.

Another very important information is the current accuracy of obtained results. You can get it using the HeadingAccuracy property of the CompassReading class. It can take one out of four values, namely Unknown, Unreliable, Approximate, and High. Depending on this value, you can inform the user whether the calibration is necessary.

After running the application on a smartphone or a tablet, you should see a result similar to the one presented in the following screenshot:

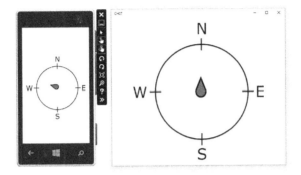

Remember that if a device does not support the compass sensor, you will not see any rotation of the compass indicator while rotating a device.

See also

- The *Detecting motion using an accelerometer* recipe
- The *Obtaining the orientation of a device* recipe
- The *Reading data from a light sensor* recipe
- The *Reading NFC tags* recipe
- The *Animating the rotation of an element* recipe in `Chapter 5`, *Animations and Graphics*

Obtaining the orientation of a device

A smartphone or a tablet can be placed in various orientations, such as with the screen faced down, up, or rotated. Fortunately, it is possible to easily get to know which orientation is currently being used and to adjust the design of the page if necessary. In this recipe, you will learn how to use the `SimpleOrientationSensor` class to get such information.

As an example, you will create a simple page with information about the current orientation. Of course, such content will be updated automatically as soon as the reading has changed.

Getting ready

To step through this recipe, you only need the automatically generated project.

How to do it...

To prepare an example presenting an information about the current orientation of the device, perform the following steps:

1. Add to the page the header (with the icon and the **Device orientation** text) and the label where the current orientation state is presented by modifying the content of the `MainPage.xaml` file as follows:

```
<Page (...)>
    <StackPanel Padding="20">
        <StackPanel Orientation="Horizontal">
            <SymbolIcon Symbol="Orientation" (...) />
            <TextBlock Text="Device orientation:" (...) />
        </StackPanel>
        <TextBlock
            x:Name="LblOrientation"
            Text="Unknown" (...) />
    </StackPanel>
</Page>
```

2. Add a private field representing an orientation sensor by adding the following line of code to the `MainPage.xaml.cs` file:

```
private SimpleOrientationSensor _orientation;
```

3. Modify the constructor of the `MainPage` class to configure the simple orientation sensor to obtain values and call the `Orientation_OrientationChanged` method when the value has changed. You can do so by modifying the code in the `MainPage.xaml.cs` file, as shown in the following code:

```
public MainPage()
{
    InitializeComponent();
```

```
_orientation = SimpleOrientationSensor.GetDefault();
if (_orientation != null)
{
    _orientation.OrientationChanged +=
        Orientation_OrientationChanged;
}
}
```

4. Add the `Orientation_OrientationChanged` method to get the current orientation value when the reading has changed, and update the text. You can do so by modifying the content of the `MainPage.xaml.cs` file, as follows:

```
private async void Orientation_OrientationChanged(
    SimpleOrientationSensor sender,
    SimpleOrientationSensorOrientationChangedEventArgs args)
{
    string orientation = GetText(args.Orientation);
    await Dispatcher.RunAsync(
        CoreDispatcherPriority.Normal,
        () => LblOrientation.Text = orientation);
}
```

5. Define the method that returns a textual representation of the orientation type by adding the following code snippet to the `MainPage.xaml.cs` file:

```
private string GetText(SimpleOrientation orientation)
{
    switch (orientation)
    {
        case SimpleOrientation.Faceup:
            return "Face-up";
        case SimpleOrientation.Facedown:
            return "Face-down";
        case SimpleOrientation.NotRotated:
            return "Not rotated";
        case SimpleOrientation.
            Rotated90DegreesCounterclockwise:
            return "Rotated 90° counter-clockwise";
        case SimpleOrientation.
            Rotated180DegreesCounterclockwise:
            return "Rotated 180° counter-clockwise";
        case SimpleOrientation.
            Rotated270DegreesCounterclockwise:
            return "Rotated 270° counter-clockwise";
        default: return "Unknown";
    }
}
```

How it works...

The way of obtaining information about the current orientation is very similar to the approaches already described in this chapter. For this reason, it will not be analyzed in detail in this recipe.

However, it is worth mentioning the `SimpleOrientation` enumeration, which contains values indicating possible orientations:

- `Faceup`: Face up, that is, screen is visible to the user
- `Facedown`: Face down, that is, screen is invisible to the user
- `NotRotated`: Not rotated
- `Rotated90DegreesCounterclockwise`: Rotated 90° counter-clockwise
- `Rotated180DegreesCounterclockwise`: Rotated 180° counter-clockwise
- `Rotated270DegreesCounterclockwise`: Rotated 270° counter-clockwise

See also

- The *Detecting motion using an accelerometer* recipe
- The *Reading data from a compass* recipe
- The *Reading data from a light sensor* recipe
- The *Reading NFC tags* recipe

Reading data from a light sensor

Does your smartphone have a lighter screen if you are outdoors in a sunny place and a darker one in case you are using it at night? It is a really nice feature that makes its usage significantly more comfortable for your eyes. Can you apply the same mechanism to your application and adjust the design depending on lighting conditions? Of course! You will learn how to do it in the current recipe.

As an example, you will prepare a simple page with the `Audio` icon as the logo and the **Let's play music!** title. Its design will be adjusted depending on the current lighting condition, as shown in the following rules:

- If the light value is high:
    - Background color will be set to white

- Foreground color will be set to black
- If the light value is medium:
    - Background color will be set to gray
    - Foreground color will be set to black
- If the light value is low:
    - Background color will be set to black
    - Foreground color will be set to light gray

Getting ready

To step through this recipe, you only need the automatically generated project.

How to do it...

To prepare an example with the page whose design is adjusted depending on the current lighting conditions, perform the following steps:

1. Prepare the simple page with the `Audio` symbol as the logo and the `Let's play music!` caption by modifying the content of the `MainPage.xaml` file, as shown in the following code snippet:

```xml
<Page x:Name="Page" (...)>
    <StackPanel
        Padding="20"
        VerticalAlignment="Center"
        HorizontalAlignment="Center">
        <Viewbox MaxWidth="200">
            <SymbolIcon
                x:Name="Symbol"
                Symbol="Audio" />
        </Viewbox>
        <TextBlock
            x:Name="Text"
            Text="Let's play music!" (...) />
    </StackPanel>
</Page>
```

2. Define possible light states as the `LightStateEnum` enumeration in the `LightStateEnum.cs` file, as follows:

```
public enum LightStateEnum
```

```
{
    Low,
    Medium,
    High
}
```

3. Add a private field representing a light sensor by adding the following line of code to the `MainPage.xaml.cs` file:

```
private LightSensor _sensor;
```

4. Modify the constructor of the `MainPage` class to configure the light sensor to call the `Sensor_ReadingChanged` method when a new reading is available by modifying the code in the `MainPage.xaml.cs` file, as follows:

```
public MainPage()
{
    InitializeComponent();
    _sensor = LightSensor.GetDefault();
    if (_sensor != null)
    {
        _sensor.ReportInterval = Math.Max(
            16, _sensor.MinimumReportInterval);
        _sensor.ReadingChanged += Sensor_ReadingChanged;
    }
}
```

5. Add the `Sensor_ReadingChanged` method to get the current LUX value and set a proper design mode. You can do so by modifying the content of the `MainPage.xaml.cs` file, as follows:

```
private async void Sensor_ReadingChanged(
    LightSensor sender,
    LightSensorReadingChangedEventArgs args)
{
    float lux = args.Reading.IlluminanceInLux;
    LightStateEnum state = GetState(lux);
    await Dispatcher.RunAsync(
        CoreDispatcherPriority.Normal,
        () => ChangeMode(state));
}
```

6. Define the `GetState` method (in the `MainPage.xaml.cs` file) that converts the current LUX value into the `LightStateEnum` enumeration value, as presented in the following code snippet:

```
private LightStateEnum GetState(float lux)
{
    if (lux < 50)
    {
        return LightStateEnum.Low;
    }
    else if (lux < 1500)
    {
        return LightStateEnum.Medium;
    }
    else
    {
        return LightStateEnum.High;
    }
}
```

7. Prepare the `ChangeMode` method (in the `MainPage.xaml.cs` file) to update the design mode based on the current light state, as shown in the following code snippet:

```
private void ChangeMode(LightStateEnum state)
{
    Color background = Colors.White;
    Color foreground = Colors.Black;
    switch (state)
    {
        case LightStateEnum.Medium:
            background = Colors.Gray;
            foreground = Colors.Black;
            break;
        case LightStateEnum.Low:
            background = Colors.Black;
            foreground = Colors.LightGray;
            break;
    }
    Page.Background = new SolidColorBrush(background);
    Symbol.Foreground = new SolidColorBrush(foreground);
    Text.Foreground = new SolidColorBrush(foreground);
}
```

How it works...

Getting the current value of illuminance in LUX is very similar to reading the current values from an accelerometer or a compass. Thus, it should not require a detailed description in this recipe.

A small explanation could be useful regarding the way of translating the LUX value into the LightStateEnum value. Such a task is performed by the GetState method. If the obtained illuminance value is in the range [0, 50), the Low value is chosen. When it is in the range [50, 1500), the Medium value is chosen. Otherwise, the High value is chosen.

After running the application, you should get a result similar to the presented in the following screenshots, depending on the lighting conditions (from the left: dark, medium, and light):

 Remember that if a device does not support the light sensor, you will not see any change in the user interface in different lighting conditions.

See also

- The *Detecting motion using an accelerometer* recipe
- The *Reading data from a compass* recipe
- The *Obtaining the orientation of a device* recipe
- The *Reading NFC tags* recipe

Launching vibrations

Vibrating a smartphone is one of the possible approaches to inform a user about important events. In this recipe, you will learn how to programmatically start vibrations.

As an example, you will prepare a simple page with the **Start vibrations** button. After clicking on it, the vibrations should be started only for 1 second.

Getting ready

To step through this recipe, you only need the automatically generated project.

How to do it...

To prepare an example that launches vibrations, perform the following steps:

1. Add a reference to **Windows Mobile Extensions for the UWP**. To do so, choose **Add | Reference...** from the context menu of the project node in the **Solution Explorer** window, click on **Universal Windows | Extensions** in the **Reference Manager** window on the left, and choose a version of **Windows Mobile Extensions for the UWP**, such as **10.0.10240.0**, as shown in the following screenshot:

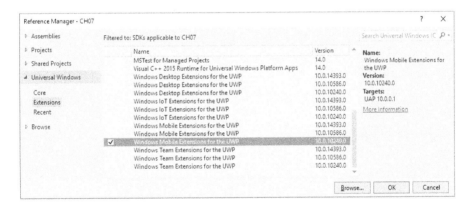

2. Add the button to launch the vibrations by modifying the content of the `MainPage.xaml` file, as shown in the following code snippet:

```
<Page (...)>
    <Grid>
        <Button
            Content="Start vibrations" (...)
            Click="BtnStart_Click" />
    </Grid>
</Page>
```

3. Add a private field representing a vibration device by adding the following line of code to the `MainPage.xaml.cs` file, as follows:

```
private VibrationDevice _vibration;
```

 Do not forget to add the necessary `using` statement for the `Windows.Phone.Devices.Notification` namespace.

4. Override the `OnNavigatedTo` method in the `MainPage` class to get a default vibration device. You can do so by modifying the code in the `MainPage.xaml.cs` file, as shown in the following code snippet:

```
protected override void OnNavigatedTo(
    NavigationEventArgs e)
{
    if (ApiInformation.IsApiContractPresent(
        "Windows.Phone.PhoneContract", 1, 0))
    {
        _vibration = VibrationDevice.GetDefault();
    }
}
```

 Do not forget to add the `using` statement for the `Windows.Foundation.Metadata` namespace.

5. Launch vibrations for one second after pressing the button by defining the `BtnStart_Click` method in the `MainPage.xaml.cs` file, as follows:

```
private void BtnStart_Click(
    object sender, RoutedEventArgs e)
{
    if (_vibration != null)
    {
        _vibration.Vibrate(TimeSpan.FromSeconds(1));
    }
}
```

How it works...

Launching vibrations in a smartphone is possible using the `VibrationDevice` class. First of all, you need to get its instance by calling the `GetDefault` static method. The next step is related to starting the vibrations. This task is very simple because you only need to call the `Vibrate` method, passing an instance of `TimeSpan` to indicate a period of time for which the vibrations should be engaged.

What is important is that you should check whether such a feature is available, because you could run the same application on various devices, not only smartphones. You can perform the necessary check by calling the `IsApiContractPresent` method, as shown in the following code snippet:

```
if (ApiInformation.IsApiContractPresent(
    "Windows.Phone.PhoneContract", 1, 0))
{
    _vibration = VibrationDevice.GetDefault();
}
```

Reading NFC tags

Have you ever thought about the proximity features available in some applications that allow, for example, using a phone as a loyalty card? Have you ever seen NFC tags available in various forms, such as stickers? If so, you can ask yourself a quite simple question: *Can I use them to perform some operations in an automatic way, just after touching such a tag with a smartphone?* The answer is really simple: *yes*. What is more, the development of such a feature is convenient due to the availability of a set of classes, as you will see in this recipe.

As an example, you will create an application that allows opening a website after reading an NFC tag by touching it with a phone. Of course, the website address will be stored in the NFC tag. Thus, you can create a collection of favorite websites as stickers and open websites directly in your application, just by touching tags!

Getting ready

To step through this recipe, you only need the automatically generated project.

How to do it...

To prepare an example that opens a website after reading an NFC tag, perform the following steps:

1. Enable the **Proximity** capability by double-clicking on the `Package.appxmanifest` file in the **Solution Explorer** window, choosing the **Capabilities** tab, and selecting the **Proximity** checkbox.

2. Add the `WebView` control, allowing you to present a website directly in your application, and an additional caption to the page by modifying the content of the `MainPage.xaml` file, as shown in the following code snippet:

```
<Page (...)>
    <Grid>
        <WebView
            x:Name="Website"
            DefaultBackgroundColor="White" />
        <TextBlock
            x:Name="Information"
            Text="Touch an NFC tag" (...) />
    </Grid>
</Page>
```

3. Add two private fields, one storing a unique identifier of the subscription for messages from the NFC tags (`_subscriptionId`), and another representing a proximity device (`_proximity`), to the `MainPage` class. You can do so by adding the following lines of code to the `MainPage.xaml.cs` file:

```
private long _subscriptionId;
private ProximityDevice _proximity;
```

4. Override the `OnNavigatedTo` method in the `MainPage` class to configure the proximity sensor to subscribe for the **NFC Data Exchange Format** (**NDEF**) messages, and call the `TagRead` method when the tag is read. You can do so by modifying the code in the `MainPage.xaml.cs` file as follows:

```
protected override void OnNavigatedTo(
    NavigationEventArgs e)
{
    _proximity = ProximityDevice.GetDefault();
    if (_proximity != null)
    {
        _subscriptionId =
            _proximity.SubscribeForMessage("NDEF", TagRead);
    }
```

```
    }
```

5. Override the `OnNavigatedFrom` method in the `MainPage` class to stop subscribing NDEF messages while going away from the page. You can do so by adding the following part of code to the `MainPage.xaml.cs` file:

```
protected override void OnNavigatedFrom(
    NavigationEventArgs e)
{
    if (_subscriptionId > 0)
    {
        _proximity.StopSubscribingForMessage(_subscriptionId);
    }
}
```

6. Add the `TagRead` method, which will be called when any NDEF tag is found. In such a case, the content of the tag will be read. If it is a website address, the `WebView` control will navigate to it. The suitable code should be added to the `MainPage.xaml.cs` file, as follows:

```
private async void TagRead(ProximityDevice sender,
    ProximityMessage message)
{
    string uri = message.DataAsString.Replace("\0", "");
    if (uri.StartsWith("http://")
        || uri.StartsWith("https://"))
    {
        await Dispatcher.RunAsync(
            Windows.UI.Core.CoreDispatcherPriority.Normal,
            () =>
            {
                Website.Navigate(new Uri(uri));
                Information.Visibility =
                    Visibility.Collapsed;
            });
    }
}
```

How it works...

As you could see, using the NFC tags is not a complex task. What is more, it is also similar to the way of obtaining data from already described sensors such as the accelerometer and the compass. However, to make it more clear, a short explanation is provided here.

Let's start with the modifications introduced in the `MainPage.xaml.cs` file, where you programmatically support reading the NFC tags. First of all, you create two private fields. One of them (`_subscriptionId`) stores a unique identifier of the subscription for tags. The other (`_proximity`) is an instance of the class representing the proximity device that will be used to read the NFC tags.

One of the most important operations is performed after navigating to the page, that is, in the `OnNavigatedTo` method. Here, you get an instance of `ProximityDevice` as well as subscribe to messages written in the NDEF format using the `SubscribeForMessage` method. It returns an identifier of the subscription. When any tag is read, the `TagRead` method will be called.

The already stored subscription identifier is used while navigating away from the page to stop subscription, that is, in the `OnNavigatedFrom` method. You can do it by calling the `StopSubscribingForMessage` method, passing such an identifier as a parameter.

Some clarification is necessary in the case of the `TagRead` method, which takes two parameters, one regarding the proximity device (`sender`) and the other regarding the read tag (`message`). At the beginning, you get the content of the tag, formatted as string, by using the `DataAsString` property. Unfortunately, as you could see using the debugger, such a value contains many `\0` characters. To get the correct content, you can just remove them from the string, as follows:

```
string uri = message.DataAsString.Replace("\0", "");
```

In the remaining part of the method, you check whether the read content starts with `http://` or `https://`. Only in such cases, the website is presented directly in your application using the `WebView` control. You can easily navigate to a given website by calling the `Navigate` method.

You can find more information about the `WebView` control in the *Presenting a website within a page* recipe in `Chapter 8`, *Internet-based Scenarios*.

If you do not have any NFC tags with the website addresses stored within them in the NDEF format, you can easily test the application using the additional features built in the emulator, as shown in the following screenshot:

To do so, you should click on the arrows icon next to the emulator to open the **Additional Tools** window. Within it, select the **NFC** tab. Then, choose **NDEF** as a message type, enter a website address (such as `http://jamro.biz`) in the following field, and click on **Send**. That is all! Thus, you can easily test scenarios where the emulator *touches* various NFC tags.

Remember that if a device does not support NFC tags, you will not get any results after touching a tag. If there are any problems, ensure that the NFC feature is also enabled in the system.

See also

- The *Detecting motion using an accelerometer* recipe
- The *Reading data from a compass* recipe
- The *Obtaining the orientation of a device* recipe
- The *Reading data from a light sensor* recipe
- The *Presenting a website within a page* recipe in `Chapter 8`, *Internet-based Scenarios*

Obtaining the current GPS location

Very often, smartphones are equipped with GPS receivers that allow you to get the current GPS coordinates. Of course, you can use such a sensor while developing applications. Due to the availability of a built-in mechanism, obtaining coordinates is really easy, as you will see in this recipe.

As an example, you will create a page with the map presenting an outline of Poland. The current location of the user will be shown on such a map as a black circle. What is more, the circle indicating the current status of the mechanism of obtaining the GPS coordinates will be presented on the page.

Getting ready

To step through this recipe, you only need the automatically generated project.

How to do it...

To prepare an example that presents the current location of the user on the map, perform the following steps:

1. Add the `Map.png` file to the `Assets` directory. The file is available together with the code attached to this chapter.
2. Enable the **Location** capability by double-clicking on the `Package.appxmanifest` file in the **Solution Explorer** window, choosing the **Capabilities** tab, and selecting the **Location** checkbox.
3. Design the page by modifying the `MainPage.xaml` file, as follows:

```
<Page (...)>
    <Grid (...)>
        <Grid VerticalAlignment="Center">
            <Image Source="/Assets/Map.png" />
            <Canvas>
                <Ellipse
                    x:Name="EllUser"
                    Width="10" Height="10"
                    Fill="Black"
                    Visibility="Collapsed" />
            </Canvas>
        </Grid>
        <Border x:Name="BorStatus" (...) />
```

```
<HyperlinkButton
    x:Name="BtnNoAccess" (...)
    NavigateUri="ms-settings:privacy-location"
    Visibility="Collapsed">
    <TextBlock
        Text="The application cannot use location.
            Click here to change settings."
        TextWrapping="Wrap"
        FontSize="16" />
</HyperlinkButton>
    </Grid>
</Page>
```

4. Add a private field representing an instance of the `Geolocator` class by adding the following line of code to the `MainPage.xaml.cs` file:

```
private Geolocator _geolocator;
```

5. Override the `OnNavigatedTo` method in the `MainPage` class to request access to location services and configure the mechanism of obtaining the current GPS coordinates of the user. You can do so by modifying the code in the `MainPage.xaml.cs` file, as shown in the following code snippet:

```
protected async override void OnNavigatedTo(
    NavigationEventArgs e)
{
    GeolocationAccessStatus status =
        await Geolocator.RequestAccessAsync();
    if (status == GeolocationAccessStatus.Denied)
    {
        BtnNoAccess.Visibility = Visibility.Visible;
    }

    _geolocator = new Geolocator
    {
        DesiredAccuracyInMeters = 100,
        ReportInterval = 5000
    };
    _geolocator.PositionChanged += Geolocator_PositionChanged;
    _geolocator.StatusChanged += Geolocator_StatusChanged;
}
```

6. Add the `Geolocator_StatusChanged` method to get the current status of the mechanism and change the color of the indicator when the status has changed. You can do so by modifying the content of the `MainPage.xaml.cs` file, as follows:

```
private async void Geolocator_StatusChanged(
    Geolocator sender, StatusChangedEventArgs args)
{
    Color color = GetColorForStatus(args.Status);
    await Dispatcher.RunAsync(
        CoreDispatcherPriority.Normal,
        () => BorStatus.Background =
            new SolidColorBrush(color));
    if (args.Status == PositionStatus.Ready)
    {
        await Dispatcher.RunAsync(
            CoreDispatcherPriority.Normal,
            () => BtnNoAccess.Visibility =
                Visibility.Collapsed);
    }
}
```

7. Prepare the `GetColorForStatus` method (in the `MainPage.xaml.cs` file) that returns a color depending on the status of the mechanism of obtaining GPS coordinates, as follows:

```
private Color GetColorForStatus(PositionStatus status)
{
    switch (status)
    {
        case PositionStatus.Ready:
            return Colors.GreenYellow;
        case PositionStatus.Initializing:
            return Colors.Yellow;
        case PositionStatus.NoData:
            return Colors.OrangeRed;
        case PositionStatus.Disabled:
            return Colors.Red;
        case PositionStatus.NotInitialized:
            return Colors.Gray;
        default: return Colors.Black;
    }
}
```

8. Add the `Geolocator_PositionChanged` method to get the current GPS coordinates when they have changed. What is more, it should place the indicator in a proper location on the map. To do so, modify the content of the `MainPage.xaml.cs` file, as shown in the following code snippet:

```
private async void Geolocator_PositionChanged(
    Geolocator sender, PositionChangedEventArgs args)
{
    double lat = args.Position.Coordinate.Latitude;
    double lon = args.Position.Coordinate.Longitude;

    double latMin = 49.0;
    double latMax = 54.84;
    double lonMin = 14.12;
    double lonMax = 24.15;

    double relX = (lon - lonMin) / (lonMax - lonMin);
    double relY = (latMax - lat) / (latMax - latMin);

    await Dispatcher.RunAsync(
        CoreDispatcherPriority.Normal,
        () =>
        {
            if (relX >= 0 && relX <= 1
                && relY >= 0 && relY <= 1)
            {
                Canvas canvas = (Canvas)EllUser.Parent;
                EllUser.Margin = new Thickness(
                    relX * canvas.ActualWidth,
                    relY * canvas.ActualHeight,
                    0,
                    0);
                EllUser.Visibility = Visibility.Visible;
            }
            else
            {
                EllUser.Visibility = Visibility.Collapsed;
            }
        });
}
```

How it works...

Obtaining the current GPS coordinates is possible using the `Geolocator` class. Its new instance is created after navigating to the page and stored as a value of the `_geolocator` private field. It is worth mentioning that you can specify values of its various properties, such as a desired accuracy in meters (`DesiredAccuracyInMeters`, 100 meters in the example) or a report interval in milliseconds (`ReportInterval`, 5 seconds).

What is more, you can handle various events, such as the ones fired when a new reading is available (`PositionChanged`) or when the status of the mechanism has been updated (`StatusChanged`). The suitable part of code is as follows:

```
_geolocator = new Geolocator
{
    DesiredAccuracyInMeters = 100,
    ReportInterval = 5000
};
_geolocator.PositionChanged += Geolocator_PositionChanged;
_geolocator.StatusChanged += Geolocator_StatusChanged;
```

You should not forget to request the user to get access to use location services for the application. You can do it by calling the `RequestAccessAsync` static method. The user will be asked only once, so it is beneficial to check whether the access has not been already denied. In such a case, you can present additional information to the user. In the example, when access is denied, the special hyperlink button will be shown. It will allow the user to navigate to the page with the location settings (`ms-settings:privacy-location`). The related part of code is as follows:

```
GeolocationAccessStatus status =
    await Geolocator.RequestAccessAsync();
if (status == GeolocationAccessStatus.Denied)
{
    BtnNoAccess.Visibility = Visibility.Visible;
}
```

The next group of operations is related to checking the status of the mechanism of obtaining the current GPS coordinates. As soon as the status has changed, the `Geolocator_StatusChanged` method is called and the indicator is colored with a suitable brush, according to the color returned by the `GetColorForStatus` method. For example, when the mechanism is ready, the indicator is in the green-yellow color. If it is disabled, the color is changed to red.

The most complex part of the code is located in the `Geolocator_PositionChanged` method. Within it, you get the current latitude and longitude, as follows:

```
double lat = args.Position.Coordinate.Latitude;
double lon = args.Position.Coordinate.Longitude;
```

In the next lines, the x and y values (`relX` and `relY`, in range [0,1]) are calculated to find a location on the map, on which the point should be added. The [0,0] point is located in the top-left corner, while [1,1] in the bottom-right corner. For calculations, the points with the highest and lowest longitude and latitude of Poland are taken into account, namely about 54°50' N (top), 49°00' N (bottom), 14°07' E (left), and 24°09' E (right), according to the following source:

```
https://pl.wikipedia.org/wiki/Geografia_Polski
```

At the end, the calculated values are used to adjust a margin of the `Ellipse` control representing the current location. Of course, the mechanism checks whether the current location is within the rectangle specified by the minimum and maximum latitude and longitude. Otherwise, the user indicator is hidden.

In the next chapter, you will learn how to use an online map directly in your application, as well as how to place a marker in a given location.

When the code is ready, you can run the application on a real device equipped with the GPS receiver and with the location services switched on. You can also launch it in the emulator to use some extra features that significantly simplify debugging of GPS-based applications. To use them, you should click on the arrows icon located next to the emulator.

In the newly opened **Additional Tools** window, you should choose the **Location** tab, as follows:

Then you can easily choose the current location by clicking on a suitable place on the map, such as **Rzeszow**, as in the example. It will be automatically used as the current location in the emulator, so you will see the black indicator placed in the correct place on the map presenting the borderline of Poland.

Remember that if a device does not support GPS, you will not see an indicator on the map in the current location of the user.

See also

- The *Arranging controls in absolute positions* recipe in `Chapter 2`, *Designing a User Interface*
- The *Opening a map in an external application, Showing a map within a page, Drawing icons, polylines, and polygons on a map, Adding a custom marker to a map,* and *Getting the coordinates of a clicked point on a map* recipes from `Chapter 8`, *Internet-based Scenarios*

Disabling switching off the screen

When the screen is not touched by a user for a long period of time, it could be switched off, depending on the current system settings. Of course, such a situation may be unacceptable in some scenarios, thus it is beneficial to learn how to disable it. You will learn how to do it in this recipe.

As an example, you will prepare a page with the **Toggle switching off** button. After pressing it, the mechanism of switching off the screen will be disabled or enabled. To simplify your understanding of the current state, the background of the page will be changed to yellow when the mechanism of switching off the screen is disabled.

Getting ready

To step through this recipe, you only need the automatically generated project.

How to do it...

To prepare an example that toggles the mechanism of switching off the screen in an automatic way, perform the following steps:

1. Add the button to toggle switching off the screen by modifying the content of the `MainPage.xaml` file, as follows:

    ```
    <Page (...) x:Name="Page">
        <Grid>
            <Button
                Content="Toggle switching off" (...)
                Click="BtnToggle_Click" />
        </Grid>
    </Page>
    ```

2. Add private fields representing a display request (`_displayRequest`) and a value indicating whether the mechanism of switching off the screen is disabled (`_isRequested`). You can do so by adding the following lines of code to the `MainPage.xaml.cs` file:

    ```
    private DisplayRequest _displayRequest;
    private bool _isRequested = false;
    ```

Do not forget to add the `using` statement for the
`Windows.System.Display` namespace.

3. Modify the constructor of the `MainPage` class to create an instance of the
   `DisplayRequest` class. You can do so by modifying the code in the
   `MainPage.xaml.cs` file, as shown in the following part of code:

```
public MainPage()
{
    InitializeComponent();
    _displayRequest = new DisplayRequest();
}
```

4. Disable or enable the possibility of switching off the screen after clicking on the
   Toggle switching off button by adding the `BtnToggle_Click` method to the
   `MainPage.xaml.cs` file, as follows:

```
private void BtnToggle_Click(
    object sender, RoutedEventArgs e)
{
    if (_isRequested)
    {
        _displayRequest.RequestRelease();
        Page.Background =
            new SolidColorBrush(Colors.White);
    }
    else
    {
        _displayRequest.RequestActive();
        Page.Background =
            new SolidColorBrush(Colors.Yellow);
    }
    _isRequested = !_isRequested;
}
```

How it works...

Enabling and disabling switching off the screen is possible using the `DisplayRequest` class. When you want to disable the mechanism of switching off the screen in an automatic way in case of no user operation, you just need to call the `RequestActive` method on the `DisplayRequest` instance. When the mechanism should be switched on again, you need to call the `RequestRelease` method.

 Do not forget to call the `RequestRelease` method as soon as the switched on screen is no longer necessary.

8
Internet-based Scenarios

In this chapter, the following recipes will be covered:

- Opening a website in a default browser
- Presenting a website within a page
- Composing an e-mail message
- Starting a phone call
- Launching a Skype call
- Opening a map in an external application
- Showing a map within a page
- Drawing icons, polylines, and polygons on a map
- Adding a custom marker to a map
- Getting the coordinates of a clicked point on a map
- Launching GPS-based navigation
- Calling API methods
- Downloading a file from the Internet

Introduction

Could you imagine your daily life without the Internet? It is used by many people, almost non-stop, for browsing websites, sending e-mails, calling, using maps, and navigation, as well as sharing diverse content using social media. Of course, people also use the Internet connection for downloading applications from mobile stores.

For these reasons, it is crucial to learn how to introduce Internet-based scenarios into your UWP applications that can be run on a smartphone, a tablet, or a desktop. Such topics are presented in the current chapter, together with examples.

First of all, you will get to know two ways of opening a website, namely in a default web browser in the system and using a control that allows presenting it directly within the application. In the next recipe, you will see how to open an e-mail client with a given configuration regarding recipients, subject, body, and even attachments. The following part of this chapter is related to calling, both by starting a traditional phone call and by calling a Skype user, using the external application installed in the device.

The next few recipes are connected with maps and navigation as important features in GPS-based applications. To start with, you will learn how to open a map in the external application along with setting a proper center point and zoom level. However, the most interesting part is presented in the succeeding recipes and shows how to use the map directly in your application as well as how to add polylines, polygons, and icons. What is more, you will learn how to add a marker on the map in the current GPS-based location of the user. Then the topics of getting coordinates of a clicked point on a map, as well as starting navigation to the given coordinates, are taken into account.

When you are developing a project that consists of many parts, including a web application for management, it is often necessary to connect a mobile application to an **Application Programming Interface** (**API**) to get or send some data. Of course, such a task can be performed in the case of UWP applications, as you will see in this chapter. The topic of sending GET-based and POST-based requests is presented together with reading JSON-formatted responses. While obtaining content from API, it is sometimes required to download additional files, such as images and movies, from the Internet. This topic is also shown and explained in this chapter.

Opening a website in a default browser

In the first recipe, you will learn how to open a given website in a default browser available in the system. Such a task is really easy and just requires you to provide a URL of the website for the `LaunchUriAsync` method. Let's start!

Getting ready

To step through this recipe, you need only the automatically generated project.

How to do it...

To prepare an example that opens a website in a default browser available in the system, perform the following steps:

1. Add a button (opening a website in a default web browser) to the page by modifying the content of the `MainPage.xaml` file, as follows:

```
<Page (...)>
    <StackPanel (...)>
        <Button
            Content="Open website" (...)
            Click="BtnOpenWebsite_Click" />
    </StackPanel>
</Page>
```

2. Define the `BtnOpenWebsite_Click` method to open the `http://jamro.biz` website in a default web browser after clicking on the button by adding the following code snippet to the `MainPage.xaml.cs` file:

```
private async void BtnOpenWebsite_Click(
    object sender, RoutedEventArgs e)
{
    await Launcher.LaunchUriAsync(
        new Uri("http://jamro.biz"));
}
```

How it works...

The task of opening a website in a default web browser is really simple and takes only one line of code. Thus, it requires just a very small explanation. As you could see in the recipe, the given address is passed as a parameter of the constructor of the `Uri` class, and its instance is passed as a parameter of the `LaunchUriAsync` method.

After running the application and clicking on the **Open website** button, you will see a result similar to the one shown in the following screenshot:

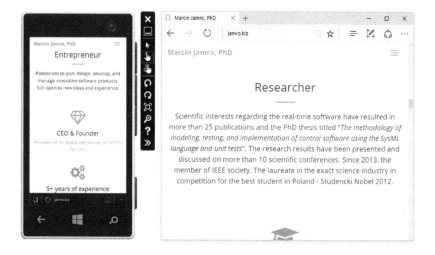

See also

- The *Presenting a website within a page* recipe
- The *Calling API methods* recipe
- The *Downloading a file from the Internet* recipe

Presenting a website within a page

As you saw in the previous recipe, opening a website in an external browser is really simple. However, it is also possible to embed the web browser directly in your application and present the website on the page, without the necessity of navigating a user away from your application. You can do it using the WebView control, as you will see in this recipe. What is more, such a control allows you to execute some additional code when navigation to another page is started or completed.

As an example, you will create a simple application that presents `http://jamro.biz` in the `WebView` control and only allows navigating to specific pages, the addresses of which start with `http://jamro.biz`. Thus, the user cannot use the application to freely browse the Internet. You will also learn how to read the address of the loaded website, as well as you will get to know whether the website has opened successfully. If it has not, its address should be presented in red.

Getting ready

To step through this recipe, you need only the automatically generated project.

How to do it...

To prepare an example that presents a website within a page, perform the following steps:

1. Add the `WebView` control (which will present a website) and the `TextBlock` control (with an address of the website) to the page. You can do so by modifying the content of the `MainPage.xaml` file, as follows:

```
<Page (...)>
    <Grid>
        <Grid.RowDefinitions>
            <RowDefinition Height="*" />
            <RowDefinition Height="Auto" />
        </Grid.RowDefinitions>
        <WebView
            x:Name="Web"
            Grid.Row="0"
            NavigationStarting="Web_NavigationStarting"
            NavigationCompleted="Web_NavigationCompleted" />
        <TextBlock
            x:Name="TxtAddress"
            Grid.Row="1" (...) />
    </Grid>
</Page>
```

2. Override the `OnNavigatedTo` method in the `MainPage` class to show `http://jamro.biz` in the `WebView` control. You can do so by modifying the code in the `MainPage.xaml.cs` file, as follows:

```
protected override void OnNavigatedTo(
    NavigationEventArgs e)
```

```
    {
        Web.Navigate(new Uri("http://jamro.biz"));
    }
```

3. Do not allow a user to navigate to any website that does not start with the `http ://jamro.biz` address. To do so, define the `Web_NavigationStarting` method that is called while the navigation is being started and allows cancelling the navigation. The following part of code should be added to the `MainPage.xaml.cs` file:

```
private void Web_NavigationStarting(WebView sender,
    WebViewNavigationStartingEventArgs args)
{
    if (!args.Uri.AbsoluteUri.StartsWith("http://jamro.biz"))
    {
        args.Cancel = true;
    }
}
```

4. Present the address of the website that is currently shown in the `WebView` control, and indicate whether any errors exist by adjusting the color of the address shown below the website. To do so, define the `Web_NavigationCompleted` method that is called when the navigation is completed. The following part of code should be added to the `MainPage.xaml.cs` file:

```
private void Web_NavigationCompleted(WebView sender,
    WebViewNavigationCompletedEventArgs args)
{
    TxtAddress.Text = args.Uri.AbsoluteUri;
    TxtAddress.Foreground =
        new SolidColorBrush(args.IsSuccess ?
            Colors.Black : Colors.Red);
}
```

How it works...

Opening a website in a web browser presented directly within the application is a bit more difficult than using an external web browser, as shown in the previous recipe. For this reason, a short, but comprehensive, explanation is provided here.

First of all, let's take a look at the XAML code. Here, you add the `WebView` control, specify its name, and handle two events, namely `NavigationStarting` and `NavigationCompleted`. The first is fired when a user starts navigation to another page, but at this time, it is still possible to cancel the navigation. The other is fired when the navigation is completed. The relevant snippet of the XAML code is as follows:

```
<WebView
    x:Name="Web" (...)
    NavigationStarting="Web_NavigationStarting"
    NavigationCompleted="Web_NavigationCompleted" />
```

By adding the `WebView` control, no page is loaded by default. You can navigate to a given website by calling the `Navigate` method, as follows:

```
Web.Navigate(new Uri("http://jamro.biz"));
```

An interesting part of code is located in the `Web_NavigationStarting` method. Within it, you check whether an address of the target website starts with `http://jamro.biz`. If not, you cancel the navigation and leave the user on the current page by setting a value of the `Cancel` property (of `WebViewNavigationStartingEventArgs`) to `true`. The related part of code is presented as follows:

```
if (!args.Uri.AbsoluteUri.StartsWith("http://jamro.biz"))
{
    args.Cancel = true;
}
```

As already mentioned, the `Web_NavigationCompleted` method is called when the navigation is completed. Here, you present the address of the current website and set its color to red (if it has not been loaded successfully) or black (otherwise), as follows:

```
TxtAddress.Text = args.Uri.AbsoluteUri;
TxtAddress.Foreground = new SolidColorBrush(
    args.IsSuccess ? Colors.Black : Colors.Red);
```

After running the application, you will see a result similar to the following:

See also

- The *Opening a website in a default browser* recipe
- The *Calling API methods* recipe
- The *Downloading a file from the Internet* recipe

Composing an e-mail message

While developing UWP applications, it is also possible to programmatically open an external e-mail client. Of course, you can configure a new message by setting its recipients, subject, body, or even choosing files that should be attached. In this recipe, you will learn how to compose an e-mail message with a few variants.

As an example, you will create an application that composes a new e-mail message in a few ways, namely with various recipients (as To, CC, and BCC), a predefined subject, a body, and importance, as well as with an attachment selected by the user from the `.jpg` files available on the device.

Getting ready

To step through this recipe, you need only the automatically generated project.

How to do it...

To prepare an example that composes new e-mail messages, perform the following steps:

1. Add three buttons (opening an external application to send e-mail messages in various configurations) to the page by modifying the content of the `MainPage.xaml` file, as follows:

```
<Page (...)>
    <StackPanel (...)>
        <Button
            Content="Send to one recipient" (...)
            Click="BtnSendOneRecipient_Click" />
        <Button
            Content="Send to many recipients" (...)
            Click="BtnSendManyRecipients_Click" />
        <Button
            Content="Send with an attachment" (...)
            Click="BtnSendWithAttachment_Click" />
    </StackPanel>
</Page>
```

2. Open an external application to send an e-mail message to one recipient with a predefined subject and body by defining the `BtnSendOneRecipient_Click` method in the `MainPage.xaml.cs` file, as shown in the following code snippet:

```
private async void BtnSendOneRecipient_Click(
    object sender, RoutedEventArgs e)
{
    EmailMessage message = new EmailMessage();
    EmailRecipient recipient = new EmailRecipient(
        "marcin@jamro.biz", "Marcin Jamro");
    message.To.Add(recipient);
    message.Body = "It is a message sent from an
        application.";
    message.Subject = "Subject of the message";
    await EmailManager.ShowComposeNewEmailAsync(message);
}
```

3. Open an external application to send an e-mail message to four recipients (two as To, one as CC, and one as BCC) with a predefined subject, body, and importance by defining the `BtnSendManyRecipients_Click` method in the `MainPage.xaml.cs` file, as shown in the following part of code:

```
private async void BtnSendManyRecipients_Click(
    object sender, RoutedEventArgs e)
{
    EmailMessage message = new EmailMessage();
    EmailRecipient recipientFirst = new EmailRecipient(
        "marcin@jamro.biz", "Marcin Jamro");
    EmailRecipient recipientSecond = new EmailRecipient(
        "marcin@tituto.com");
    message.To.Add(recipientFirst);
    message.To.Add(recipientSecond);

    EmailRecipient recipientCC = new EmailRecipient(
        "copies@jamro.biz");
    message.CC.Add(recipientCC);

    EmailRecipient recipientBCC = new EmailRecipient(
        "hidden@jamro.biz");
    message.Bcc.Add(recipientBCC);

    message.Body = "It is a message sent from an
        application to a few recipients.";
    message.Subject = "Subject of the message";
    message.Importance = EmailImportance.High;
    await EmailManager.ShowComposeNewEmailAsync(message);
}
```

4. Open an external application to send an e-mail message to one recipient with a predefined subject and body, as well as with the possibility of choosing a `.jpg` file as an attachment. You can do so by defining the `BtnSendWithAttachment_Click` method in the `MainPage.xaml.cs` file, as follows:

```
private async void BtnSendWithAttachment_Click(
    object sender, RoutedEventArgs e)
{
    FileOpenPicker picker = new FileOpenPicker();
    picker.FileTypeFilter.Add(".jpg");
    StorageFile file = await picker.PickSingleFileAsync();
    if (file != null)
    {
        EmailMessage message = new EmailMessage();
```

```
EmailRecipient recipient = new EmailRecipient(
    "marcin@jamro.biz", "Marcin Jamro");
message.To.Add(recipient);
message.Body = "It is a message with an attachment,
    sent from an application.";
message.Subject = "Subject of the message";

RandomAccessStreamReference stream =
    RandomAccessStreamReference.CreateFromFile(file);
EmailAttachment attachment =
    new EmailAttachment(file.Name, stream);
message.Attachments.Add(attachment);

await EmailManager.ShowComposeNewEmailAsync(
    message);
    }
}
```

How it works...

The preceding code, despite being quite long, is not so difficult to understand. However, to make it even clearer, a detailed explanation is given here.

Let's start with the `EmailMessage` class, which contains a set of properties. By setting their values, you can configure a new e-mail message. First of all, you can set the recipients of the message using one of the following properties:

- `To`: A direct recipient
- `CC` (**Carbon Copy**): A recipient that will receive a copy
- `BCC` (**Blind Carbon Copy**): A recipient that will receive a hidden copy

Of course, you can add more than one recipient in each variant. Each recipient is represented as an instance of the `EmailRecipient` class. It allows specifying either only an e-mail address or an e-mail address along with a display name.

Among another properties, you can find the following ones:

- `Subject`: A default subject
- `Body`: A default body
- `Importance`: An importance, such as high
- `Attachments`: A collection of attachments added to the message

An additional comment is necessary in the case of adding an attachment to the message. Such a task is accomplished by creating a new instance of the `EmailAttachment` class and passing its name and a stream as a parameter. The instance should be added to the collection in the `Attachments` property. Of course, you can use a file picker to allow a user to choose a suitable file that should be attached to the e-mail message, as shown in the preceding code.

> Attaching a file while composing an e-mail message using the preceding code could not be available in some e-mail clients.

In the end, you should call the `ShowComposeNewEmailAsync` static method of the `EmailManager` class to navigate to the e-mail client for composing a message.

See also

- The *Choosing a file to open* recipe in `Chapter 6`, *Multimedia*

Starting a phone call

A UWP application, launched on a smartphone, allows showing a dialog to start a call with a given number. Such a task requires just one line of code. Of course, you should also take care about devices that do not support calling. You will learn how to achieve this goal in the current recipe.

As an example, you will create a simple page with a button. After clicking on it, a dialog should be presented that allows calling a given phone number. Of course, you will handle a scenario of not supporting such a feature. In such a case, a message is shown.

Getting ready

To step through this recipe, you need only the automatically generated project.

How to do it...

To prepare an example that allows starting a phone call, perform the following steps:

1. Add reference to **Windows Mobile Extensions for the UWP**. To do so, choose **Add | Reference...** from the context menu of the project node in the **Solution Explorer** window, click on **Universal Windows | Extensions** in the **Reference Manager** window on the left, and choose a version of **Windows Mobile Extensions for the UWP**, such as **10.0.10240.0**.

2. Add a button (that should open a dialog to confirm starting a call) to the page by modifying the content of the `MainPage.xaml` file, as follows:

```
<Page (...)>
    <Grid>
        <Button
            Content="Call me!" (...)
            Click="BtnCall_Click" />
    </Grid>
</Page>
```

3. Open a dialog to confirm starting a call after clicking on the button if such a feature is available. Otherwise, just present a dialog with information that the device does not support calling. To do so, define the `BtnCall_Click` method in the `MainPage.xaml.cs` file, as follows:

```
private async void BtnCall_Click(
    object sender, RoutedEventArgs e)
{
    if (ApiInformation.IsApiContractPresent(
        "Windows.Phone.PhoneContract", 1, 0))
    {
        PhoneCallManager.ShowPhoneCallUI(
            "+48 000-000-000", "Marcin Jamro");
    }
    else
    {
        ContentDialog dialog = new ContentDialog()
        {
            Content = "We are sorry, but the device
                does not support calling.",
            PrimaryButtonText = "OK"
        };
        await dialog.ShowAsync();
    }
}
```

How it works...

Opening a dialog for calling a given number requires just calling the `ShowPhoneCallUI` method of the `PhoneCallManager` class, as follows:

```
PhoneCallManager.ShowPhoneCallUI("Number", "Display name");
```

Of course, you should check whether the application is launched on a phone. You can do it using the `IsApiContractPresent` method, as follows:

```
ApiInformation.IsApiContractPresent(
    "Windows.Phone.PhoneContract", 1, 0)
```

If such an expression is evaluated to `false`, the dialog with information is shown. To do so, the `ContentDialog` class is used. You can easily specify the content of the dialog by setting a value of the `Content` property, while the button text is defined as a value of the `PrimaryButtonText` property. At the end, you just need to call the `ShowAsync` method to present the dialog.

After running the application on a smartphone, a tablet or a desktop, you will get a result similar to the ones shown in the following screenshot:

See also

- The *Launching a Skype call* recipe

Launching a Skype call

Apart from starting a traditional phone call, you can easily launch a call to a given Skype user using the external application installed on the device. You will learn how to do it in this recipe. Similar to the case of opening a website in a default web browser, such a task just requires specifying a proper `Uri` instance and passing it as a parameter to the `LaunchUriAsync` method of the `Launcher` class.

Getting ready

To step through this recipe, you need only the automatically generated project.

How to do it...

To prepare an example that allows launching a Skype call, perform the following steps:

1. Add a button (starting a call to a given Skype user) to the page by modifying the content of the `MainPage.xaml` file, as follows:

```
<Page (...)>
    <StackPanel (...)>
        <Button
            Content="Start call" (...)
            Click="BtnStartCall_Click" />
    </StackPanel>
</Page>
```

2. Define the `BtnStartCall_Click` method to call a particular Skype user after clicking on the button. You can do so by adding the following part of code to the `MainPage.xaml.cs` file:

```
private async void BtnStartCall_Click(
    object sender, RoutedEventArgs e)
{
    Uri uri = new Uri("skype:marcinjamro?call");
    await Launcher.LaunchUriAsync(uri);
}
```

How it works...

To launch the Skype call, you need to specify a `Uri` instance in the following form:

```
skype:username?call
```

Then, you should use the `Launcher` class to launch the mentioned `Uri`. That's all! The Skype application, if installed, is launched, and a user can easily start a call to a specified contact.

See also

- The *Starting a phone call* recipe

Opening a map in an external application

After learning how to open a website, compose an e-mail message, and start a call, it is beneficial to get to know how to use maps in your applications. In the beginning, you will see how to open an external application that allows centering a map in a given location and deciding the region of the map to be presented.

As an example, you will create a simple page with three buttons. The first two will open the map centered in the location of Rzeszow's Town Hall in two modes (2D and rotated, further named 3D), while the other presents the region of Rzeszow's Market Square.

Getting ready

To step through this recipe, you need only the automatically generated project.

How to do it...

To prepare an example that opens the map in an external application, perform the following steps:

1. Add three buttons (opening an external application to view maps in various configurations) to the page by modifying the content of the `MainPage.xaml` file, as follows:

```
<Page (...)>
    <StackPanel (...)>
        <Button
            Content="Rzeszow's Town Hall on 2D map" (...)
            Click="BtnTownHall2D_Click" />
        <Button
            Content="Rzeszow's Town Hall on 3D map" (...)
            Click="BtnTownHall3D_Click" />
        <Button
            Content="Rzeszow's Market Square" (...)
            Click="BtnMarketSquare_Click" />
    </StackPanel>
</Page>
```

2. Open an external application to present a map centered in the location of Rzeszow's Town Hall, that is, the center point (ce) set to 50.037348°N 22.003998°E (cp) with the zoom level equal to 18 (lvl). To do so, define the BtnTownHall2D_Click method in the MainPage.xaml.cs file, as shown in the following code snippet:

```
private async void BtnTownHall2D_Click(
    object sender, RoutedEventArgs e)
{
    Uri uri = new Uri(
        "bingmaps:?cp=50.037348~22.003998&lvl=18");
    await Launcher.LaunchUriAsync(uri);
}
```

3. Open an external application to present a map in the 3D mode by setting a pitch (pit) value to 60 degrees centered in the location of Rzeszow's Town Hall, that is, the center point (ce) set to 50.037348°N 22.003998°E (cp) with the zoom level equal to 18 (lvl). To do so, define the BtnTownHall3D_Click method in the MainPage.xaml.cs file, as follows:

```
private async void BtnTownHall3D_Click(
    object sender, RoutedEventArgs e)
{
    Uri uri = new Uri(
        "bingmaps:?cp=50.037348~22.003998&lvl=18&pit=60");
    await Launcher.LaunchUriAsync(uri);
}
```

4. Open an external application to present a region of the map with Rzeszow's Market Square by setting a proper bounding box (bb). Its north-west corner is specified in the location 50.037860°N 22.003736°E, while the south-east corner is located in 50.037178°N 22.005581°E. To do so, define the `BtnMarketSquare_Click` method in the `MainPage.xaml.cs` file, as shown in the following part of code:

```
private async void BtnMarketSquare_Click(
    object sender, RoutedEventArgs e)
{
    Uri uri = new Uri(
      "bingmaps:?bb=50.037178_22.003736~50.037860_22.005581");
    await Launcher.LaunchUriAsync(uri);
}
```

How it works...

You specify a way of presenting the map using a proper `Uri` instance passed as a parameter to the `LaunchUriAsync` method of the `Launcher` class. Of course, a format of the parameter of the `Uri` constructor depends on the variant of a chosen map presentation mode.

If you want to present the map in the traditional 2D mode by setting the center point (cp) together with the zoom level (lvl), you can use the following string:

```
bingmaps:?cp=[latitude]~[longitude]&lvl=[zoom]
```

Of course, [latitude], [longitude], and [zoom] placeholders should be replaced with correct values, as shown in the preceding example.

The external application also supports 3D mode, which can be achieved by setting a proper value of pitch (pit). To do so, you just need to add another parameter that specifies such a value, as follows:

```
bingmaps:?cp=[latitude]~[longitude]&lvl=[zoom]&pit=[pitch]
```

A different format is used for choosing a region that should be presented on the map instead of specifying a particular center point. In such a case, you should apply the following string as `Uri`:

```
bingmaps:?bb=[min-lat]_[min-lon]~[max-lat]_[max-lon]
```

You should get the coordinates of the north-west and south-east corners and place their latitudes and longitudes according to the preceding syntax.

After running the application and clicking on the **Rzeszow's Town Hall on 3D map** button, you will see a result similar to presented in the following screenshot:

See also

- The *Showing a map within a page* recipe
- The *Drawing icons, polylines, and polygons on a map* recipe
- The *Adding a custom marker to a map* recipe
- The *Getting the coordinates of a clicked point on a map* recipe
- The *Launching GPS-based navigation* recipe
- The *Obtaining the current GPS location* recipe in `Chapter 7`, *Built-in Sensors*

Showing a map within a page

Presenting a map in the external application is a really nice feature that can be implemented in a very easy way. However, it is significantly more interesting to have a map shown directly in your application, isn't it? Fortunately, your applications can use the `MapControl` control to achieve this goal, as you will see in this recipe and a few following recipes.

As an example, you will create a page with the map and two buttons. The first will show Rzeszow Castle on the map, while the other makes it possible to present the airport located near Rzeszow. What is more, just after opening the page, the map will be centered in a specified location with a given zoom level. You will also see how to enable or disable the presentation of various features on the map. Let's start!

Getting ready

To step through this recipe, you need only the automatically generated project.

How to do it...

To prepare an example that presents the map directly within the application, perform the following steps:

1. Add the `MapControl` control (presenting the map), as well as two buttons (navigating to suitable locations on the map) to the page. To do so, modify the content of the `MainPage.xaml` file, as follows:

```
<Page (...)
    xmlns:Maps="using:Windows.UI.Xaml.Controls.Maps" (...)>
    <Grid>
        <Maps:MapControl x:Name="Map" />
        <StackPanel (...)>
            <Button
                Content="Go to a castle" (...)
                Click="BtnShowCastle_Click" />
            <Button
                Content="Go to an airport" (...)
                Click="BtnShowAirport_Click" />
        </StackPanel>
    </Grid>
</Page>
```

 Do not forget to add the `using` statement for the `Windows.UI.Xaml.Controls.Maps` namespace.

2. Override the `OnNavigatedTo` method in the `MainPage` class to configure the map shown on the page. First of all, the map is centered in the point 50.0406°N 21.9995°E (the `Center` property) and a zoom level is set to 15 (`ZoomLevel`). What

is more, a light color scheme is selected (ColorScheme), the map is not rotated (Heading), and landmarks (including business ones, LandmarksVisible and BusinessLandmarksVisible), pedestrian features (PedestrianFeaturesVisible), traffic flow (TrafficFlowVisible), and transit features (TransitFeaturesVisible) are visible. To do so, modify the MainPage.xaml.cs file, as shown in the following code snippet:

```
protected override void OnNavigatedTo(
    NavigationEventArgs e)
{
    BasicGeoposition center = new BasicGeoposition()
    {
        Latitude = 50.0406,
        Longitude = 21.9995
    };
    Map.Center = new Geopoint(center);
    Map.ZoomLevel = 15;
    Map.ColorScheme = MapColorScheme.Light;
    Map.Heading = 0;
    Map.BusinessLandmarksVisible = true;
    Map.LandmarksVisible = true;
    Map.PedestrianFeaturesVisible = true;
    Map.TrafficFlowVisible = true;
    Map.TransitFeaturesVisible = true;
}
```

Before sending the application to the Windows Store, you should not forget to specify a value of the MapServiceToken property. You will learn how to obtain a token in the *Obtaining a map token* recipe in Chapter 9, *Testing and Submission*.

3. Programmatically center the map (with an animation) in the location of Rzeszow Castle (50.0325°N 22.0007°E). To do so, call TrySetViewAsync in the BtnShowCastle_Click method in the MainPage.xaml.cs file, as shown in the following code snippet:

```
private async void BtnShowCastle_Click(
    object sender, RoutedEventArgs e)
{
    BasicGeoposition center = new BasicGeoposition()
    {
        Latitude = 50.0325,
        Longitude = 22.0007
    };
    await Map.TrySetViewAsync(new Geopoint(center));
```

```
    }
```

4. Programmatically show a region of the map with an airport located near
   Rzeszow. To do so, call `TrySetViewBoundsAsync` in the
   `BtnShowAirport_Click` method in the `MainPage.xaml.cs` file, as shown in
   the following part of code:

```
private async void BtnShowAirport_Click(
    object sender, RoutedEventArgs e)
{
    GeoboundingBox bounds = new GeoboundingBox(
        new BasicGeoposition()
        {
            Latitude = 50.1146,
            Longitude = 22.0015
        },
        new BasicGeoposition()
        {
            Latitude = 50.1092,
            Longitude = 22.0463
        });
    await Map.TrySetViewBoundsAsync(bounds, null,
        MapAnimationKind.Default);
}
```

How it works...

It is possible to show a map directly in your application by adding the `MapControl` control
from the `Windows.UI.Xaml.Controls.Maps` namespace. This control contains a set of
properties that can be set either in XAML or programmatically in the C# language, as you
can see in the example.

You can specify a center point of the map by setting the value of the `Center` property of
`MapControl`. First, create an instance of the `BasicGeoposition` class, set the values of its
`Latitude` and `Longitude` properties, and pass this instance as a parameter of the
`Geopoint` constructor. The relevant part of code is as follows:

```
BasicGeoposition center = new BasicGeoposition()
{
    Latitude = 50.0406,
    Longitude = 21.9995
};
Map.Center = new Geopoint(center);
```

Of course, the `Center` property is not the only one defined in `MapControl`. Among others, the following can be used to adjust the map:

- `ZoomLevel`: An integer value indicating the zoom level
- `ColorScheme`: A used color scheme, such as light
- `Heading`: A heading of the map

What is more, you can easily show or hide additional layers with information that could be useful for a user, such as the following:

- Landmarks (`LandmarksVisible` and `BusinessLandmarksVisible`)
- Features for pedestrians (`PedestrianFeaturesVisible`)
- Traffic flow (`TrafficFlowVisible`)
- Transit information (`TransitFeaturesVisible`)

After configuring a map, it is crucial to learn how to move the map to a given location. What is interesting is that moving the map is performed with an animation and provides a user with a really nice experience. To do so, you need to create the `Geopoint` instance representing a target location on the map. This instance should be passed to the `TrySetViewAsync` method, as follows:

```
BasicGeoposition center = new BasicGeoposition() { /* ... */ };
await Map.TrySetViewAsync(new Geopoint(center));
```

A bit more complex code is necessary to present a region of the map. In such a case, you need to create an instance of the `GeoboundingBox` class, passing two instances of the `BasicGeoposition` class, representing the north-west and south-east corners of the region. Then, the `GeoboundingBox` instance should be passed as the first parameter of the `TrySetViewBoundsAsync` method, as shown in the following code snippet:

```
GeoboundingBox bounds = new GeoboundingBox(
    new BasicGeoposition() { /* ... */ },
    new BasicGeoposition() { /* ... */ });
await Map.TrySetViewBoundsAsync(
    bounds, null, MapAnimationKind.Default);
```

After running the application and clicking on the buttons, you will see results similar to the following screenshot:

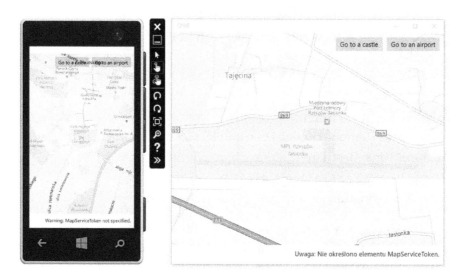

The first presents a map on a smartphone, centered in the location of Rzeszow Castle, thus prepared after clicking on the first button. The other shows a region of the airport located near Rzeszow.

You could see the red text at the bottom of the map. It informs you that the map service token has not been specified. As already mentioned, you will learn how to obtain such a token in the next chapter of this book.

See also

- The *Opening a map in an external application* recipe
- The *Drawing icons, polylines, and polygons on a map* recipe
- The *Adding a custom marker to a map* recipe
- The *Getting the coordinates of a clicked point on a map* recipe
- The *Launching GPS-based navigation* recipe
- The *Obtaining the current GPS location* recipe in `Chapter 7`, *Built-in Sensors*

Drawing icons, polylines, and polygons on a map

It is often necessary to present additional content on the map, such as icons, polylines, and even polygons. Thus, you can easily show some interesting points, indicate a route, as well as mark regions important for a user. In this recipe, you will learn how to perform such tasks using `MapControl`.

As an example, you will add three icons on the map, presenting Rzeszow Castle, Rzeszow Town Hall, and Farny Church. Apart from them, you will draw a polyline marking the 3rd May Street in Rzeszow. At the end, you will draw a polygon that indicates a border of Rzeszow Castle.

Getting ready

To step through this recipe, you need only the automatically generated project.

How to do it...

To prepare an example that adds icons, a polyline, and a polygon on the map, perform the following steps:

1. Add the `MapControl` control (presenting the map) to the page. To do so, modify the content of the `MainPage.xaml` file, as follows:

```
<Page (...)
    xmlns:Maps="using:Windows.UI.Xaml.Controls.Maps"  (...)>
    <Grid>
        <Maps:MapControl x:Name="Map" />
    </Grid>
</Page>
```

2. Override the `OnNavigatedTo` method in the `MainPage` class to center the map in the point 50.0406°N 21.9995°E (the `Center` property) with a zoom level set to 15 (`ZoomLevel`), and draw a polygon, icons, and a polyline using the `AddPolygon`, `AddIcons`, and `AddPolyline` methods (defined later). To do so, modify the code in the `MainPage.xaml.cs` file, as follows:

```
protected override void OnNavigatedTo(
    NavigationEventArgs e)
```

```
{
    BasicGeoposition center = new BasicGeoposition()
    {
        Latitude = 50.0406,
        Longitude = 21.9995
    };
    Map.Center = new Geopoint(center);
    Map.ZoomLevel = 15;
    AddPolygon();
    AddIcons();
    AddPolyline();
}
```

3. Add a polygon that presents the border of Rzeszow Castle, by specifying a list of four coordinates (the `Path` property, starting with 50.032739°N 22.000116°E and ending with 50.032846°N 22.001002°E) and using the `MapPolygon` class. The polygon should have the `WhiteSmoke` color (`FillColor`) and an orange dashed border (`StrokeColor` and `StrokeDashed`) with 3-pixel width (`StrokeThickness`). To do so, define the `AddPolygon` method in the `MainPage.xaml.cs` file, as follows:

```
private void AddPolygon()
{
    MapPolygon polygon = new MapPolygon()
    {
        Path = new Geopath(new List<BasicGeoposition>()
        {
            new BasicGeoposition() {
                Latitude = 50.032739, Longitude = 22.000116 },
            (...)
            new BasicGeoposition() {
                Latitude = 50.032846, Longitude = 22.001002 }
        }),
        FillColor = Colors.WhiteSmoke,
        StrokeColor = Colors.Orange,
        StrokeThickness = 3,
        StrokeDashed = true
    };
    Map.MapElements.Add(polygon);
}
```

4. Add icons to the map (using the built-in mechanism with the `MapIcon` class) in the location of Rzeszow Castle (50.0325°N 22.0007°E), Rzeszow Town Hall (50.0373°N 22.0039°E), and Farny Church (50.0378°N 22.0018°E). To do so, define the `AddIcons` method in the `MainPage.xaml.cs` file, as shown in the following code snippet:

```
private void AddIcons()
{
    MapIcon iconCastle = new MapIcon()
    {
        Title = "Rzeszow Castle",
        Location = new Geopoint(new BasicGeoposition()
            { Latitude = 50.0325, Longitude = 22.0007 }),
        CollisionBehaviorDesired =
            MapElementCollisionBehavior.RemainVisible,
        NormalizedAnchorPoint = new Point(0.5, 1.0)
    };
    MapIcon iconTownHall = new MapIcon() { (...) };
    MapIcon iconFarnyChurch = new MapIcon() { (...) };
    Map.MapElements.Add(iconCastle);
    Map.MapElements.Add(iconTownHall);
    Map.MapElements.Add(iconFarnyChurch);
}
```

5. Add a polyline that presents the 3rd May Street in Rzeszow by specifying a list of coordinates (the `Path` property, starting with 50.037612°N 22.001645°E and ending with 50.034408°N 22.001018°E) and using the `MapPolyline` class. The polyline should have its width set to 5 pixels (`StrokeThickness`) and its color set to blue (`StrokeColor`). To do so, define the `AddPolyline` method in the `MainPage.xaml.cs` file, as follows:

```
private void AddPolyline()
{
    MapPolyline line = new MapPolyline()
    {
        Path = new Geopath(new List<BasicGeoposition>()
        {
            new BasicGeoposition() {
                Latitude = 50.037612, Longitude = 22.001645 },
            (...)
            new BasicGeoposition() {
                Latitude = 50.034408, Longitude = 22.001018 }
        }),
        StrokeColor = Colors.RoyalBlue,
        StrokeThickness = 5
    };
    Map.MapElements.Add(line);
}
```

How it works...

You can place elements in specific locations on the map by adding them to the collection stored in the `MapElements` property of `MapControl`. However, which objects should be added? You will find an answer to this question in the explanation that follows.

First of all, let's take a look at the method responsible for adding an icon. Each is represented by the `MapIcon` instance, as shown in the following code snippet:

```
MapIcon icon = new MapIcon()
{
    Title = "Title of the point",
    Location = new Geopoint(new BasicGeoposition() { /* ... */ },
    CollisionBehaviorDesired =
        MapElementCollisionBehavior.RemainVisible,
    NormalizedAnchorPoint = new Point(0.5, 1.0)
};
Map.MapElements.Add(icon);
```

The `MapIcon` class contains a set of properties, such as the following:

- `Title`: A textual value shown next to the icon
- `Location`: A location on the map (latitude and longitude)
- `CollisionBehaviorDesired`: A value indicating whether the icon should disappear when it collides with another element or should remain visible
- `NormalizedAnchorPoint`: A point indicating an anchor placed on the map

The `NormalizedAnchorPoint` property requires some additional clarification. It specifies a point of the icon that should be located exactly in the given location on the map. It means that while moving and, more importantly, changing the zoom level, the given point will still be located in a proper location on the map. The anchor point is specified by two values, namely *x* and *y* coordinates normalized to [0, 1] range, as presented in the following screenshot:

The default map icon contains an indicator at the bottom, centered horizontally. For this reason, the normalized anchor point should be set to (0.5, 1.0).

Another object that can be placed on a map is a **polyline**. It is defined as a list of points connected by straight lines. Of course, you can set the proper color and width of the polyline, as shown in the example. The relevant part of code is as follows:

```
MapPolyline line = new MapPolyline()
{
    Path = new Geopath(new List<BasicGeoposition>()
    {
        new BasicGeoposition() {  /* ... */ }, (...)
        new BasicGeoposition() {  /* ... */ }
    }),
    StrokeColor = Colors.RoyalBlue,
    StrokeThickness = 5
};
Map.MapElements.Add(line);
```

The last element is a polygon with a given location on the map, a specified fill color, as well as a chosen stroke width, color, and a value indicating whether it should be dashed. The polygon is defined similarly as a polyline, as a list of BasicGeoposition instances. The suitable part of code is as follows:

```
MapPolygon polygon = new MapPolygon()
{
    Path = new Geopath(new List<BasicGeoposition>()
    {
        new BasicGeoposition() { /* ... */ },
        new BasicGeoposition() { /* ... */ }
    }),
    FillColor = Colors.WhiteSmoke,
    StrokeColor = Colors.Orange,
    StrokeThickness = 3,
    StrokeDashed = true
};
Map.MapElements.Add(polygon);
```

After running the application, you will see a result similar to the following screenshot, showing the project in smartphone and desktop-based versions:

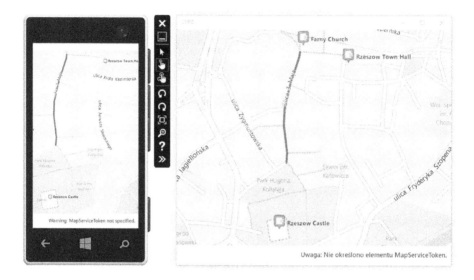

See also

- The *Opening a map in an external application* recipe
- The *Showing a map within a page* recipe
- The *Adding a custom marker to a map* recipe
- The *Getting the coordinates of a clicked point on a map* recipe
- The *Launching GPS-based navigation* recipe
- The *Obtaining the current GPS location* recipe in `Chapter 7`, *Built-in Sensors*

Adding a custom marker to a map

A default map icon, presented in the previous recipe, could not be suitable in all applications. For example, it could not match the design that is applied in the project. Thus, it should be replaced with another one, which is consistent with the overall visual identity. In this recipe, you will learn how to place a custom marker on the map.

As an example, you will prepare an application that obtains the current location of the user using the GPS receiver. Then it will center the map on this location and place a custom image representing the user.

Getting ready

To step through this recipe, you need only the automatically generated project.

How to do it...

To prepare an example that adds a custom marker on the map in the current location of the user, perform the following steps:

1. Enable the `Location` capability by double-clicking on the `Package.appxmanifest` file in the **Solution Explorer** window, choosing the **Capabilities** tab, and selecting the **Location** checkbox.

2. Add the `Marker.png` file to the `Assets` directory. The relevant `.png` file is available together with the code attached to this chapter.

3. Add the `MapControl` control (presenting the map) to the page. To do so, modify the content of the `MainPage.xaml` file, as follows:

```
<Page (...)
    xmlns:Maps="using:Windows.UI.Xaml.Controls.Maps"  (...)>
    <Grid>
        <Maps:MapControl x:Name="Map" />
    </Grid>
</Page>
```

4. Override the `OnNavigatedTo` method in the `MainPage` class to request access to location services and, if allowed, get the current GPS coordinates of the user, center the map, and place an image-based marker at that location. To do so, modify the code in the `MainPage.xaml.cs` file, as follows:

```
protected override async void OnNavigatedTo(
    NavigationEventArgs e)
{
    GeolocationAccessStatus status =
        await Geolocator.RequestAccessAsync();
    if (status == GeolocationAccessStatus.Allowed)
    {
        Geolocator geolocator = new Geolocator();
```

```
Geoposition position =
    await geolocator.GetGeopositionAsync();
Map.Center = position.Coordinate.Point;
Map.ZoomLevel = 15;

Image marker = new Image();
marker.Source = new BitmapImage(
    new Uri("ms-appx:///Assets/Marker.png",
        UriKind.Absolute));
marker.Height = 64;
Map.Children.Add(marker);
MapControl.SetLocation(marker,
    position.Coordinate.Point);
MapControl.SetNormalizedAnchorPoint(marker,
    new Point(0.5, 1.0));
    }
}
```

How it works...

In this recipe, a few tasks are combined together to create a real-world scenario:

- Obtaining the current GPS coordinates of a user
- Centering the map in the current location and setting the right zoom level
- Adding the custom marker in the current location

The first task is performed using the `Geolocator` class and its `GetGeopositionAsync` method. After calling it, you will wait for obtaining the one-time location. The relevant part of code is shown in the following code snippet:

```
Geolocator geolocator = new Geolocator();
Geoposition position = await geolocator.GetGeopositionAsync();
```

The second task is accomplished by setting values of `Center` and `ZoomLevel` properties of `MapControl`, as already explained. The last task, regarding the addition of a custom marker, is significantly more interesting. Here, you create a new image in a programmatic way, set its source to the `Marker.png` file from the `Assets` directory, and specify its height to a desired value. At the end, you set a location on the map and choose a normalized anchor point. The code is as follows:

```
Image marker = new Image();
marker.Source = new BitmapImage(
    new Uri("ms-appx:///Assets/Marker.png", UriKind.Absolute));
marker.Height = 64;
```

```
Map.Children.Add(marker);
MapControl.SetLocation(marker, position.Coordinate.Point);
MapControl.SetNormalizedAnchorPoint(marker, new Point(0.5, 1.0));
```

After running the application, it will wait until the current GPS location is obtained. Then the map will be centered on this place and an image-based marker will be added, as shown in the following screenshot:

See also

- The *Opening a map in an external application* recipe
- The *Showing a map within a page* recipe
- The *Drawing icons, polylines, and polygons on a map* recipe
- The *Getting the coordinates of a clicked point on a map* recipe
- The *Launching GPS-based navigation* recipe
- The *Obtaining the current GPS location* recipe in Chapter 7, *Built-in Sensors*

Getting the coordinates of a clicked point on a map

The MapControl control, available for UWP applications, supports various ways of user interaction. For example, you can handle an event that is fired when the user presses the map. Of course, you can get the latitude and longitude of this location. In this recipe, you will learn how to perform this task.

As an example, you will create an application that presents the map. After clicking on it, an ellipse should be added in the clicked point. Of course, such ellipses should be shown correctly regardless of the location and the zoom level of the map.

Getting ready

To step through this recipe, you need only the automatically generated project.

How to do it...

To prepare an example that adds an ellipse on the map in the location pressed by a user, perform the following steps:

1. Add the MapControl control (presenting the map) to the page and handle the event of tapping the map (MapTapped). To do so, modify the content of the MainPage.xaml file, as shown in the following part of code:

```
<Page (...)
    xmlns:Maps="using:Windows.UI.Xaml.Controls.Maps"  (...)>
    <Grid>
        <Maps:MapControl
            x:Name="Map"
            MapTapped="Map_MapTapped" />
    </Grid>
</Page>
```

2. Place an ellipse in the location tapped by the user by adjusting the code of the Map_MapTapped method in the MainPage.xaml.cs file, as follows:

```
private void Map_MapTapped(
    MapControl sender, MapInputEventArgs args)
{
    Geopoint point = args.Location;
```

```
Ellipse ellipse = new Ellipse()
{
    Height = 10,
    Width = 10,
    Fill = new SolidColorBrush(Colors.Red)
};
Map.Children.Add(ellipse);
MapControl.SetLocation(ellipse, point);
MapControl.SetNormalizedAnchorPoint(ellipse,
    new Point(0.5, 0.5));
}
```

How it works...

The most interesting part of code is shown in the `Map_MapTapped` method. It is called when a user clicks on the map. First of all, you read the coordinates of the clicked point, which are stored in the `Location` property of `MapInputEventArgs`. In the following part of code, you create a new instance of the `Ellipse` class, specify its fill color, add to the collection of map elements, and set a location on the map and a normalized anchor point.
These operations are similar to the ones described in the previous recipe.

After running the application and clicking on various locations on the map, you can get results similar to those presented in the following screenshot:

See also

- The *Opening a map in an external application* recipe
- The *Showing a map within a page* recipe
- The *Drawing icons, polylines, and polygons on a map* recipe
- The *Adding a custom marker to a map* recipe
- The *Launching GPS-based navigation* recipe
- The *Obtaining the current GPS location* recipe in `Chapter 7`, *Built-in Sensors*

Launching GPS-based navigation

Do you know that you can launch the built-in navigation directly from your application to allow a user to be navigated to the target? You will learn how to do it in this recipe.

As an example, you will create a page with two text boxes (for the latitude and longitude of the destination) and a button. After clicking on the button, the values from the textboxes will be read and used for launching navigation to the target point.

Getting ready

To step through this recipe, you need only the automatically generated project.

How to do it...

To prepare an example that launches the GPS-based navigation to the given coordinates, perform the following steps:

1. Add two text boxes (where a user can type the latitude and longitude of the destination) and a button (starting navigation) to the page by modifying the content of the `MainPage.xaml` file, as follows:

```
<Page (...)>
    <StackPanel (...)>
        <TextBox
            x:Name="TxtLatitude" (...)
            Header="Destination latitude" (...) />
        <TextBox
            x:Name="TxtLongitude" (...)
```

```
        Header="Destination longitude" (...) />
    <Button
        Content="Start navigation to the destination"
        (...) Click="BtnNavigate_Click" />
</StackPanel>
</Page>
```

2. Start the built-in navigation mechanism after clicking on the button. To do so, define the `BtnNavigate_Click` method in the `MainPage.xaml.cs` file, as shown in the following code snippet:

```
private async void BtnNavigate_Click(
    object sender, RoutedEventArgs e)
{

    float latitude;
    float longitude;
    string latitudeString =
        TxtLatitude.Text.Replace(",", ".");
    string longitudeString =
        TxtLongitude.Text.Replace(",", ".");
    if (float.TryParse(latitudeString, NumberStyles.Float,
        new NumberFormatInfo(), out latitude)
        && float.TryParse(longitudeString,
        NumberStyles.Float, new NumberFormatInfo(),
        out longitude))
    {
        string uri = string.Format(
            "ms-drive-to:?destination.latitude={0}
            &destination.longitude={1}&destination.name={2}",
            latitude.ToString(new NumberFormatInfo()),
            longitude.ToString(new NumberFormatInfo()),
            "Destination for navigation");
        await Launcher.LaunchUriAsync(new Uri(uri));
    }
}
```

How it works...

Launching navigation to a given location is possible using the `LaunchUriAsync` method, similarly to opening a website or launching a Skype call. In this case, you need to provide the string in the following format:

```
ms-drive-to:?destination.latitude=[latitude]
    &destination.longitude=[longitude]&destination.name=[name]
```

Of course, you should specify the latitude and longitude of the destination (in the [latitude] and [longitude] placeholders) and its name (as [name]).

A short explanation is necessary for the code that prepares the Uri string. First of all, you get values from the textboxes and replace a comma with a dot. Such a part of code is used to support languages (for example, Polish), in which a comma is used in the textual representation of floating point values. In the following part, you check (using the TryParse method) whether it is possible to parse a string representing a floating point value to float. Only in such a case, the navigation is started.

After running the application, providing the correct latitude and longitude of the destination, and clicking on the button, the external application is launched and the navigation is started, as shown in the following screenshot:

See also

- The *Opening a map in an external application* recipe
- The *Showing a map within a page* recipe
- The *Drawing icons, polylines, and polygons on a map* recipe
- The *Adding a custom marker to a map* recipe
- The *Getting the coordinates of a clicked point on a map* recipe
- The *Obtaining the current GPS location* recipe in Chapter 7, *Built-in Sensors*

Calling API methods

Many projects are prepared as distributed systems with not only mobile applications. Very often, a set of web applications is used as well, for example, to enter data by users. Of course, such data also needs to be shown in mobile applications along with the possibility of updating them just after modification in the web-based part. What is more, some external data, for example, obtained from the sensors of mobile devices, may need to be entered into the system. These are only a few reasons why APIs are developed as a way of exchanging data between various parts of the system. In this chapter, you will learn how to send GET and POST-based requests to the API and obtain JSON-encoded results.

As an example, you will create the page that contains two buttons and a text block for presenting the results. After clicking on the first button, the GET request will be sent to the API. As a result, the JSON-encoded data of users will be returned. Then, the number of users, together with an average age, will be presented in the user interface. When the user presses the second button, the POST-based API method will be called along with passing JSON-encoded parameters. This method will return JSON-encoded search results, taking into account the parameters.

Getting ready

To step through this recipe, you need only the automatically generated project.

How to do it...

To prepare an example that sends requests to the API, as well as reads JSON-formatted responses, perform the following steps:

1. Install the `Newtonsoft.Json` library using the NuGet Package Manager.
2. Add two buttons (to send GET and POST requests), as well as the `TextBlock` control (where results will be shown) to the page by modifying the `MainPage.xaml` file, as shown in the following part of code:

```
<Page (...)>
    <StackPanel (...)>
        <Button
            Content="Call the GET-based API method" (...)
            Click="BtnGET_Click" />
        <Button
            Content="Call the POST-based API method" (...)
            Click="BtnPOST_Click" />
```

```
    <TextBlock x:Name="TxtResult" (...) />
  </StackPanel>
</Page>
```

3. Define the `SearchUser` class representing the data of a single user returned from the API. To do so, adjust the code of the class in the `SearchUser.cs` file, as shown in the following code snippet:

```
public class SearchUser
{
    [JsonProperty("login")]
    public string Login { get; set; }

    [JsonProperty("age")]
    public int Age { get; set; }
}
```

4. Define the `SearchResponse` class representing the data of the API response. To do so, adjust the code of the class in the `SearchResponse.cs` file, as shown in the following part of code:

```
public class SearchResponse
{
    [JsonProperty("users")]
    public List<SearchUser> Users { get; set; }
}
```

5. Define the `SearchRequestParameters` class representing the data of parameters passed to the POST-based API method. To do so, adjust the code of the class in the `SearchRequestParameters.cs` file, as follows:

```
public class SearchRequestParameters
{
    [JsonProperty("login")]
    public string Login { get; set; }

    [JsonProperty("min_age")]
    public int MinimumAge { get; set; }

    [JsonProperty("max_age")]
    public int MaximumAge { get; set; }
}
```

6. Send a GET request, read a response, and present a calculated result. To do so, define the `BtnGET_Click` method in the `MainPage.xaml.cs` file, as shown in the following code snippet:

```
private async void BtnGET_Click(
    object sender, RoutedEventArgs e)
{
    try
    {
        HttpClient client = new HttpClient();
        HttpResponseMessage responseMessage =
            await client.GetAsync(
                new Uri("http://jamro.biz/book/users.php"));
        string responseJson = await
            responseMessage.Content.ReadAsStringAsync();
        SearchResponse response =
            JsonConvert.DeserializeObject<SearchResponse>(
                responseJson);
        TxtResult.Text = string.Format(
            "{0} user(s) found with {1:F2}
             as an average age.",
            response.Users.Count,
            response.Users.Average(u => u.Age));
    }
    catch (HttpRequestException)
    {
        TxtResult.Text = "Cannot get the results.";
    }
    catch (JsonReaderException)
    {
        TxtResult.Text = "Cannot parse the response.";
    }
}
```

 Do not forget to add the necessary `using` statement for the `System.Linq` namespace.

7. Send a POST request by passing JSON-encoded parameters, read the response, and present the calculated result. To do so, define the `BtnPOST_Click` method in the `MainPage.xaml.cs` file, as follows:

```
private async void BtnPOST_Click(
    object sender, RoutedEventArgs e)
{
    try
    {
        SearchRequestParameters parameters =
            new SearchRequestParameters()
            {
```

```
                    Login = "mar",
                    MinimumAge = 25,
                    MaximumAge = 30
                };
                string parametersJson =
                    JsonConvert.SerializeObject(parameters);
                StringContent stringContent =
                    new StringContent(parametersJson,
                        Encoding.UTF8, "application/json");
                HttpClient client = new HttpClient();
                HttpResponseMessage responseMessage =
                    await client.PostAsync(
                        new Uri("http://jamro.biz/book/users.php"),
                        stringContent);
                string responseJson = await
                    responseMessage.Content.ReadAsStringAsync();
                SearchResponse response =
                    JsonConvert.DeserializeObject<SearchResponse>(
                        responseJson);
                TxtResult.Text = string.Format(
                    "{0} user(s) found with {1:F2}
                     as an average age.",
                    response.Users.Count,
                    response.Users.Average(u => u.Age));
            }
            catch (HttpRequestException)
            {
                TxtResult.Text = "Cannot get the results.";
            }
            catch (JsonReaderException)
            {
                TxtResult.Text = "Cannot parse the response.";
            }
        }
```

How it works...

Sending requests to an API is possible using the `HttpClient` class. It contains a set of methods, including `GetAsync` and `PostAsync`, that allow sending a request with a proper type, namely GET and POST. The necessary code is really short and self-explanatory, but a comprehensive explanation is added here to make it even easier to understand.

First of all, let's take a look at the calling of a GET-based method. In such a case, you just provide an address, such as `http://jamro.biz/book/users.php`.

Of course, you can provide additional parameters by the query string, such as in the following example:
`http://jamro.biz/book/users.php?year=2016`

By calling the awaitable `GetAsync` method, you get the `HttpResponseMessage` instance representing a response obtained from the server. The relevant code snippet is as follows:

```
HttpClient client = new HttpClient();
HttpResponseMessage responseMessage =
    await client.GetAsync(
        new Uri("http://jamro.biz/book/users.php"));
```

You can easily read the content of the response as a string value by calling the `ReadAsStringAsync` method on the `Content` property, as follows:

```
string responseJson =
    await responseMessage.Content.ReadAsStringAsync();
```

Depending on an API configuration, data can be returned in various ways, such as using XML, JSON, or even custom format. In the current example, you assume that a JSON-encoded response is returned. The sample result with the data of four users is presented as follows:

```
{
  "users": [
    {
      "login": "marcin",
      "age": 27
    },
    {
      "login": "david",
      "age": 35
    },
    {
      "login": "mary155",
      "age": 24
    },
    {
      "login": "claudia9",
      "age": 20
    }
  ]
}
```

The next part of the example uses data already obtained from the API. In the beginning, you deserialize the JSON-encoded response and store it as the `SearchResponse` instance. The last instruction presents the total number of users and an average age.

Sending a POST request and passing additional data is a bit more complex. In such a case, you need to call the `PostAsync` method by passing two parameters, namely an address and the `StringContent` instance representing additional data for the request. The relevant code snippet is as follows:

```
HttpResponseMessage responseMessage =
    await client.PostAsync(
        new Uri("http://jamro.biz/book/users.php"),
        stringContent);
```

First, you need to prepare such additional data. In the beginning, you create a new instance of the `SearchRequestParameters` class, which represents such data, set values of its properties, serialize it, and use in the constructor of `StringContent`, as follows:

```
SearchRequestParameters parameters = new SearchRequestParameters()
{
    Login = "mar",
    MinimumAge = 25,
    MaximumAge = 30
};
string parametersJson = JsonConvert.SerializeObject(parameters);
StringContent stringContent = new StringContent(
    parametersJson, Encoding.UTF8, "application/json");
```

The sample JSON-encoded string representing parameters is as follows:

```
{
    "login": "mar",
    "min_age": 25,
    "max_age": 30
}
```

The remaining part of code is similar to the one explained earlier for the GET request.

See also

- The *Presenting a website within a page* recipe
- The *Downloading a file from the Internet* recipe

Downloading a file from the Internet

When your application needs to present content in the offline mode, it is necessary to download data from the Internet and store them on the device. Of course, such content could consist of text, images, or even movies. However, how can you download images and movies, as well as save them in a device? You will learn it in this recipe.

As an example, you will create a page with the **Download a photo** button. After clicking on it, you will download a file from a given address and save locally. Of course, you will also handle a scenario when a user does not have an Internet connection or when a remote file does not exist.

Getting ready

To step through this recipe, you need only the automatically generated project.

How to do it...

To prepare an example that downloads a file from the Internet and saves it locally, perform the following steps:

1. Add a button to the page by modifying the content of the `MainPage.xaml` file, as follows:

```
<Page (...)>
    <Grid (...)>
        <Button
            Content="Download a photo" (...)
            Click="BtnDownloadPhoto_Click" />
    </Grid>
</Page>
```

2. Programmatically download a file from the Internet and save it in the device. To do so, define the `BtnDownloadPhoto_Click` method in the `MainPage.xaml.cs` file, as shown in the following code snippet:

```
private async void BtnDownloadPhoto_Click(
    object sender, RoutedEventArgs e)
{
    string url = "http://jamro.biz/img/researcher-2.jpg";
    try
    {
```

```
HttpClient httpClient = new HttpClient();
StorageFile file =
    await ApplicationData.Current.LocalFolder.
        CreateFileAsync("Photo.jpg",
            CreationCollisionOption.ReplaceExisting);
using (Stream fileStream =
    await file.OpenStreamForWriteAsync())
{
    using (Stream urlStream =
        await httpClient.GetStreamAsync(url))
    {
        await urlStream.CopyToAsync(fileStream);
    }
}
}
catch (Exception exception)
{
    Debug.WriteLine("Cannot download the file {0} -
        exception: {1}", url, exception);
}
}
```

Do not forget to add the necessary `using` statement for the `System.Net.Http` namespace.

How it works...

The code necessary to download a file from the Internet and save it in the device is not very complicated. For this purpose, you use two streams, represented by the following `Stream` instances:

- A readable stream of a downloaded file (`urlStream` in the preceding example)
- A writeable stream of a file where you should save the result (`fileStream`)

The most important task is to copy the readable stream (representing the downloaded file) to the writeable one (of the target file). You can achieve this goal by calling the `CopyToAsync` method as follows:

```
using (Stream fileStream = await file.OpenStreamForWriteAsync())
{
    using (Stream urlStream =
        await httpClient.GetStreamAsync(url))
    {
        await urlStream.CopyToAsync(fileStream);
    }
}
```

When it is impossible to download a file, the suitable information is presented in the **Output** window in the IDE. You can achieve this goal using the `WriteLine` method of the `Debug` class.

See also

- The *Presenting a website within a page* recipe
- The *Calling API methods* recipe

9
Testing and Submission

In this chapter, the following recipes will be covered:

- Creating a unit test
- Running a set of tests
- Adding a project to the Windows Dev Center
- Associating an application with the store
- Adjusting the manifest file
- Obtaining a map token
- Receiving push notifications
- Preparing files for submission
- Submitting the application
- Updating the application
- Generating promotional codes
- Browsing reviews and ratings
- Analyzing acquisitions

Introduction

In the previous eight chapters, you learned a lot about the development of
UWP applications, starting with creating a new project, adding pages, navigating between
them, as well as running the application either with or without debugging. You also learned
how to add controls to pages using the XAML language, apply styles, and localize the
application. Then, the subject of using the MVVM design pattern, view models and binding,
and storing data in files and a database have been introduced. You have already learned
how to add animations, graphics, and multimedia to your application, as well as obtain
data from various built-in sensors.

In the previous chapter, you learned how to support Internet-based scenarios, such as composing e-mail messages, opening websites, showing maps, or launching GPS-based navigation. So what's next? It is high time that we prepare an application for submission to the Windows Store and make it available to people all over the world!

In the current chapter, you will start with applying unit tests to your application. Thus, you will be able to introduce automatic testing that could significantly increase software quality and make finding bugs much simpler and faster. Also, the provided information could be used while developing applications according to the **Test-Driven Development (TDD)** paradigm.

When your solution is properly tested, you can proceed to the process of configuring and submitting the project to the Windows Store. Thus, in this chapter, you will also learn how to create a project in the Windows Dev Center available via a web browser. Using this tool, you can easily manage all your Windows Store-based applications. In the next step, you will associate the developed project in the IDE with the application specified in the Windows Dev Center.

In the following set of recipes, you will get to know how to adjust the manifest file with various pieces of information about the application as well as what kind of graphics you should prepare.

If you want to use maps or push notifications in an application, you will learn how to obtain the necessary credentials. They include a map token for handling maps and an application secret and a package SID for supporting push notifications. Such values are available in external web applications, as you will see in this chapter.

Then, you will learn how to prepare a `.appxupload` file and submit it to the Windows Store to make the application available to users from all over the world. Of course, you will also get to know how to update the already submitted application after you introduce some changes.

What is more, some additional features regarding the promotion and analytics of your newly published application will be taken into account. You will see how to generate promotional code to grant free access to a paid application or organize beta-testing of the project with limited availability in the store. At the end, you will learn how to browse the reviews and ratings of your application as well as how to analyze its acquisitions.

Creating a unit test

While developing applications, you might make various mistakes in the implementation that could lead to incorrect software operations, such as showing improper data, navigating to a different screen than planned, or even crashing. Of course, you should try to limit such situations, but how can you find such problems and fix them before deployment? The natural answer is *by testing*, but what do you mean by *testing*?

Will you just launch the application in an emulator or a real device and use it as a potential user? Of course, such a testing process is really useful and important. However, what will you do after you make the changes in the project? Will you introduce such testing again and again? It seems to be very time-consuming and not so interesting, doesn't it?

In this chapter, you will get to know another approach and learn how to create a unit test to introduce automatic testing for your application.

Getting ready

To step through this recipe, you need a project that could be tested. As an example, an application for calculating the average fuel consumption is taken into account. It allows you to enter multiple amounts of data consisting of used liters of fuel and completed distance in kilometers. The application should present all of the typed data and the calculated average fuel consumption per 100 kilometers. It should also allow you to remove a particular entry. An example design of this, both on a smartphone and a desktop, is shown in the following screenshot:

The application contains only one page, namely `MainPage`. The `MainViewModel` instance is used as a data context, as specified in the `MainPage.xaml.cs` file from the `Views` directory. Some parts of the `MainPage.xaml.cs` file are as follows:

```
public sealed partial class MainPage : Page
{
    private MainViewModel _vm = null;
    public MainPage() { (...) }

    private void BtnDelete_Click(object sender, RoutedEventArgs e)
    {
        Button button = (Button)sender;
        Consumption consumption = (Consumption)button.DataContext;
        _vm.DeleteConsumption(consumption);
    }
}
```

 You can find the entire code of the example in the files attached to this chapter.

The most important parts of the `MainPage.xaml` file are as follows:

```
<Page (...)>
    <Page.Resources> (...) </Page.Resources>
    <Grid> (...)
        <Grid (...)> (...)
            <TextBox (...)
                Text="{Binding Fuel, Mode=TwoWay}" /> (...)
            <TextBox (...)
                Text="{Binding Distance, Mode=TwoWay}" /> (...)
            <Button (...)
                Command="{Binding CmdAdd}"
                Content="+" />
        </Grid>
        <TextBlock (...)>
            <Run Text="The average fuel consumption is" />
            <Run Text="{Binding Calculator.Average}" (...) />
            <Run Text="liters per 100 km" />
        </TextBlock> (...)
        <ItemsControl (...)
            ItemsSource="{Binding Calculator.Consumptions}"
            Visibility="{Binding Calculator.Consumptions.Count,
                Converter={StaticResource IntToVisibility}}"> (...)
            <ItemsControl.ItemTemplate>
                <DataTemplate>
```

```
<Border (...)>
    <Grid> (...)
        <TextBlock (...)>
            <Run Text="{Binding Fuel}" />
            <Run Text="l for" />
            <Run Text="{Binding Distance}" />
            <Run Text="km" />
        </TextBlock>
        <Button (...)
            Click="BtnDelete_Click"
            Content="x" />
    </Grid>
</Border>
                    </DataTemplate>
                </ItemsControl.ItemTemplate>
            </ItemsControl> (...)
        </Grid>
    </Page>
```

The code of the `MainViewModel` class is as follows:

```
[ImplementPropertyChanged]
public class MainViewModel
{
    public float Distance { get; set; } = 0.0f;
    public float Fuel { get; set; } = 0.0f;
    public ConsumptionCalculator Calculator { get; set; }
    public ICommand CmdAdd { get; set; }

    public MainViewModel()
    {
        Calculator = new ConsumptionCalculator();
        CmdAdd = new RelayCommand(
            () => Calculator.Add(Distance, Fuel));
    }

    public void DeleteConsumption(Consumption consumption)
    {
        Calculator.Delete(consumption);
    }
}
```

The `Distance` and `Fuel` properties are bound to the `Text` properties of the textboxes with the data of a new entry, regarding used fuel and completed distance. Another property, namely `Calculator`, is an instance of the `ConsumptionCalculator` class. It contains the business logic regarding calculating the average fuel consumption. You will learn how to test this class in the following part of the recipe.

The code of the `ConsumptionCalculator` class is shown as follows:

```
[ImplementPropertyChanged]
public class ConsumptionCalculator
{
    public ObservableCollection<Consumption> Consumptions
        { get; private set; }
    public float Average { get; private set; }

    public ConsumptionCalculator()
    {
        Consumptions = new ObservableCollection<Consumption>();
    }

    public void Add(float distance, float fuel)
    {
        if (distance > 0 && fuel > 0)
        {
            Consumption consumption = new Consumption()
            {
                Distance = distance,
                Fuel = fuel
            };
            Consumptions.Add(consumption);
            CalculateAverage();
        }
    }

    public void Delete(Consumption consumption)
    {
        Consumptions.Remove(consumption);
        CalculateAverage();
    }

    public void CalculateAverage()
    {
        float distance = Consumptions.Sum(c => c.Distance);
        float fuel = Consumptions.Sum(c => c.Fuel);
        float average = 0.0f;
        if (distance > 0.0f)
        {
            average = (fuel * 100) / distance;
        }
        Average = (float)Math.Round(average, 2);
    }
}
```

The class contains two properties, an observable collection of entries (`Consumptions`) and calculated average fuel consumption per 100 kilometers (`Average`). What is more, the class allows you to add a new entry (`Add`), delete the existing one (`Delete`), and calculate the average value (`CalculateAverage`). It is worth mentioning that the data of a single entry, regarding used fuel and completed distance, is represented by an instance of the `Consumption` class, and the code for this is as follows:

```
[ImplementPropertyChanged]
public class Consumption
{
    public float Distance { get; set; }
    public float Fuel { get; set; }
}
```

When the project is prepared, you can proceed to the following part of this recipe.

How to do it...

To prepare a set of tests for the exemplary application, perform the following steps:

1. Add a unit test application to the solution. To do so, navigate to **Add** | **New Project...** from the context menu of the solution node in the **Solution Explorer** window. Then, go to **Installed** | **Visual C#** | **Windows** | **Universal** in the tree on the left-hand side and choose the **Unit Test App (Universal Windows)** option in the central part of the window. Also, specify a name for the project (such as `CH09.Tests`), as shown in the following screenshot:

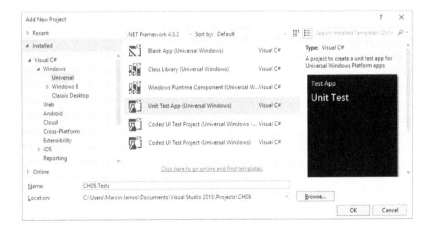

2. Press **OK**. If the additional window with a possibility of choosing the target and minimum supported platform version appears, choose the proper values and click on **OK**. The project will be created automatically.

3. Add a reference to the project that will be tested (CH09 in the example) to the unit test application (CH09.Tests). To do so, choose **Add Reference...** from the context menu of the **References** node of the CH09.Tests group in the **Solution Explorer** window. Then, go to **Projects | Solution** in the tree on the left-hand side and select the main project (such as CH09), as shown in the following screenshot. At the end, press **OK**.

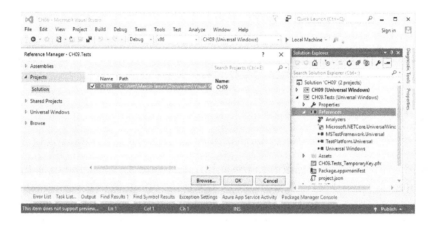

4. Create the first test that verifies there are no entries just after you create an instance of the ConsumptionCalculator class. To do so, use the already added UnitTest.cs file but rename it to ConsumptionCalculatorTest.cs and modify its content as follows:

```
[TestClass]
public class ConsumptionCalculatorTest
{
    [TestMethod]
    public void CreateInstance_ShouldHaveNoItems()
    {
        ConsumptionCalculator calculator =
            new ConsumptionCalculator();
        Assert.AreEqual(0, calculator.Consumptions.Count);
    }
}
```

How it works...

First of all, let's take a look at the exemplary test specified in the
ConsumptionCalculatorTest class. Its code is as follows:

```
[TestClass]
public class ConsumptionCalculatorTest
{
    [TestMethod]
    public void CreateInstance_ShouldHaveNoItems()
    {
        ConsumptionCalculator calculator =
            new ConsumptionCalculator();
        Assert.AreEqual(0, calculator.Consumptions.Count);
    }
}
```

As you could see, the class with test cases is associated with the TestClass attribute.
Similarly, each method that represents a single test case is associated with TestMethod.

> You should not forget about using TestClass and TestMethod attributes
> while adding new test cases. Of course, more than one test case can be
> defined in a single file. You can also use many classes with various groups
> of tests.

It is a good idea to prepare simple test cases with one clear goal that is visible in the name of
the method representing the test case. As an example, the first test ensures that there are no
entries (ShouldHaveNoItems) just after you create a new instance of the
ConsumptionCalculator class (CreateInstance).

Now you know how to name methods that represent test cases, but how can you check
whether a part of the system will operate as expected? To do so, you can use the Assert
class and a set of methods defined within it. Let's take a look at some of them.

In the example, you could see the AreEqual method. It checks whether its two parameters
(namely expected and actual values) are equal, that is, the number of items in the collection
(the Consumption property) is equal to 0. If not, the test fails. Otherwise, the test is
continued until the next assertion or the end.

What is important is that the AreEqual method exists in various versions that differ with
the number and types of parameters. For instance, there is a version dedicated to string
values with an additional parameter indicating whether a string case should be ignored
(that is, marcin will be equal to MaRcIn), as follows:

```
public static void AreEqual(
```

```
        string expected, string actual, bool ignoreCase);
```

Among other variants, you will see the version dedicated to `double` values that takes into account a delta value for accepting a bit smaller or bigger value than expected, as shown here:

```
public static void AreEqual(
    double expected, double actual, double delta);
```

Some versions of the `AreEqual` method make it possible to pass an additional message, which is presented when the assertion is not passed. Such messages could be useful while finding the source of the problem when a test fails.

Of course, the `AreEqual` method is not the only one that can be useful for verifying whether the application will operate as expected. Among others, the `AreNotEqual` method exists, which operates in opposition to `AreEqual`, that is, it checks whether the values given as parameters are not equal. If they are equal, the test fails. Some versions of this method are presented as follows:

```
public static void AreNotEqual(
    object notExpected, object actual);
public static void AreNotEqual(
    float notExpected, float actual, float delta);
public static void AreNotEqual(string notExpected, string actual,
    bool ignoreCase, CultureInfo culture);
```

Other interesting methods are `IsTrue` and `IsFalse`. They check whether the condition is equal to `true` or `false`, respectively. The related part of the code is as follows:

```
public static void IsTrue(bool condition);
public static void IsFalse(bool condition);
```

If you want to check whether the value is equal to `null` or not, you can use either the `IsTrue` or `IsFalse` method. However, this task can be performed even in a simpler way using `IsNull` or `IsNotNull` methods. The first method checks whether the given parameter is equal to `null`, while the other checks whether it is not equal to `null`. If these conditions are not satisfied, the test fails. The `IsNull` and `IsNotNull` methods are shown as follows:

```
public static void IsNull(object value);
public static void IsNotNull(object value);
```

Among other methods that represent assertions, it is worth mentioning
`IsInstanceOfType` and `IsNotInstanceOfType`. The first checks whether the given
object (the first parameter) is an instance of the given type (the second parameter). The
other works in the opposite way. These methods are presented as follows:

```
public static void IsInstanceOfType(
    object value, Type expectedType);
public static void IsNotInstanceOfType(
    object value, Type wrongType);
```

What is more, the `Assert` class can be used to check whether a given exception is thrown
while executing an action. When the exception is not thrown, the test fails. To do so, you
can use the following `ThrowsException` method:

```
public static T ThrowsException<T>(Action action)
    where T : Exception;
```

At the end, let's take a look at the `Fail` and `Inconclusive` methods:

```
public static void Fail();
public static void Inconclusive();
```

The first just informs that the test has failed with or without an additional message. The
other indicates that the result is inconclusive, that is, you do not have sufficient information
to decide whether the test has passed or failed. You can use this method just after you
define the test method but before you add any test code.

See also

- The *Running a set of tests* recipe
- The *Running the application, Breakpoints-based debugging, Step-by-step debugging,
  Executing code while debugging,* and *Logging information while debugging* recipes in
  Chapter 1, *Getting Started*
- The *Creating the view model for a page* recipe in Chapter 3, *MVVM and Data Binding*

Running a set of tests

In the previous recipe, you learned how to define the first unit test. However, only one test is not enough to thoroughly test the solution. For this reason, you should specify a set of them as well as run them frequently to ensure that newly introduced changes do not cause any regression, that is, new features do not cause problems with the existing modules. In this recipe, you will learn how to add a few other test cases as well as how to run them to check whether all of them have passed.

Getting ready

To step through this recipe, you need the project from the previous recipe.

How to do it...

To learn how to run a set of tests, perform the following steps:

1. Create a set of tests to thoroughly test the `ConsumptionCalculator` class. As the second test, let's check whether after adding the correct data, the number of consumption entries is equal to one. The suitable test case is presented in the following code snippet:

```
[TestMethod]
public void AddCorrectData_ShouldBeAdded()
{
    ConsumptionCalculator calculator =
        new ConsumptionCalculator();
    calculator.Add(120.0f, 8.9f);
    Assert.AreEqual(1, calculator.Consumptions.Count);
}
```

2. Add other tests, for instance, to check the calculation of an average value for a few added entries as well as to ensure that removing an already added item would work as expected. To keep things simple, the code regarding the set of other tests is presented in the following part of this recipe.

3. Run the tests by navigating to **Test** | **Run** | **All Tests** from the main menu. When the tests are completed, you will see the **Test Explorer** window with the test results as well as information about their status and the amount of time they had taken, as shown in the following screenshot:

You can launch all the tests in the solution by pressing *Ctrl + R + A*.

How it works...

As already mentioned, the first test, presented in the previous recipe, is not enough to thoroughly test the `ConsumptionCalculator` class. For this reason, in this recipe, you could see which additional tests can be defined to check it more accurately.

Your tests should check whether the application operates correctly both in correct and incorrect circumstances. It means that you should test not only the expected operation while passing correct values of parameters, but also handle non-planned scenarios with incorrect values or improper control by a user.

One of the important tests checks whether it is impossible to add incorrect data, such as a negative distance or a negative amount of consumed fuel. As an example, let's see a test case regarding adding a negative distance. In such a case, a new entry should not be added to the collection, as follows:

```
[TestMethod]
public void AddNegativeDistance_ShouldBeRejected()
{
    ConsumptionCalculator calculator =
        new ConsumptionCalculator();
```

```
    calculator.Add(-5.2f, 12.1f);
    Assert.AreEqual(0, calculator.Consumptions.Count);
}
```

It is worth mentioning that the preceding test can be divided into three parts, forming the AAA structure (**Arrange-Act-Assert**):

- Preparing the system for testing (*Arrange*) by creating an instance of the class
- Performing the tested operation (*Act*) by adding an entry with incorrect data
- Checking whether the system operates as expected (*Assert*) by ensuring that the number of entered data is still equal to zero

You can find more information about AAA at `http://wiki.c2.com/?Arra ngeActAssert`.

So far, you have tested that it is possible to add one piece of correct data, but what about adding more? This should also be tested by a unit test, as follows:

```
[TestMethod]
public void AddTwoCorrectData_ShouldBeAdded()
{
    ConsumptionCalculator calculator =
        new ConsumptionCalculator();
    calculator.Add(120.0f, 8.9f);
    calculator.Add(15.0f, 2.5f);
    Assert.AreEqual(2, calculator.Consumptions.Count);
}
```

After testing the process of adding new entries that is reflected in the total number of items within the collection, you could ask yourself a really good question, *Wait, you have tested the addition of elements, but what about calculating an average value?* This is a really good question! Such a feature should be addressed in a set of tests as well.

In the first one, you can try to calculate the average value when no entries are added. A suitable test case is shown in the following part of code:

```
[TestMethod]
public void CalculateAverageWithoutData_ShouldBeZero()
{
    ConsumptionCalculator calculator =
        new ConsumptionCalculator();
    calculator.CalculateAverage();
    Assert.AreEqual(0.0f, calculator.Average);
```

```
    }
```

In the next set of tests, you could check the result of calculating the average value for one or two added entries as well as in case of introducing many of them. The last scenario is addressed in the following test case that uses 1,000 entries:

```
[TestMethod]
public void CalculateAverageWithManyData_ShouldBeCorrect()
{
    ConsumptionCalculator calculator =
        new ConsumptionCalculator();
    for (int i = 1; i < 1000; i++)
    {
        calculator.Add(120.5f * i, 9.8f * i);
    }
    calculator.CalculateAverage();
    Assert.AreEqual(8.13f, calculator.Average);
}
```

The next feature is removing an already added item. In such a case, you could check various scenarios, such as removing a correct item, deleting an already removed item, or removing an item that has not been added yet. As an example, let's take a look at the following test case for removing an item that was correctly added earlier:

```
[TestMethod]
public void RemoveCorrectItem_ShouldBeRemoved()
{
    ConsumptionCalculator calculator =
        new ConsumptionCalculator();
    calculator.Add(120.5f, 9.8f);
    calculator.Delete(calculator.Consumptions[0]);
    Assert.AreEqual(0, calculator.Consumptions.Count);
}
```

Of course, the mentioned tests are not the only possible ones, so you could think on your own about others that can be applied in this example.

There's more...

The topic of unit testing is strongly related to the TDD paradigm. It significantly changes the development process because it requires you to prepare tests before writing the actual implementation. Thus, tests are used to ensure that newly added features would remain consistent with the requirements. What is more, a comprehensive set of tests is really useful for regression testing to ensure that newly added or modified modules do not cause problems in the software.

Do you want to know how to apply the TDD approach for introducing a new feature for your application? If so, let's follow the steps shown here:

1. Implement a test for checking a new feature.
2. Run the test to ensure that it fails.
3. Perform the following two operations until the test is passed:
    - Adjust the implementation of the system
    - Run the test
4. Refactor the code to improve its quality without changing its behavior.
5. Run the test to ensure that the refactoring does not cause any regression.

See also

- The *Creating a unit test* recipe

Adding a project to the Windows Dev Center

Apart from developing a project in the IDE, it is also necessary to add the application to the Windows Dev Center. This tool is available via a web browser and makes it possible to perform a lot of operations regarding your applications. At the beginning, you need to specify a new project, and you will learn how to do this while reading the recipe.

How to do it...

To add a project to the Windows Dev Center, perform the following steps:

1. Open `https://developer.microsoft.com/en-us/store/publish-apps`. If you do not have a developer account, create it according to the instructions presented on the website.
2. Click on the **Dashboard** option at the top of the website and log in using the Microsoft account.
3. Click on the **Create a new app** button.
4. Reserve a name for the application by proposing a name in the textbox and clicking on the **Reserve product name** button, as shown in the following screenshot. Of course, you should enter a name that has not been reserved yet:

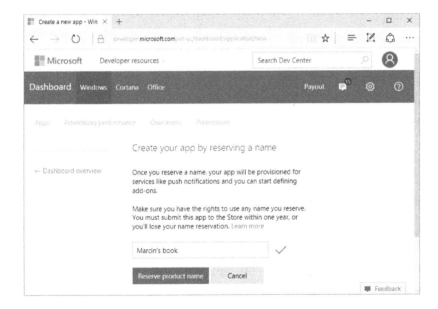

See also

- The *Associating an application with the store* recipe
- The *Adjusting the manifest file* recipe
- The *Obtaining a map token* recipe
- The *Receiving push notifications* recipe
- The *Preparing files for submission* recipe

- The *Submitting the application* recipe
- The *Updating the application* recipe
- The *Generating promotional codes* recipe
- The *Browsing reviews and ratings* recipe
- The *Analyzing acquisitions* recipe
- The *Creating a new project* recipe in `Chapter 1`, *Getting Started*

Associating an application with the store

When the application is created in the Windows Dev Center, you should associate your project in the IDE with this application. Fortunately, such a process is really straightforward and can be performed directly from the IDE without writing even one line of code, as you will see in this recipe.

Getting ready

To step through this recipe, you need the project that you want to associate with the store. You should have an application created in the Windows Dev Center as well.

How to do it...

To associate an application with the store, perform the following steps:

1. Right-click on the project node in the **Solution Explorer** window and go to **Store | Associate App with the Store**.
2. Press **Next** in the **Associate Your App with the Windows Store** window.
3. Choose the application name from the list and press **Next**.
4. When the information about values that will be added to the manifest file is presented, click on the **Associate** button.

How it works...

When the described process is completed, you can take a look at the
`Package.StoreAssociation.xml` file created in the project directory. It contains various
pieces of information regarding the application defined in the Windows Dev Center, as
shown in the following part of code:

```xml
<?xml version="1.0" encoding="utf-8"?>
<StoreAssociation
  xmlns="http://schemas.microsoft.com/appx/2010/storeassociation">
  <Publisher>CN=(...)</Publisher>
  <PublisherDisplayName>(...)</PublisherDisplayName> (...)
  <SupportedLocales> (...)
    <Language Code="en" InMinimumRequirementSet="true" /> (...)
    <Language Code="pl" InMinimumRequirementSet="true" /> (...)
  </SupportedLocales>
  <ProductReservedInfo>
    <MainPackageIdentityName>(...)</MainPackageIdentityName>
    <ReservedNames>
      <ReservedName>Marcin's book</ReservedName>
    </ReservedNames>
  </ProductReservedInfo>
  <AccountPackageIdentityNames>
    <MainPackageIdentityName>(...)</MainPackageIdentityName>
    <MainPackageIdentityName>(...)</MainPackageIdentityName> (...)
  </AccountPackageIdentityNames> (...)
</StoreAssociation>
```

As you could see, the `Package.StoreAssociation.xml` file contains data stored in the
XML format. Among them, you can find the data of a publisher (the `Publisher` and
`PublisherDisplayName` nodes), supported language codes (`SupportedLocales`),
identity and reserved names (`MainPackageIdentityName` and `ReservedNames`,
respectively), and the identity names of other applications registered from the same
developer account (`AccountPackageIdentityNames`).

See also

- The *Adding a project in Windows Dev Center* recipe
- The *Adjusting the manifest file* recipe
- The *Obtaining a map token* recipe
- The *Receiving push notifications* recipe
- The *Preparing files for submission* recipe

- The *Submitting the application* recipe
- The *Updating the application* recipe
- The *Generating promotional codes* recipe
- The *Browsing reviews and ratings* recipe
- The *Analyzing acquisitions* recipe

Adjusting the manifest file

Various pieces of information about the application is stored in the `Package.appxmanifest` file, located in the main directory of the project. Many settings have default values, but it is beneficial to learn how to adjust them. In this recipe, you will get to know how to configure the application using the **Application**, **Visual Assets**, **Capabilities**, **Declarations**, **Content URIs**, and **Packaging** tabs presented in the visual editor of the manifest file.

Getting ready

To step through this recipe, you only need the automatically generated project.

How to do it...

To adjust the manifest file, perform the following steps:

1. Double-click on the `Package.appxmanifest` file in the project node in the **Solution Explorer** window to open it in the visual editor.

2. Choose the **Application** tab, shown in the following screenshot, to adjust basic information about the application, including a display name and description, a code of the default language, supported orientations of the device (in order to restrict them), or configuration of tile updates:

By configuring the tile update feature, a tile of the application may be updated periodically (such as every 30 minutes, every hour, or once per day) according to the data returned as a response for the GET request sent to the given URI.

3. Choose the **Visual Assets** tab, presented in the following screenshot, to specify the various assets used by the application. What is more, you could also set a name of the tile, its background color, as well as specify when a name should be visible, depending on the tile size:

A set of default images is automatically generated and located in the `Assets` directory. Of course, you should replace them with your version consistent with the visual identity of the application. To simplify this task, there is a list of names and dimensions of default graphics, as follows:

- `LockScreenLogo.scale-200.png`: 48 x 48 pixels
- `SplashScreen.scale-200.png`: 1240 x 600 pixels
- `Square44x44Logo.scale-200.png`: 88 x 88 pixels
- `Square44x44Logo.targetsize-24_altform-unplated.png`: 24 x 24 pixels
- `Square150x150Logo.scale-200.png`: 300 x 300 pixels
- `StoreLogo.png`: 50 x 50 pixels
- `Wide310x150Logo.scale-200.png`: 620 x 300 pixels

4. Choose the **Capabilities** tab, presented in the following screenshot, to decide which features or devices your application can use. What is interesting is that you can select a suitable item from the **Capabilities** list and read its description to get to know whether this is really necessary in the case of your application.

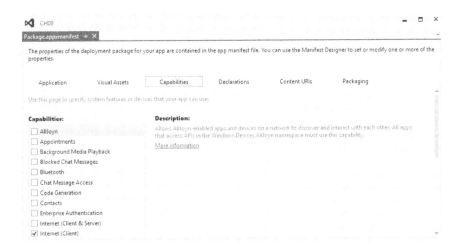

5. Choose the **Declarations** tab, presented in the following screenshot, to specify the declarations used by the application:

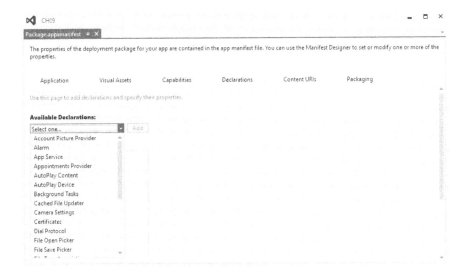

By supporting declarations, your application may interact with the system. For example, you can present results returned by your application in the system's search results (the **Search** declaration). You can also register a URL protocol to be handled by the application (such as `mailto`, the **Protocol** declaration). What is more, you can use the application as a share target, where users can publish various types of content (the **Share Target** declaration).

6. Choose the **Content URIs** tab, presented in the following screenshot, to specify the addresses of websites that could send the `ScriptNotify` event to the application. Thus, you could be informed when a process is completed or when some special event has occurred in the embedded web browser.

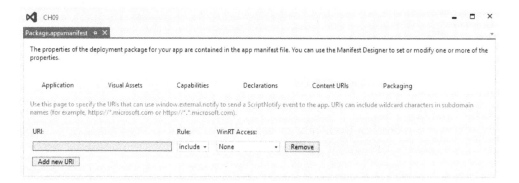

7. Choose the **Packaging** tab, presented in the following screenshot, to specify the details of the deployment package, such as its name and version:

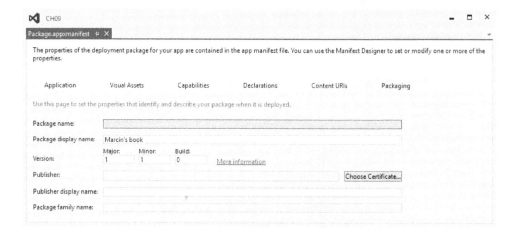

Such data will be modified while associating your project with the application created in Windows Dev Store, as presented in the previous recipe.

See also

- The *Associating an application with the store* recipe
- The *Preparing files for submission* recipe
- The *Submitting the application* recipe
- The *Updating the application* recipe

Obtaining a map token

As you learned in the previous chapter, you can show a map directly in your application. Unfortunately, by default, it informs a user that the map service token has not been specified. You can solve this problem by generating a map token using the Bing Maps Dev Center portal, as you will see in this recipe. Then, the obtained token should be set as a value of the `MapServiceToken` property of `MapControl`.

Getting ready

To step through this recipe, you need a project that contains a page with the `MapControl` control. You could use an application developed as an example in the *Showing a map within a page* recipe from `Chapter 8`, *Internet-based Scenarios*.

How to do it...

To obtain a map token, perform the following steps:

1. Log in to the Windows Dev Center, as already explained in the recipe titled *Adding a project to the Windows Dev Center*.
2. Click on the application name in the dashboard.
3. Go to **Services** | **Maps** from the menu on the left-hand side.

4. According to the information presented on the website, click on the **Bing Maps Dev Center** link, which will redirect you to `https://www.bingmapsportal.com`.
5. Sign in to Bing Maps Dev Center. Then, go to **My account | My Keys** from the menu at the top.
6. Press **Click here to create a new key** just below the **My keys** header.
7. Enter an **Application name** as well as choose a suitable **Key type** and **Application type**, as shown in the following screenshot:

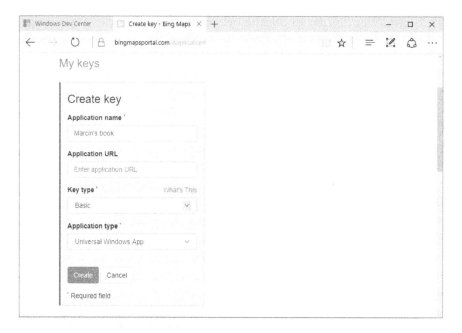

8. Click on the **Create** button. The **Key created successfully** message should be presented and a new application should appear in the list.
9. Copy the key and use it while configuring the `MapControl` control.

See also

- The *Adding a project in Windows Dev Center* recipe
- The *Associating an application with the store* recipe
- The *Showing a map within a page, Drawing icons, polylines, and polygons on a map, Adding a custom marker to a map,* and *Getting the coordinates of a clicked point on a map* recipes in `Chapter 8`, *Internet-based Scenarios*

Receiving push notifications

You could be accustomed to receiving various notifications on your smartphone, for example, after obtaining a new e-mail message or after publishing a post on your profile in social media. So do you think it is possible to add such a feature to your application as well and receive notifications in circumstances related to your project, such as when a new message has been received or when a user has been followed by another?

Of course, this is possible. However, adding support for push notifications requires a bit more development effort because preparing both the server side and client side is necessary. The client-side solution is presented and explained in the current recipe, but the server-side implementation is out of the scope of this recipe.

In this recipe, you will learn how to use **Windows Push Notification Services** (WNS), including generating necessary configuration data using the **Live Services site** as well as preparing the implementation to obtain the channel URI to which the server-side part should send the data of a push notification.

Getting ready

To step through this recipe, you only need the automatically generated project.

How to do it...

To configure an application to receive push notifications, perform the following steps:

1. Log in to the Windows Dev Center, as already explained in the recipe titled *Adding a project to the Windows Dev Center*.
2. Click on the application name in the dashboard.
3. Select **Push notifications** under **Services** from the menu on the left-hand side.
4. Go to **WNS | MPNS** from the menu on the left-hand side, located just below the **Push notifications** option.
5. According to the information presented on the website, click on the **Live Services site** link, which will redirect you to another portal.
6. Copy one of the application secrets as well as the package SID. These values will be necessary to properly configure the server-side part that should send requests to WNS.
7. At the end, click on **Save**. Now you can log out and close the web browser.

8. Get the channel URI while opening the main page by overriding the `OnNavigatedTo` method in the `MainPage.xaml.cs` file, as follows:

```
protected override async void OnNavigatedTo(
    NavigationEventArgs e)
{
    MessageDialog dialog = new MessageDialog(string.Empty);
    dialog.Title = "Push notifications";
    try
    {
        PushNotificationChannel channel =
         await PushNotificationChannelManager.
          CreatePushNotificationChannelForApplicationAsync();
        dialog.Content = "The channel URI is: " +
            channel.Uri;
    }
    catch (Exception)
    {
        dialog.Content = "Cannot get the channel URI";
    }
    await dialog.ShowAsync();
}
```

How it works...

The process of adding support for push notifications requires a bit more clarification. To make it clearer, an additional image is shown here:

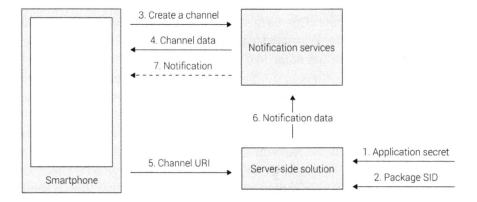

First of all, you need to get the necessary configuration data, namely an application secret and package SID. These values should be set in the server-side implementation, as shown by arrows **1** and **2**. Of course, a separate application secret and package SID are both necessary for each application that needs to receive push notifications.

The following operations are related to the client-side implementation. Here, you need to create the push notification channel for a given application (arrow **3**). You can do this by calling the `CreatePushNotificationChannelForApplicationAsync` method. It returns an instance of the `PushNotificationChannel` class (arrow **4**), which contains a set of properties, including `Uri` that stores the URI of the channel. This is a unique value for each application instance and should be passed to the server-side implementation (arrow **5**). As you could see in the preceding code, the `try-catch` block is used to handle exceptions that may be thrown when the channel cannot be created, for example, when a user does not have an Internet connection.

 It is worth mentioning that the channel URI can change during consecutive launches of the application. For this reason, it is necessary to create a new channel each time the application starts to be certain that the up-to-date channel URI is being used.

The next step (arrow **6**) presents an operation taken by the server-side solution. It prepares XML-based data of a notification and sends them to WNS. At the end, a smartphone, a tablet, or a desktop receives the notification and presents it to the user (arrow **7**).

There's more...

As already mentioned, the server-side implementation is out of the scope of this recipe. However, you could easily prepare it using the PushSharp library (`https://github.com/Redth/PushSharp`), which allows you to send push notifications to various devices, including those with the Windows 10 operating system.

See also

- The *Adding a project in Windows Dev Center* recipe
- The *Associating an application with the store* recipe
- The *Adjusting the manifest file* recipe

Preparing files for submission

When an application is developed in the IDE and created in the Windows Dev Center, and the manifest file is configured properly, it is high time that you prepare files for submission to the Windows Store. In this chapter, you will learn how to do this.

Getting ready

To step through this recipe, you need the project that you want to submit to the Windows Store.

How to do it...

To generate files for submission to the Windows Store, perform the following steps:

1. Right-click on the project node in the **Solution Explorer** window and go to **Store | Create App Packages...**.
2. When the wizard asks you whether you want to build packages to upload to the Windows Store, choose the answer **Yes (as [name] by [user])**. Then, click on the **Next** button.
3. Specify the output location (by default set to the AppPackages directory in the project folder), adjust the version, and choose the architectures, as shown in the following screenshot:

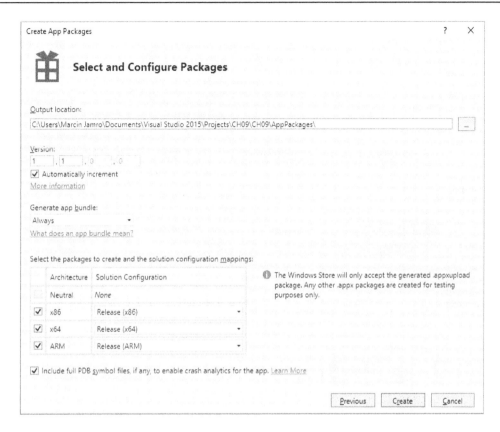

4. Click on the **Create** button and wait until the project is built in the chosen configurations. It could take some time.

5. When the information **Package Creation Completed** is shown, you should test whether the application complies with the requirements of the Windows Store. To do so, click on **Launch Windows App Certification Kit**.

6. Select all the certification tests and press **Next**. Do not take any actions until all the tests have been completed. If all tests pass successfully, you are ready to submit the generated package to the Windows Store.

7. Close Windows App Certification Kit.

How it works...

By default, the files are generated in the AppPackages directory in the project folder. Within it, you could find a directory whose name ends with Test (such as CH09_1.1.0.0_Test) as well as the .appxupload file (such as CH09_1.1.0.0_x86_x64_arm_bundle.appxupload). While submitting the project to the store, you should choose only the .appxupload file, as you will see in the next recipe.

See also

- The *Adding a project to the Windows Dev Center* recipe
- The *Associating an application with the store* recipe
- The *Adjusting the manifest file* recipe
- The *Submitting the application* recipe
- The *Updating the application* recipe

Submitting the application

Now, after reading more than 100 recipes discussed in this book, you are ready to submit a developed application to the Windows Store and make it available to people from various countries all over the world! So, let's start a new submission, configure it, and upload the .appxupload file. You will learn how to perform these tasks in this recipe.

Getting ready

To step through this recipe, you need only the project ready for submission to the Windows Store.

How to do it...

To submit an application to the Windows Store, perform the following steps:

1. Log in to the Windows Dev Center, as already explained in the recipe titled *Adding a project to the Windows Dev Center*.
2. Click on the application name in the dashboard.

3. Press the **Start your submission** button. The website with information about the submission will be presented automatically, as follows:

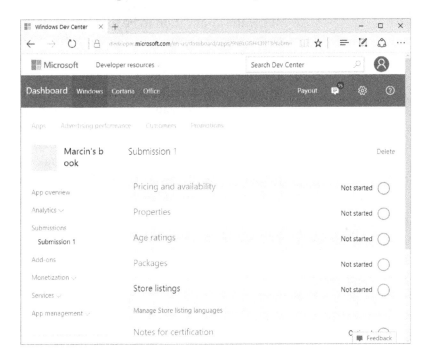

4. Specify the pricing and availability of your application by clicking on **Pricing and availability** and configuring the following settings:
   - Select the base price for the application, such as **Free** or **9.99 USD**.
   - Select the option to provide a free trial, such as **No free trial** or **15 days**.
   - Select custom prices for particular markets by pressing **Show options**, next to the **Market and custom prices** header, and specifying the prices for each market.
   - You can choose time-limited price reduction by pressing the **New Sale** button, located below the **Sale pricing** header, and providing a name of the sale, price tier, as well as the start and end date and hour. Once you do this, ensure you click on **Done**.
   - Decide on the visibility of the application in the store by choosing a proper option after pressing the **Show options** link in the **Distribution and visibility** group. Here are the options:
      - Choose the **Make this app available in the Store** option to make the application searchable and downloadable by users.

- Select the **Hide this app in the Store. Customers with a direct link to the app's listing can still download it, except on Windows 8 and Windows 8.1** option to not allow the application to be found by searching in the store. Users can still download it using a direct link.
- Select **Hide this app and prevent acquisition. Customers with a direct link can see the app's listing, but can only download the app if they have a promotional code and are using a Windows 10 device** to not allow the application to be found by searching in the store. However, make it possible for all the users with a direct link to see the app's listing as well as allow people to download with the correct promotional code (see the *Generating promotional codes* recipe for more information).

- There is a possibility that the application will be acquired in volumes by organizations. You can set this up by pressing the **Show options** link in **Organization licensing group** and choosing the proper checkboxes.
- You can select the publication date by choosing a proper option in the **Publish date** group to specify whether the application should be published as soon as it passes certification, manually by a developer, or not sooner than the given date.

5. Click on **Next**. Then, specify the properties of the submission by clicking on **Properties** and configuring the following settings:
    - A category (such as **Entertainment**) and subcategory (if applicable) in the **Category and subcategory** section
    - Additional declarations in the **Product declarations** group, such as support for installation on alternate drives or removable storage
    - Required (**Minimum hardware**) or recommended hardware (**Recommended hardware**) for the application, such as a touchscreen, camera, or a specified amount of memory

6. Click on **Next**. Then, complete the questionnaire regarding the age ratings. To do so, select **I'm ready to complete the International Age Rating Coalition (IARC) questionnaire** and choose the type of the application from the set provided on the website. Next, answer the set of additional questions, such as regarding violent material in the application.

7. Proceed to the next step, namely **Packages**, to submit the already generated `.appxupload` file. To do so, click on the **browse your files** link and choose a file.

You can also review the availability of your application on various platforms using the **Device family availability** option.

8. Click on **Save**. Next, manage the app's listing in various languages in the **Store listings** option. For each supported language, you can specify the following:
    - A description and release notes
    - Various screenshots, such as for desktop and mobile versions
    - Optional promotional artworks
    - Application features
    - Additional system requirements
    - Keywords describing the application
    - Information about the copyright and trademark
    - Additional license terms
    - An address to the website
    - A website or e-mail address regarding support
    - An address to the privacy policy

9. Click on **Save** and proceed to the **Notes for certification** part. Here, you should provide testers with various information that will be useful for them while testing your application.

10. Press the **Submit to the Store** button on the page with information about the submission, below **Notes for certification**. You will be navigated to the page with information about the certification process of the submission.

11. If necessary, change the publication date by clicking on the **Change publish date** link below the current certification state.

How it works...

After submitting the application to the Windows Store, you should wait until its certification is completed. Of course, you will be notified if any problems occurred or when the application passes the certification without any errors.

See also

- The *Adding a project in Windows Dev Center* recipe
- The *Associating an application with the store* recipe
- The *Adjusting the manifest file* recipe
- The *Preparing files for submission* recipe

- The *Updating the application* recipe
- The *Generating promotional codes* recipe
- The *Browsing reviews and ratings* recipe
- The *Analyzing acquisitions* recipe

Updating the application

After the publication of the application, it is often necessary to submit updates that either fix the bugs discovered in the project or add new features. In such a case, you can just send an update to the already published application, as you will see in this recipe.

Getting ready

To step through this recipe, you need a project that has already been published in the Windows Store. You should also have an updated version of the .appxupload file.

How to do it...

To update the application already submitted to the store, perform the following steps:

1. Log in to the Windows Dev Center, as already explained in the recipe titled *Adding a project to the Windows Dev Center*.
2. Click on the application name in the dashboard.
3. Press the **Update** link next to the information about the current submission. The next submission will be started automatically.
4. Proceed in the same way as in the case of submitting a new application, but just change the content that has been modified in the new version.

See also

- The *Adding a project in Windows Dev Center* recipe
- The *Associating an application with the store* recipe
- The *Adjusting the manifest file* recipe
- The *Preparing files for submission* recipe
- The *Submitting the application* recipe

- The *Generating promotional codes* recipe
- The *Browsing reviews and ratings* recipe
- The *Analyzing acquisitions* recipe

Generating promotional codes

After publishing the application to the Windows Store, you may face a few challenges, such as how to grant free-of-charge access to a paid application or how to distribute the application to beta-testers when its visibility is limited. Both these problems can be easily solved by promotional codes, which you can generate using the Windows Dev Center. Then, you can send them to particular users, for instance, via e-mail messages.

In this recipe, you will learn how to generate a set of promotional codes for the published application as well as how to download the `.tsv` file with the data of such codes.

Getting ready

To step through this recipe, you need a project that has already been published in the Windows Store.

How to do it...

To generate promotional codes, perform the following steps:

1. Log in to the Windows Dev Center, as already explained in the recipe titled *Adding a project to the Windows Dev Center*.
2. Click on the application name in the dashboard.
3. Go to **Monetization** | **Promotional codes** from the menu on the left-hand side.
4. Press the **Order codes** button.
5. Provide the necessary information regarding the new order. Follow these steps:
    1. Choose the application
    2. Type a name of the order
    3. Decide whether each code can be used once or multiple times
    4. Set a number of codes that should be generated
    5. Decide whether the codes should be active immediately
    6. Specify when the codes should expire

6. Click on the **Order codes** button. You will be navigated to the list of orders.

7. Press the **Download** link located next to the given order name. Then, you will be able to download the .tsv file with the data of generated codes.

 You can open the .tsv file using a text editor or Microsoft Excel.

See also

- The *Submitting the application* recipe
- The *Updating the application* recipe
- The *Browsing reviews and ratings* recipe
- The *Analyzing acquisitions* recipe

Browsing reviews and ratings

While your application is getting more and more popular, a number of reviews and ratings could increase. Of course, it is a good idea to take a look at the feedback from the users as well as prepare the next versions of the application to suit their needs. With the usage of the Windows Dev Center, you can easily browse reviews and ratings as well as download the report, as you will see in this recipe.

Getting ready

To step through this recipe, you need a project that has already been published in the Windows Store.

How to do it...

To browse the reviews and ratings regarding the application, perform the following steps:

1. Log in to the Windows Dev Center, as already explained in the recipe titled *Adding a project to the Windows Dev Center*.

2. Click on the application name in the dashboard.

3. To read the reviews as well as download a report, navigate to **Analytics |
Reviews** from the menu on the left-hand side.

4. To see information about ratings, including their total number and calculated
average value, as well as to download a report, go to **Analytics | Ratings** from
the menu on the left-hand side.

See also

- The *Submitting the application* recipe
- The *Updating the application* recipe
- The *Generating promotional codes* recipe
- The *Analyzing acquisitions* recipe

Analyzing acquisitions

Applications published in the Windows Store can be available for various markets all over
the world. However, is it possible to get to know the countries from where users have
downloaded the application? Of course! Suitable data are shown in the analytics module
within the Windows Dev Center, as you will see in the current recipe.

Getting ready

To step through this recipe, you need a project that has already been published in the
Windows Store.

How to do it...

To analyze the acquisitions of the application, perform the following steps:

1. Log in to the Windows Dev Center, as already explained in the recipe titled
Adding a project to the Windows Dev Center.

2. Click on the application name in the dashboard.

3. To get detailed information about acquisitions as well as download a report, go to
Analytics | Acquisitions from the menu on the left-hand side.

4. Browse the various parts of the website to get the acquisition data depending on the market and OS version as well as the customer demographic.

See also

- The *Submitting the application* recipe
- The *Updating the application* recipe
- The *Generating promotional codes* recipe
- The *Browsing reviews and ratings* recipe

Useful Resources

The book presents many topics regarding development of **Universal Windows Platform (UWP)** applications. However, it is worth mentioning additional resources, where you can find more information, especially about the topics mentioned in the book.

Getting started

You can find more information about the IDE, its various features, creating a UWP project, as well as running and debugging an application at the following websites:

- The Visual Studio Community IDE is presented at:
    - https://www.visualstudio.com/vs/community/
- Various features of the IDE, including managing solutions and projects, writing code, debugging, and profiling tools are shown at:
    - https://msdn.microsoft.com/library/b142f8e7.aspx
    - https://msdn.microsoft.com/library/efc4xwkb.aspx
    - https://msdn.microsoft.com/library/sc65sadd.aspx
    - https://msdn.microsoft.com/library/mt210448.aspx
- An explanation what is a UWP application is provided at:
    - https://msdn.microsoft.com/windows/uwp/get-started/whats-a-uwp
- A set of resources regarding developing UWP applications is available at:
    - https://developer.microsoft.com/windows/apps/develop
- A few device families are explained at:
    - https://msdn.microsoft.com/library/windows/apps/dn706137.aspx

- The API reference is available at:
  - https://msdn.microsoft.com/library/windows/apps/bg
    124285.aspx
- The process of placing controls on a page, setting their names and properties, as well as creating event handlers is described at:
  - https://msdn.microsoft.com/windows/uwp/controls-and-patt
    erns/controls-and-events-intro
- The layouts of UWP applications are introduced at:
  - https://msdn.microsoft.com/windows/uwp/layout/index
- The XAML platform is presented at:
  - https://msdn.microsoft.com/windows/uwp/xaml-platform/xam
    l-overview
- Events are described at:
  - https://msdn.microsoft.com/windows/uwp/xaml-platform/eve
    nts-and-routed-events-overview
- The attached properties are explained at:
  - https://msdn.microsoft.com/windows/uwp/xaml-platform/att
    ached-properties-overview
- The app lifecycle is introduced at:
  - https://msdn.microsoft.com/windows/uwp/launch-resume/ind
    ex
  - https://msdn.microsoft.com/windows/uwp/launch-resume/app
    -lifecycle
- Navigation between pages is explained at:
  - https://msdn.microsoft.com/library/windows/apps/mt
    187344.aspx
- The back button navigation is shown at:
  - https://msdn.microsoft.com/library/windows/apps/mt
    465734.aspx
- The process of deploying and debugging UWP applications, as well as testing them using the smartphone-based emulator, are presented at:
  - https://msdn.microsoft.com/windows/uwp/debug-test-perf/d
    eploying-and-debugging-uwp-apps
  - https://msdn.microsoft.com/windows/uwp/debug-test-perf/t
    est-with-the-emulator

Designing a User Interface

More information about various XAML controls, styles, and localization can be found at the following websites:

- The list of controls is presented at:
  - `https://msdn.microsoft.com/windows/uwp/controls-and-patt erns/index`
- Description of some controls, such as buttons and lists, is provided at:
  - `https://msdn.microsoft.com/windows/uwp/controls-and-patt erns/buttons`
  - `https://msdn.microsoft.com/windows/uwp/controls-and-patt erns/text-block`
  - `https://msdn.microsoft.com/windows/uwp/controls-and-patt erns/text-box`
  - `https://msdn.microsoft.com/windows/uwp/controls-and-patt erns/password-box`
  - `https://msdn.microsoft.com/windows/uwp/controls-and-patt erns/checkbox`
  - `https://msdn.microsoft.com/windows/uwp/controls-and-patt erns/toggles`
  - `https://msdn.microsoft.com/windows/uwp/controls-and-patt erns/lists`
  - `https://msdn.microsoft.com/windows/uwp/controls-and-patt erns/images-imagebrushes`
- Arranging controls is mentioned at:
  - `https://msdn.microsoft.com/windows/uwp/layout/layout-pan els`
  - `https://msdn.microsoft.com/windows/uwp/layout/layouts-wi th-xaml`
- Styling controls is described at:
  - `https://msdn.microsoft.com/windows/uwp/controls-and-patt erns/styling-controls`
- The brushes are presented at:
  - `https://msdn.microsoft.com/windows/uwp/graphics/using-br ushes`
- A difference between margin and padding is explained at:
  - `https://msdn.microsoft.com/windows/uwp/layout/alignment- margin-padding`

- Using controls for choosing date and time is described at:
    - https://msdn.microsoft.com/windows/uwp/controls-and-patterns/date-and-time
    - https://msdn.microsoft.com/windows/uwp/controls-and-patterns/calendar-view
    - https://msdn.microsoft.com/windows/uwp/controls-and-patterns/calendar-date-picker
    - https://msdn.microsoft.com/windows/uwp/controls-and-patterns/date-picker
    - https://msdn.microsoft.com/windows/uwp/controls-and-patterns/time-picker
- Using app bars is presented at:
    - https://msdn.microsoft.com/windows/uwp/controls-and-patterns/app-bars
- Showing dialogs is covered at:
    - https://msdn.microsoft.com/windows/uwp/controls-and-patterns/dialogs
- The localization topics are mentioned at:
    - https://msdn.microsoft.com/windows/uwp/globalizing/globalizing-portal
    - https://msdn.microsoft.com/windows/uwp/globalizing/put-ui-strings-into-resources

MVVM and data binding

There are various additional resources regarding the data binding mechanism. You can read more about such topics at the following websites:

- General description of the MVVM design pattern is presented at:
    - https://msdn.microsoft.com/library/hh848246.aspx
- The data binding mechanism is introduced at:
    - https://msdn.microsoft.com/windows/uwp/data-binding/index
    - https://msdn.microsoft.com/windows/uwp/data-binding/data-binding-quickstart
    - https://msdn.microsoft.com/windows/uwp/data-binding/data-binding-in-depth

- The `IValueConverter` interface is presented at:
  - https://msdn.microsoft.com/library/windows/apps/windows.ui.xaml.data.ivalueconverter.aspx
- The controls presenting progress are shown at:
  - https://msdn.microsoft.com/windows/uwp/controls-and-patterns/progress-controls
- The controls that show a list are described at:
  - https://msdn.microsoft.com/windows/uwp/controls-and-patterns/lists
- The `Hub` control is presented at:
  - https://msdn.microsoft.com/windows/uwp/controls-and-patterns/hub
- The asynchronous programming is introduced at:
  - https://msdn.microsoft.com/windows/uwp/threading-async/asynchronous-programming-universal-windows-platform-apps

Data storage

More information about managing files and directories, writing and reading files, as well as about using a SQLite database can be found at the following websites:

- Various topics regarding files, folders, and libraries are provided at:
  - https://msdn.microsoft.com/windows/uwp/files/index
  - https://msdn.microsoft.com/windows/uwp/files/quickstart-listing-files-and-folders
  - https://msdn.microsoft.com/windows/uwp/files/quickstart-reading-and-writing-files
  - https://msdn.microsoft.com/windows/uwp/files/quickstart-getting-file-properties
  - https://msdn.microsoft.com/windows/uwp/files/access-the-sd-card
- The `XDocument` class is described at:
  - https://msdn.microsoft.com/library/system.xml.linq.xdocument.aspx
- The code for converting an object into JSON-formatted string and to convert a JSON-formatted string to an object, using the `Json.NET` library, is presented at:
  - http://www.newtonsoft.com/json/help/html/SerializingJSON.htm

- The site of the `SQLite.Net PLC` library is available at:
  - `https://github.com/oysteinkrog/SQLite.Net-PCL`

Animations and graphics

You can find additional resources regarding animations, drawing shapes, and rendering 3D graphics using **DirectX** at the following websites:

- The animations are described at:
  - `https://msdn.microsoft.com/windows/uwp/graphics/animations-overview`
- The subject of drawing various shapes is mentioned at:
  - `https://msdn.microsoft.com/windows/uwp/graphics/drawing-shapes`
- The topic of touch interactions is introduced at:
  - `https://msdn.microsoft.com/windows/uwp/input-and-devices/touch-interactions`
- Transformations, such as regarding scaling and rotation, are shown at:
  - `https://msdn.microsoft.com/windows/uwp/graphics/transforms-overview`
- Information about creating 3D graphics is available at:
  - `https://msdn.microsoft.com/windows/uwp/gaming/index`
  - `https://msdn.microsoft.com/windows/uwp/gaming/an-introduction-to-3d-graphics-with-directx`
  - `https://msdn.microsoft.com/windows/uwp/gaming/tutorial-create-your-first-metro-style-directx-game`
  - `https://msdn.microsoft.com/windows/uwp/gaming/directx-and-xaml-interop`

Multimedia

There are various interesting resources about creating the multimedia applications. You can find more information about such a topic at the following websites:

- Playing audio and video files is described at:
  - `https://msdn.microsoft.com/windows/uwp/audio-video-camera/play-audio-and-video-with-mediaplayer`

- https://msdn.microsoft.com/windows/uwp/controls-and-patt
  erns/media-playback

- The `FlipView` control is presented at:
  - https://msdn.microsoft.com/windows/uwp/controls-and-patt
    erns/flipview
- The `WriteableBitmapEx` library is shown at:
  - https://github.com/teichgraf/WriteableBitmapEx/
- The file pickers are mentioned at:
  - https://msdn.microsoft.com/windows/uwp/files/quickstart-
    using-file-and-folder-pickers
  - https://msdn.microsoft.com/windows/uwp/files/quickstart-
    save-a-file-with-a-picker
- Various features regarding using audio, video, and camera in UWP applications
  are indicated at:
  - https://msdn.microsoft.com/windows/uwp/audio-video-camer
    a/index
- Using camera in an application is explained at:
  - https://msdn.microsoft.com/windows/uwp/audio-video-camer
    a/camera
- The `ZXing.Net.Mobile` library is presented at:
  - https://github.com/Redth/ZXing.Net.Mobile
- The speech synthesis and recognition features are described at:
  - https://msdn.microsoft.com/windows/uwp/input-and-devices
    /speech-interactions
  - https://msdn.microsoft.com/windows/uwp/input-and-devices
    /speech-recognition
  - https://msdn.microsoft.com/windows/uwp/input-and-devices
    /define-custom-recognition-constraints

Built-in sensors

You can find more information about using the sensors within the UWP application at the following websites:

- Various sensors (such as an accelerometer, a compass, and a light sensor) that can be used from UWP applications are presented at:
    - `https://msdn.microsoft.com/windows/uwp/devices-sensors/sensors`
    - `https://msdn.microsoft.com/windows/uwp/devices-sensors/calibrate-sensors`
    - `https://msdn.microsoft.com/windows/uwp/devices-sensors/use-the-accelerometer`
    - `https://msdn.microsoft.com/windows/uwp/devices-sensors/use-the-compass`
    - `https://msdn.microsoft.com/windows/uwp/devices-sensors/use-the-light-sensor`
    - `https://msdn.microsoft.com/windows/uwp/devices-sensors/use-the-orientation-sensor`
- A description of how to vibrate a smartphone is shown at:
    - `https://msdn.microsoft.com/library/windows/apps/xaml/dn611853.aspx`
- The example of using the `SubscribeForMessage` method from the `ProximityDevice` class is available at:
    - `https://msdn.microsoft.com/library/windows/apps/windows.networking.proximity.proximitydevice.subscribeformessage`
- An instruction how to get the user's current location is presented at:
    - `https://msdn.microsoft.com/windows/uwp/maps-and-location/get-location`
- The `DisplayRequest` class is described at:
    - `https://msdn.microsoft.com/library/windows/apps/windows.system.display.displayrequest`

Internet-based scenarios

More information about opening a website, composing an e-mail message, using a map, launching the navigation, as well as sending HTTP requests, are shown as follows:

- Launching a default web browser is mentioned at:
  - https://msdn.microsoft.com/windows/uwp/launch-resume/launch-default-app#http-uri-scheme
- Presenting a website within a page is described at:
  - https://msdn.microsoft.com/windows/uwp/controls-and-patterns/web-view
- Composing an e-mail message is presented at:
  - https://msdn.microsoft.com/windows/uwp/contacts-and-calendar/sending-email
- Opening a default e-mail client is explained at:
  - https://msdn.microsoft.com/windows/uwp/launch-resume/launch-default-app#email-uri-scheme
- Composing an SMS message is shown at:
  - https://msdn.microsoft.com/windows/uwp/contacts-and-calendar/sending-an-sms-message
- The PhoneCallManager class is described at:
  - https://msdn.microsoft.com/library/windows/apps/dn624832
- The Skype URIs are indicated at:
  - https://msdn.microsoft.com/library/office/dn745878.aspx
- Launching an external application to present a map is shown at:
  - https://msdn.microsoft.com/windows/uwp/launch-resume/launch-maps-app
- Presenting the map within an application is described at:
  - https://msdn.microsoft.com/windows/uwp/maps-and-location/controls-map
  - https://msdn.microsoft.com/windows/uwp/maps-and-location/display-maps
  - https://msdn.microsoft.com/windows/uwp/maps-and-location/display-poi

- Various topics regarding a network-enabled application are available at:
    - `https://msdn.microsoft.com/windows/uwp/networking/networking-basics`
    - `https://msdn.microsoft.com/windows/uwp/networking/which-networking-technology`
    - `https://msdn.microsoft.com/windows/uwp/networking/httpclient`

Testing and submission

There are various additional resources regarding the process of submitting the application to the Windows Store, as well as analyzing many data about the already published project. You can read more about such topics at the following websites:

- The topic of unit testing is mentioned at:
    - `https://www.visualstudio.com/docs/test/developer-testing/getting-started/getting-started-with-developer-testing`
- The capabilities are described at:
    - `https://msdn.microsoft.com/windows/uwp/packaging/app-capability-declarations`
- A way of obtaining an authentication key for a map is explained at:
    - `https://msdn.microsoft.com/windows/uwp/maps-and-location/authentication-key`
- The Windows Push Notification Services are presented at:
    - `https://msdn.microsoft.com/windows/uwp/controls-and-patterns/tiles-and-notifications-windows-push-notification-services-wns-overview`
- Preparing the project for submission to the Windows Store is described at:
    - `https://msdn.microsoft.com/windows/uwp/packaging/packaging-uwp-apps`

- Usage of the Windows Dev Center portal is presented at:
  - `https://msdn.microsoft.com/windows/uwp/publish/using-the-windows-dev-center-dashboard`
  - `https://msdn.microsoft.com/windows/uwp/publish/create-your-app-by-reserving-a-name`
  - `https://msdn.microsoft.com/windows/uwp/publish/app-management-and-services`
  - `https://msdn.microsoft.com/windows/uwp/publish/analytics`
  - `https://msdn.microsoft.com/windows/uwp/publish/app-promotion-and-customer-engagement`
  - `https://msdn.microsoft.com/windows/uwp/publish/app-submissions`

- The Windows App Certification Kit is introduced at:
  - `https://msdn.microsoft.com/windows/uwp/debug-test-perf/windows-app-certification-kit`

Index

10

Extensible Markup Language (XML) 180
external application
 map, opening 392

F

Field of View (FOV) 295
file
 accessing, reference 323
 creating 185
 downloading, from Internet 421
 iterating through 188
 preparing, for submission 454, 456
 removing 196
 renaming 192
 selection, for opening 321
 selection, for saving 323
font size, element
 animating 273

G

Garbage Collector (GC) 50
global style
 defining 92
GPS-based navigation
 launching 412, 414
grayscale mode
 image, converting to 313
grid view
 collection, binding to 166
grid
 controls, arranging 98

H

Hub controls
 reference 469
hub
 collection, binding to 174
 working 177

I

icons
 adding, to app bars 109
 drawing, on map 401, 405, 406

image
 adding 76
 capturing, from camera 325
 converting, to grayscale mode 313
 modifying 310
 recoloring 315
information
 logging, while debugging 47
Integrated Development Environment (IDE)
 about 10
 installing 12
 reference 465
 setting up 11
internet-based scenarios
 references 473
Internet
 advantages 377
 file, downloading from 421
items' collection repositioning
 animating 257
IValueConverter interface
 reference 469

J

JavaScript Object Notation (JSON) file
 about 180
 reading 218
 writing 212

L

Language Integrated Query (LINQ) 238
light sensor
 data, reading from 354
list view
 collection, binding to 161
listbox
 adding 74
 working 75

M

manifest file
 adjusting 444, 445, 447
map token
 obtaining 449
map

browsing 462
rotate touch event
    handling 286, 287, 288
rotation of element
    animating 269

S

screen switch off
    disabling 373
scrollable view
    controls, adding 87
set of tests
    running 436, 440
shapes
    drawing programmatically 276
    drawing, automatically 279
size of element
    animating 264, 266
Skype call
    launching 391
Speech Recognition Grammar Specification
    (SRGS)
    reference 339
Speech Synthesis Markup Language (SSML)
    reference 335
speech
    recognizing 336
SQLite database
    creating 229, 230, 236
    data, removing 246
    data, selecting 238, 242
    data, storing 237, 238
    data, updating 245
step-by-step debugging
    performing 44
store
    application, associating with 442
structure of directories
    reading 183
Studio Community IDE
    reference 465
styles
    applying programmatically 95

T

tables
    creating 229, 236
tap touch event
    handling 281, 283
Test-Driven Development (TDD) 426
testing
    references 474
text block
    adding 60
    working 61, 65, 69
text file
    reading 201
    writing 198
Text To Speech (TTS) 335
textbox
    adding 64
    value, binding to 147
time
    selecting 105
touch interactions
    reference 470
transformations
    reference 470
two-way binding
    creating 148

U

unit test
    creating 427, 431, 435
    working 433
unit testing
    references 474
Universal Windows Platform (UWP)
    about 10, 465
    layout, reference 466
    reference 465, 466
user control
    creating 112
    using 112
    working 116
User Interface (UI)
    about 10
    designing, references 467